The Political Economy of the Han Dynasty and Its Legacy

It has been claimed that the Han Dynasty (206–9 BCE and 25–220 CE) was China's most successful empire. This book contains original essays on various aspects of the Han's political economy and its legacy, written by leading Chinese and Western scholars whose collective expertise spans economic history, history of economic thought and sinology. It offers refreshingly diverse interpretations of major events, policies and ideas that were current in what was arguably the most formative and influential period of China's history.

Topics covered in the book include the following: the identification, possible influences and evolution of various "schools" of thought (notably "Confucianism", "Legalism" and "Daoism"); monetary and fiscal thought and policy; ideas surrounding "war economy" in the early ("Western") Han; the treatment of land issues and their remarkable enduring legacy; a Western perspective on the famous "Discourses on Salt and Iron" (*Yantie lun*); and a reappraisal of the "economic" ideas of Han's celebrated contemporary historian, Sima Qian.

The book will be of interest to not only specialist economic historians and historians of economic thought but also historians of any stripe who are concerned with this remarkable period of China's history. Through its provision of explanatory and contextualising material, both in the Introduction and elsewhere, the book will also be accessible to non-specialist readers, with or without a background in China studies.

Cheng Lin is Professor and Dean of the Department of Economic History at Shanghai University of Finance and Economics, and Vice-President of the Society of the History of Chinese Economic Thought. His main research area is the history of Chinese economic thought with a particular focus on nineteenth- and early twentieth-century thought.

Terry Peach is Professor of Economics at Shanghai University of Finance and Economics and Chair of the UK History of Economic Thought Society. He has previously taught at the Universities of Manchester and Oxford. His research and publications fall within the area of history of economic thought, recently extended to include ancient Chinese and Greek thought.

Wang Fang is Professor of Economics at Shanghai University of Finance and Economics. Her main research field is the history of Chinese economic thought from ancient times to the present, with particular attention to ideas concerning land issues.

Routledge Studies in the History of Economics

For more information about this series, please visit: www.routledge.com/series/SE0341

The Political Economy of the Han Dynasty and Its Legacy

Edited by Cheng Lin, Terry Peach and Wang Fang

Routledge
Taylor & Francis Group

LONDON AND NEW YORK

First published 2019
by Routledge
2 Park Square, Milton Park, Abingdon, Oxon OX14 4RN

and by Routledge
605 Third Avenue, New York, NY 10017

First issued in paperback 2020

Routledge is an imprint of the Taylor & Francis Group, an informa business

British Library Cataloguing-in-Publication Data
A catalogue record for this book is available from the British Library

Library of Congress Cataloging-in-Publication Data
A catalog record for this book has been requested

ISBN 13: 978-0-367-72821-2 (pbk)
ISBN 13: 978-1-138-06075-3 (hbk)

Typeset in Times New Roman
by Apex CoVantage, LLC

Contents

Contributors

Cheng Lin is Professor and Dean of the Department of Economic History at Shanghai University of Finance and Economics and Vice-President of the Society of the History of Chinese Economic Thought. Publications include *Banking in China, 1859–1949* (SUFE Press, 1999); *Western Development in China, 1840–1949* (with Wang Fang and Zhang Wei) (Shanghai Peoples Press: 2007); Cheng, Peach and Wang (eds.), *The History of Ancient Chinese Economic Thought* (Routledge, 2014); "The Historical Status of Chinese Economic Thought" (with Zhang Shen and Chen Xudong) (*Research in Chinese Economic History*, 2016: 3); "The Spread of Western Economics in China: Features and Influence, 1840–1949" (with Zhang Shen) (*Frontiers of Economics in China*, 2017: 12); "Choice and Innovation: Localisation of Western Economics in Modern China" (with Zhang Shen and Chen Xudong) (*Economic Research Journal*, 2018: 7)

Gavin S.H. Chiu is Associate Professor, Jao Tsung-I Institute of Culture Studies, Shenzhen University. His research interests are in the economic history of China and history of Chinese economic thought. Publications include *Pioneer of the Free Economy in Chinese History: The Economic Thought of Sima Qian* (Taipei: Wan Juan Lou Books, 2017), *A Case Study of the History of Chinese Political Economy* (with Cheung W.P.) (Fujian: Xiamen University Press, 2010) and *The Economic Depression in the Mid-Qing Dynasty* (with Sung X.W.) (Hong Kong: Shu Yan University Press, 2004).

S.C. Kwan is Assistant Professor in the School of Humanities and Languages, Caritas Institute of Higher Education (Hong Kong). His research interests are in Chinese philosophy.

Li Chaomin is Research Fellow at Shanghai University of Finance and Economics. Publications include *A History of Defence Economics* (Shanghai: Sanlian Bookstore, 2010), *Approaches to War Finance in China (1931–1945)* (Shanghai: China Oriental Publishing Centre, 2011) and "The Influence of Ancient Chinese Thought on the Ever-Normal Granary of Henry A. Wallace", in Cheng, Peach and Wang (eds.) *The History of Ancient Chinese Economic Thought* (Routledge, 2014).

Li Wei recently obtained his PhD from Fudan University and is researching the comparison between monetary and fiscal systems in China and the West.

Ma Tao is Professor in the Department of Economics, Fudan University. Major publications include *The Confucian Tradition and the Modern Market Economy* (Fudan University Press, 2000), *A History of Economic Thought*, Volume 1 (Economic Science Press, 2013) and "Paradigm and Development of Western Economics" (*Social Sciences in China*, 2014: 10).

Terry Peach is Professor of Economics at Shanghai University of Finance and Economics. Publications include *Interpreting Ricardo* (Cambridge University Press, 1993; paperback edition 2009), *David Ricardo: Critical Responses*, vols. i–iv (ed.) (London: Routledge, 2003) and *The History of Ancient Chinese Economic Thought* (co-ed.) (London: Routledge, 2014), as well as articles in journals including the *Economic Journal, Cambridge Journal of Economics, History of Political Economy* and *Oxford Economic Papers*.

Elisa Levi Sabattini is Associate Professor of Chinese Philology at L'Orientale University of Naples and affiliated Research Fellow at the Frieberg Centre for Asian Studies at the Hebrew University of Jerusalem. Her research focuses on the intellectual history of early China, and she has published in journals including *Oriens Extremus, Extrême-Orient-Extrême-Occident, Frontiers of Philosophy in China* and *Monumenta Serica*. She is currently co-editing a book with Christian Schwermann on *Between Command and Market: Economic Thought and Practice in Early China* (Brill, *forthcoming*) and co-translating (with Paul R. Goldin) *Xinyu* by Lu Jia.

Bertram Schefold is Professor of Economics at Johann Wolfgang Goethe-University. He has held visiting positions at numerous institutions including the Universities of Cambridge (Trinity College), Rome, St. Petersburg and Stanford. Publications include more than 40 books and 250 articles. He was President of the European Society for the History of Economic Thought in 2000–2002 and has held the position of Honorary President of the Society thereafter.

Wang Fang is Professor of Economics at Shanghai University of Finance and Economics. Publications include Wang Fang, Yan Hongzhong and Gao Yu, "A Study of the Development of Regional Currency Markets in Late Qing China" (*Historical Research* 2016: 3); Wang Fang and Xiong Jin-wu, "The Relationship Between Economic Thought and System in the Transition Period of Modern China: A Case Study of the Evolution of the Land System" (*Research in Chinese Economic History*, 2015: 12); Wang Fang, Miao Degang and He Xiaobo, "Did Civilian Granaries Affect Social Stability? Empirical Evidence from the Qing Dynasty (1817–1856)" (*Frontiers of Economics in China*, 2015: 3); Zhao and Wang, *Development and Transformation – Changes in Chinese Economic Thought: 1978–2018* (Capital University of Economics and Business Press, 2018); Cheng, Peach and Wang (eds.), *The History of Ancient Chinese Economic Thought* (Routledge, 2014); and Wang Fang, *A Study of the*

Rural Land Ownership and Land Tenure in Ancient China (Fudan University Press, 2006).

Zhang Shen is Associate Research Fellow at Shanghai Academy of Social Sciences. Publications include "The Development of Chinese Theories of Industrialisation in Modern Times" (*Journal of Finance and Economics*, 2013: 12) and "The First Great Divergence of China and Western Economic Thought" (*Economic Sciences* 2017:1).

Zhong Xiangcai is Research Fellow at the Institute of Economics, Shanghai Academy of Social Sciences. Publications include *A History of Chinese Economic Thought* (Shanghai Academy of Social Sciences Press, 2016), *Ideas of Economic Reform in Modern China* (Shanghai Academy of Social Sciences Press, 2016) and *A History of Chinese Agricultural Thought* (Shanghai Jiao Tong University Press, 2017).

Acknowledgements

Among the many people who have provided assistance and support in the genesis of this book, we should like to thank our partners, colleagues, students and friends as well as our university for the generous funding of the international workshop in 2016 at which several of the contributions were first presented. Our thanks are also due to our publishers for their commitment to our project and their patience in awaiting its completion. Finally, Wang Xiaobo deserves mention for her assistance to Terry Peach in the preparation of the final manuscript.

1 The political economy of the Han

Introduction

Terry Peach

Introduction

The Han Dynasty has come to be seen by some as "China's most successful empire":[1] one that "bequeathed to China an ideal and a concept of empire that survived basically intact for two thousand years".[2] Included in the bequest was "the most persistent ideal of Chinese history", namely, the "unity of China under one leader",[3] as well as more mundane legacies "such as 'Han characters', meaning Chinese [written] characters, and the 'Han race', meaning people of northern China".[4] Comprising a "former" or "Western" Han period (206–9 BCE), which followed on from the bloody demise of the first imperial empire of Qin (221–206 BCE), and a "later" or "Eastern" Han period (25–220 CE), with Wang Mang's "New" (Xin) Dynasty in between, the Han has been revered for its development of an authoritarian system of governance, a self-justifying ideology (with "Confucian" characteristics) and a hierarchical structure of administrative controls, which were (mostly) successful in crushing internal dissent and ensuring territorial integrity over a vast land mass with a population of around 50 million. Not surprisingly, scholarly attention has been lavished on subjects including Han's politics, philosophy, literature, international relations, sociology and scientific and non-scientific beliefs, but relatively little has been written on Han's political economy and its legacy. This book is a contribution towards remedying that deficiency.

The content of the volume is previewed in the following section, and it may suffice here to note that the discussion of Han's political economy extends not only to policies that were devised and implemented in areas relating to the state's production, distribution and consumption of (material) wealth, but also to debates surrounding those policies, their relationship with various "schools of thought" and the articulation and advocacy of particular visions of economic activity (i.e. activity relating *to* the production, distribution and consumption of wealth). While there are some exceptions, it will become apparent that most of the discussion is focused on the Former Han, as is the case with other studies of the Han, for the simple reason that this is the period for which we possess the more detailed primary resources. Yet, notwithstanding this limitation, it should also become apparent that there is an abundance of topics to discuss, and debate, arising from what was arguably the most formative and influential period of China's history.

The contributions

The second chapter, "From contention to unification: Transformation of economic thought in the Han Dynasty and its heritage" by Cheng Lin and Zhang Shen, has the aim of tracing the development of economic thought from pre-Han times to what is identified as its "grand unification" in the reign of Emperor Zhao (87–74 BCE). According to the authors, the pre-Qin period (more specifically, 550–233 BCE) was characterised by a metaphorical "contention of a hundred schools of thought", the principle ones being "Confucianism", "Legalism" and "Daoism", followed by the dominance of one single "school" – that of "Legalism" – during the Qin itself (221–206 BCE).[5] Then, in the early years of Han during the reign of Emperor Gauzo (206/202–195 BCE), they allege the influence of "Huang-Lao" thought, a species of "Daoism" that is said to incorporate a non-interventionist approach to economic management combined with elements of "Confucianism". In the third phase identified by Cheng and Zhang, coinciding with the reign of Emperor Wu (141–87 BCE), we are introduced to the contributions of "two out-standing intellectuals", Dong Zhongshu (ca. 195–104 BCE)[6] and Sima Qian (ca. 145–89 BCE),[7] the former advancing his own variation on a "Confucian" theme, which is said to have exerted a great influence on economic thought and policy in later times, and the latter preparing "a solid theoretical foundation for *laissez-faire* thought" which, notwithstanding its solidity, was to exert very little influence. It was also during this third phase that "Legalism" staged a comeback under the direction of Sang Hongyang (ca. 152–80 BCE);[8] Sang presided over the imple-mentation of policies including state monopolies in the production and sale of salt, iron implements and alcohol, together with the so-called equitable distribu-tion and price equalisation systems involving the government purchase, storage and sale of commodities, including but not confined to basic necessities.

Cheng and Zhang's fourth stage of "grand unification" is dated as occurring under the reign of Emperor Zhao (87–74 BCE). As attested in the *Discourses on Salt and Iron* (*Yantie lun*),[9] the conference held in 81 BCE and presided over by the 13-year old Emperor Zhao, this phase was marked by the rejection on the part of putative "Confucians" of Sang Hongyang's policies, leading thereafter to a synthesis of "Legalist", "Daoist", "Confucian" and popular mercantile thought, characteristics of which included a privileging of collective over individual inter-ests; an emphasis on the "Confucian" values of "benevolence and righteousness" rather than benefit (or profit); stress on *ben* ("root" or "primary" economic activi-ties, especially agriculture) rather than *mo* ("branch" or "secondary" activities, including commerce and the production of non-essential goods); encouragement of frugality; and a reduction in inequality. According to Cheng and Zhang, this "unified system" of economic thought was applied in the discussion of several top-ics of pressing concern, such as the ownership and distribution of land, currency, finance and governance; and, in this process, it underwent further development and refinement. Over time, however, the privileged status that the "system" came to acquire resulted in turning what had been a mutable framework of economic thought into a fossilised orthodoxy that stifled further intellectual development until the Qing Dynasty, almost two millennia later.

The third chapter, "Dong Zhongshu and Confucian Economic Thought as State Ideology in the Western Han Dynasty" by Zhong Xiangcai, also traces the evolution of economic thought, in Zhong's study from pre-Qin times to the reign of Wang Mang in the short-lived Xin (New) Dynasty (9 BCE–23 CE). He, too, discerns the triumph of a particular "school" of thought in the late Western Han, but rather than describing this "school" as a synthesis of previously distinct sets of ideas, Zhong awards the prize to a "Confucian school" and, more precisely, to a variant of "Confucianism" that had taken shape under the influence of Dong Zhongshu.

According to Zhong's reconstruction, the "Confucianism" of pre-Qin times was characterised by a "*laissez-faire* dimension", most evident in the teachings of Mencius (370–290 BCE), and an emphasis on "individualism". This is said to have contrasted sharply with the pre-Qin "Legalism" espoused by Guan Zhong (ca. 723–645 BCE)[10] in the Spring and Autumn Period (770–480 BCE) and Shang Yang (390–338 BCE)[11] and Han Fei (280–233 BCE)[12] in the Warring States period (480–221 BCE), who had advocated state intervention and control of the economy, and had framed their arguments in terms of the interests of the state rather than the interests of individuals (described by Zhong as the methodology of "holism"). Dong Zhongshu's contribution was to absorb those characteristics of "Legalism" *within* "Confucianism". The "Confucianism" that was to become the official state ideology in the Later Han (according to Zhong) was therefore radically different from its pre-Qin namesake.

As the underlying rationale for Dong's embrace of centralised state power, Zhong singles out a radically altered conception of the role and wisdom of the "Son of Heaven" (the emperor). In pre-Qin times, he argues, the infallibility of the ruler was not taken as given; hence, the role of senior advisors (gentlemen or *junzi*) was to provide necessary guidance towards finding, and following, the ideal "way" (*Dao*) of governance. But, in Dong's revised scheme of things, the Son of Heaven is, in virtue of his paternity, *necessarily* omniscient: he alone has infallible knowledge of the "way" and of the policies required to get there. If that is true, however, it must follow that the ideal polity is one in which everything of any importance is determined centrally and *imposed* on the "little people" below.

On Zhong's account, it is perhaps not surprising that Dong Zhongshu's "revised Confucianism" should have attracted the attention of a ruler – Emperor Wu – who had himself overseen the creation of a centralised and authoritarian system of governance, nor is it surprising that Wu should have accepted Dong's proposal to abolish all "schools" of thought except for this new variant of "Confucianism": a move that calls to mind, and is strikingly similar to, Qin's earlier proscription of all literature that might be used to criticise a "Legalist" state.[13] By Wang Mang's time, Zhong reports that any distinction between "Confucian" and "Legalist" thought had evaporated, the shared objective being to pursue "national interest" and an "ideal" social and economic order, as conceived by an all-powerful, central authority that had arrogated to itself the control over people's lives and their thought. Such was the dubious legacy of Han "Confucianism".

As with the previous two chapters, the following two – "The Monetary and Fiscal System of the Western and Eastern Han Dynasties" by Ma Tao and Li Wei, and "Monetary Thought in the Han Dynasty and Three Kingdoms Period (220–280 BCE)" by Gavin S.H. Chiu and S.C. Kwan – also share an overlapping focus. Ma Tao and Li Wei provide a detailed account of the evolution of monetary thought and policy and, regarding fiscal policy, of the demands on resources (which became particularly onerous during the reign of Emperor Wu), the various measures adopted to meet those demands (including poll tax, land tax, business tax, property tax, income from the state monopolies of salt, iron and alcohol and income from the employment of unfree, or corvée, labour) and the administrative machinery that was erected to oversee fiscal management.[14] At one level, the wide array of policies and, especially with the currency, the seemingly endless changes in policy may seem to preclude a generalised explanation. But, the authors argue, the fundamental driving force was always to meet the voracious demands of a central Han state that seemed incapable of reining in its own expenses, thus providing a legacy for future dynasties of constrained development of the private economy, long-term stagnation and a plundered population.

Among the many changes in monetary policy documented by Ma Tao and Li Wei, the principal ones concerned the physical properties of the (copper) coins that constituted the chosen medium of exchange, and the regulations governing private coinage, which varied between positively encouraging private individuals to engage in coinage and imposing a strict government monopoly, with infringements to be met (in principle, but often not in practice) by capital punishment. During the early Han, it was the more "liberal" policy on coinage that mostly prevailed, the rationale being (according to Ma and Li) that the inflation thereby engendered from excessive private minting would at least have the short-term beneficial consequence of stimulating economic activity following the ravages that had accompanied the overthrow of the Qin and the internecine strife thereafter. Under Emperor Wu, however, the emphasis was decidedly on the enforcement of a government monopoly, which after several abortive attempts eventually achieved a measure of success circa 113 BCE with the minting of a coin – the *Wu Zhu Qian* – the intricate design of which deterred all but the most skilled of counterfeiters and "criminal incorrigibles", as they were described in the *Han shu*.[15] Nevertheless, by the reign of Emperor Yuan (48–33 BCE), monetary problems were again plaguing the empire, leading to (renewed) calls for the abolition of currency itself. It is the history of such "anti-monetary thought" that forms the subject matter of the fifth chapter by Chiu and Kwan.

Chiu and Kwan's thesis is that the popularity and implementation of anti-monetary ideas depended on the coincidence (or "synergy") between the articulation of those ideas and the outbreak of economic crises. People, including rulers, are *misled* into believing that the root cause of economic difficulties is the very existence of monetary transactions, even though the actual cause may have been monetary mismanagement or a non-monetary phenomenon.

Chiu and Kwan point to instances of the airing of anti-monetary sentiment (by Jia Yi[16] and Chao Cuo,[17] who held office under the reigns of Emperors Wen (180–157 BCE) and Jing (157–141 BCE)) that failed to gain support precisely because the other condition for acceptance – economic distress – was wanting. By the later Western Han, they argue that economic circumstances had deteriorated, with the result that the proposal to abolish currency from Gong Yu (123–43 BCE), deputy Prime Minister in the reign of Emperor Cheng (33–7 BCE), received a much more sympathetic hearing, even though it was not implemented. Subsequently, after Wang Mang's disastrous attempts to reform the currency, followed later by the rampant inflation from monetary mismanagement in the reign of Emperor Huan (146–168 BCE), people were sufficiently receptive to the siren calls of anti-monetarism that "natural economy" became a prominent feature of economic life, and remained that way for the next 500 years. At least in the authors' opinion, this marked yet another baleful legacy of the Han: a crippling aversion to a fully mon-etised economy with its origins in the anti-monetary thought articulated at various times throughout the dynasty.

Returning to fiscal measures, the sixth chapter, "The System of Tribute Equali-sation in the Han" by Li Chaomin, sets out to clarify the nature of the *junshu* policy (translated by Li as the "tribute equalisation" policy) introduced during the reign of Emperor Wu, as distinct from (according to Li) the *pingshun* or "balanced standard" policy with which, in Li's opinion, it has been misleadingly confounded.

The policies in question had been introduced over the period 120–110 BCE along with other expedients – including the salt and iron monopolies, sale of social ranks and government posts, payment of fees for the remission and mitiga-tion of punishments and taxes on wealth, carts and boats – in an attempt to meet skyrocketing government expenditure on military campaigns and public works: expenditure that could not be covered by more traditional fiscal measures such as poll tax, land tax and produce tax. One problem identified at the time was, undoubtedly, the uneconomical collection of taxes-in-kind from distant regions, the value of which "often did not equal the cost of transportation".[18] Hence the suggestion of Sang Hongyang, by now in control of the ministry of agriculture, that "local products commanding a high price, such as would ordinarily be carted away and sold by the traders in other regions, should be transported to the capital in lieu of taxes".[19] This, according to Li Chaomin, was one of two aspects of the *junshu* policy.

The other aspect concerned the *amount* of tax that would be collected, the answer being found, according to Li, in the *Yugong* ("Fair Levies") chapter of the Han mathematical textbook *Jiuzhang Suanshu* (*The Nine Chapters on the Math-ematical Art*), where instruction is provided for the calculation of an equalised *net* burden of taxation, taking account of factors such as differences in distance (and therefore transportation costs) from the final collection point, and differences in the local costs of tribute (grain, mostly) and labour.

While Li Chaomin's conjecture is certainly plausible, it is also understandable that the many commentators excoriated by him for their interpretative shortcomings should have identified the "tribute equalisation" policy with the more general "balanced policy" system, because that is what we find in the surviving primary literature. To take Sima Qian's account, the goods dispatched to the centre as tribute would be stored in a "balanced standard office". However, the purpose of the office, and the scheme, was to give officials "complete control over *all* the goods in the empire, selling when prices were high and buying when they were low . . . and it would be impossible for *any* commodity to rise sharply in price";[20] this suggests that "tribute equalisation" was merged with the more general "balanced standard" policy of the purchase and sale of commodities (including grain) not limited to items of tribute: something effectively conceded by Li Chaomin in the fourth point of his conclusion.

Along with other fiscal measures, one purpose of the "balanced policy" system was to fund military expenditure, probably the greatest part of which was incurred with Han's numerous attempts to secure its borders against the attacks of the northern steppe confederacy of nomads, labelled by the Chinese as X*iongnu* ("ferocious slaves"). According to Sima Qian's account, the Xiongnu had been "a source of constant worry and harm to China" ever since the Three Dynasties (Yu, Xia and Shang) of remote antiquity.[21] In more recent times, the first emperor of Qin had overruled the advice of his first minister, Li Si, and dispatched a force of 100,000 troops, led by General Meng Tian, to attack the Xiongnu and drive them back from the northern border. But the territorial gains from this hugely costly campaign were fully reversed after the collapse of Qin, the Xiongnu having reached "their peak of strength and size" under Maodun, their vigorous new leader (titled *Shanyu*).[22] Not long after, and also against ministerial advice, the first emperor of Han, Gaozu, launched another major attack on the Xiongnu (the "Pincheng campaign"), which turned out to be a spectacular failure. Thereafter, Gaozu instituted a tribute policy of sending "specified quantities of silk floss and cloth, grain, and other food stuffs each year", with an imperial princess thrown in for good measure (in the hope of subduing the *Shanyu* through ties of kinship).[23] The tribute policy is reported to have been successful to the extent that frontier raids became less frequent, and was continued under the reign of Emperor Hui and Empress Lü (195–180 BCE), possibly at an increasing cost to the Han treasury.[24]

This brings us to the seventh chapter, "War Economy during the Western Han Dynasty" by Elisa Levi Sabattini, in which Jia Yi (200–168 BCE)[25] takes centre-stage in proposing to Emperor Wu a cunning plan for the containment of the Xiongnu.

Jia Yi started from the premise that the Han state lacked the military techniques and resources to defeat the Xiongnu in steppe warfare. At the same time, he condemned the tributary arrangement as too expensive and as humiliating to the Han by suggesting that the Xiongnu had an equal if not superior status. He therefore devised a strategy – using "three models" and "five baits" – aimed at sowing dissention among the Xiongnu ranks, weakening the authority of the *Shanyu* and turning the Xiongnu into subjects of the Han who could then be used to defend the borders at the empire, all at a lower cost to the Han state.

The purpose of the "three models" was to persuade the Xiongnu people that "they can feel secure and appreciated under the Han political umbrella"; it was a form of brainwashing, to be achieved through the dissemination of state propaganda. Concurrently, the Xiongnu leaders, as distinct from the *Shanyu* himself, would be "baited" with Han produce, although on this model only *surplus* produce would be offered, thus minimising the cost to the empire.

It was an intriguing proposal, but, in the event, it was the old model of buying interludes of peace with tribute, interspersed with debilitatingly expensive military campaigns, that was followed during the reign of Emperor Wen and, with the emphasis decidedly on military force, in the reign of Emperor Wu. It was to take until the late first century CE before the Xiongnu threat was finally extinguished.

Yet another threat to the Han, this time of the internal variety, was perceived by some as the growing concentration of the ownership of land by rich families and merchants, and the resulting creation of an expropriated and impoverished rural peasantry. This phenomenon, the measures proposed to deal with it, and the extraordinary influence that the early Han discussions exerted on future generations up to the early years of the People's Republic of China, are discussed in the eighth chapter, "The 'Land Quota' System in the Han Dynasty and Its Historical Influence" by Wang Fang.

In his address to Emperor Wen of 155 BCE, Chao Cuo[26] lamented the burden that government demands, and environmental disasters, were imposing on the rural population, who were often forced to take out loans "at one hundred per cent interest" in order to pay government levies. Then, "in many cases", the result was that "fields and dwellings are sold, children and grandchildren are vended, in order to pay debts".[27] In part, this dire state of affairs was said to have arisen as a result of policies introduced in the Qin state, which had "abolished the *jing-tian* ancient well-field system of land division"[28] and allowed the sale and purchase of land.

The *jing* (or "well-field") system was one in which land would be divided into areas consisting of nine plots, as represented by "井", the Chinese character for *jing*. Each outer plot would be assigned to and worked by one family, who would have the right to consume the plot's produce and whatever they obtained in exchange for that produce. The eight families would work the central plot collectively, with the produce going to the state in full payment of the families' tribute obligations. This system was advocated in *Mencius* (II.A.3) and was evidently taken by Dong Zhongshu (if not by later scholars) as an historical reality.

According to Dong, the Han had followed the institutions of Qin without changing them. Although a return to the *jing* system would be his ideal solution, Dong acknowledged that "it would be difficult to act precipitately" by attempting a return to that system, hence his compromise suggestion that the "people's ownership of land be limited",[29] described by Wang Fang as the "land quota" proposal.

As documented by Wang Fang, discussions of the *jing* and land quota systems occurred repeatedly in the following centuries as scholars and politicians sought their own solutions to the seemingly perennial problems of land annexation and rural poverty. One arresting example is the attempt by Wang Mang during his ill-fated Xin Dynasty actually to impose a *jing* (or *jing*-like) system, backed initially by harsh penalties on those who had the temerity "to speak evil of the sage [*jing*] institution".[30] By the end of the Xin Dynasty both the *jing* system, and the associated "King's fields system"[31] (which prohibited trade in land), had been relegated once again to the status of historical curiosities.

And that, in a sense, is how Dong Zhongshu's proposals always remained: beguiling historical curiosities that attracted attention periodically but never provided successful practical solutions. But, if that is the case, why did they exert such a lasting influence? Wang Fang floats a number of possible reasons at the close of her chapter, to which it may be added that "archaism" – the desire to find historical precedents and solutions, genuine or counterfeit – has been a characteristic of Chinese intellectual life from time immemorial: something that applies with equal force to the inspiration for Dong's own proposals.

One of those proposals – the *jing* system – was rehearsed shortly after Dong's death at the *Yantie lun* (*Discourses on Salt and Iron*) conference held in 81 BCE (see above, p. 3 n.9). This fascinating debate is discussed in the ninth chapter of this collection, "A Western Perspective on the *Yantie lun*" by Bertram Schefold.

The debate was conducted in the main between, on one side, the "Capable and Good Literary Scholars", titled "Literati and Worthies" in Essen M. Gale's translation and often described (as in Schefold's chapter) as "Confucians", and, on the other side, Sang Hongyang, the "Lord Grand Secretary", who had presided in the reign of Emperor Wu over the implementation of the monopolies, and the "equable marketing" and "balanced standard" policies that were also debated along with the state monopoly of coinage.[32]

The main thrust of the critics' argument was, in brief, that government policies had legitimised profit-seeking behaviour, created a class of newly rich, wealth-flaunting government officials and robbed the people of traditional sources of employment (such as private coinage). The result had been to entice people from "primary" activities as they sought to emulate the rich, thereby destroying the idyllic rustic simplicity of fabled "Confucian" antiquity when, according to Ban Gu's description, the

> desires of the people were few and undertakings were limited. Their wealth was sufficient, and they did not vie with one another. Thereupon, those above the people guided them by means of virtue and normalised them through ceremonial rites. Hence the people had a sense of shame [and] respect; they highly esteemed rightness, but disesteemed profit.
>
> (*Han shu* 91, in Swann 1950, p. 417)

In response, Sang Hongyang countered (*inter alia*) that the policies had generated desperately needed revenue to fund national defence, provided the means to care for the people in times of need and deterred the activities of private profit-seekers. The debate ended rancorously, with no compromise in sight.

In addition to providing a summary of the exchanges, Schefold takes the step of making comparisons with ancient Greek writings, including the pre-C2 BCE pseudo-Aristotelian *Oeconomica*, and with Kaspar Klock's *De Aerario*, of 1651. He also directly confronts a question that has been mostly elided to this point: what *is* the "political economy" that forms the object of this book's enquiries (in Schefold's case, in the *Yantie lun*)?

One thing it is *not*, according to Schefold, is analytical or theoretical economics in the modern sense: for example, there are no theoretical "models", no theory of value, no analysis of growth paths and, more generally, no "recognition of the economy as an autonomous force", the workings of which can be investigated *independently* of political or any other influences. Rather, what we find are discussions of topics of a recognisably "economic" nature, such as development, production, market forms, employment, money, public finance and international trade. It is the discussions of topics such as these that form the corpus, and define the boundaries, of Han "economics" or "political economy".

Whether all scholars would agree with Schefold's judgement is another matter. Thus, in the opinion of some commentators, we do find a few instances of more sophisticated economic thinking in Han writings. Sima Qian's are a case in point, where allegedly we encounter an argument in favour of *laissez-faire* that entitles its author "to be regarded as the Chinese Adam Smith",[33] pre-dating the Scotsman's efforts by 1,600 years or so, and with the theoretical principles set out in less than half a page (in translation).

As I argue in the tenth chapter, "Sima Qian and *laissez-faire*: Satire on a 'Discordant and Degenerate Age'", there is no doubt that *Shiji* 129, "The Biographies of the Money-makers", does contain material that can be generously construed as giving (no more than) a very basic sketch of some aspects of a *laissez-faire* system.[34] However, the question I ask is not about the quality of that "analysis"; rather, it is whether Sima Qian was truly an *advocate* of such a profit-driven economic system – a question I answer in the negative. For although *Shiji* 30, taken in isolation and glossing over hints to the contrary, may suggest a pro-*laissez-faire* position, material elsewhere in the *Shiji* provides a quite different perspective, illuminating the chapter as a brilliant and cutting satire of an age that Sima Qian utterly despised. On my reading, the legacy here has been one of radical misunderstanding, although as I suggest in a Postscript to the chapter, those who have been taken in by Sima Qian's rhetorical skill could at least console themselves with the thought that they are part of a long and illustrious tradition, possibly begun by Ban Gu, the lead author of the *Han shu* (*Book of Han*).

Those are the contributions. In the following section, I offer some personal observations on the representation of Han political economy and, in particular, its identification with "schools" of thought.

Identifying the political economy of the Han: problems and perspectives

For the purposes of this discussion, I adopt a general conception of "political economy" as ideas and policies relating to a state's production, distribution and consumption of wealth (material output), in pursuit of objectives that may include (without exhausting the possibilities) the state's internal stability, territorial expansion, defence and the maintenance of a "ruling class", subject to possible influences from whatever systems of doctrine or belief ("schools of thought") are prevalent at the time. The main question I address is whether it is possible and meaningful to associate Han political economy with particular "schools of thought".

According to a much simplified version of received opinion, the political economy that was dominant in Han's predecessor dynasty, the Qin, was a form of "Legalism", which was replaced in the early Han – at some point between the founding reign of Emperor Gaozu and the reign of Emperor Wudi – with a "*laissez-faire*" approach that *may* have originated in "Huang-Lao" doctrine, incorporating elements of "Confucianism", "Legalism" and "Daoism". Then, during the reign of Wudi, "Legalism" returned with a raft of policies involving centralised state control, which was later to provoke the reversion to a "Confucian" political economy, or a political economy with a strong "Confucian" flavour, that endured for centuries thereafter. On this account, the "political economy of the Han" is a story of multiple and contending "schools of thought", of which the principal ones were "Legalism" and "Confucianism". I first consider the possibility of identifying and characterising the political economy of these two major "schools" in their pre-Han incarnations.

Of the two, pre-Qin "Legalism", as represented in the writings associated with Shang Yang (see above, p. 3 n.11) and Han Fei (see above, p. 3 n.12), is the less problematical to reconstruct.[35] A product of the autonomous evolution of individual states following the breakdown of the Western Zhou, "Legalism" was a system of disciplined central management (it is the "ruler alone" who should exercise "control of the wealth and resources of a state"[36]), with the state's directives enshrined in a comprehensive system of laws backed by harsh punishments. Within the "Legalist" state, the activities of the population would be mostly confined to agriculture and military service, where agriculture ("primary activity") is taken to include not only the production of food and raw materials but also the provision of *essential* material products, such as clothes, shelter, tools and weapons, and notably excluding "luxuries" (commodities *not* required for the conduct of agriculture or warfare).

Shang Yang and Han Fei were at pains to present themselves as "modernists" who had no wish to follow the (reputed) practices of antiquity. The proposed means of achieving their objectives was a variety of carrot-and-stick policies that would both incentivise people to pursue the state's goals and make it impossible for them to do otherwise. Thus, taking it as given that the "desire of people for riches and honour does not generally cease before their coffins are closed",[37] the state must control the "gates" through which people can satisfy those desires: agriculture must be made the sole profitable means to acquire (moderate) riches, and military achievement the sole means to obtain public honours. At the same time, the state must remove any temptation for people to emulate those who engage in other activities, notably merchants and traders, artisans who specialise in "non-essential" production and "wandering philosophers" who earn their subsistence

without performing any "useful" function and fill the heads of people with seditious ideas (that is, ideas that run counter to "Legalism"). All such people involved
in "non-essential" or "secondary" activities – the "vermin of society", to use Han
Fei's felicitous expression[38] – must be eradicated using both indirect measures
(taxation, for example) and, if necessary, direct suppression.

With no temptation or possibility of doing anything other than fight or farm,[39]
people would become "stupid" and "simple minded",[40] as intended all along, and
therefore fully compliant with the state's directives. But they would not be merci-
lessly abused. In this latter regard, whether consciously or not, Shang Yang and
Han Fei were following the advice on governance in the *Shang shu*: "A leader
should be loved. Who should be feared? *The People*".[41] The leader, and only the
leader, would ensure, and would be seen as ensuring, that the people were cared
for in times of famine[42] (by distributing supplies from state granaries[43]); state
activity and expenditure would be controlled, so the people would not be overburdened by taxation or by demands for corvée labour; and "depraved officials"
would be prevented from "gaining private profits at the expense of the people".[44]
In consequence, "the people will feel content", and the state will be secure.

The political economy of "Legalism" emerges as a set of ideas and policies for
the central control and management of what is produced (and obtained through
foreign trade, which should be conducted only for strategically important reasons,
never for obtaining luxury goods[45]), levels of consumption and the provision of
"welfare", in pursuit of objectives that include a docile, obedient and loyal population and, above all, a state that is primed for military engagement. But there is
one further area that calls for attention: the means by which produce is distributed
from where it is grown or made to where it is consumed.

Shang Yang and Han Fei were united in condemning merchants – the very
people who *did* transport produce – on the grounds that the successful ones would
beguile the people into seeking wealth from "secondary activities". In Han Fei's
case, the answer was to "wipe them out" along with the other "vermin", leaving unanswered the question of how, and by whom, distribution is to be accom-
plished in their absence. Shang Yang's proposal was more nuanced: he advocated
the replacement of private merchants by state-registered carters, whose activity
would be limited to tasks that were authorised by the state (they would be prohibited from transporting private cargo).[46] As we shall see, it was not only "Legalists" who were challenged by adopting a critical view of merchants *and* accepting
the necessity of the distributive function they performed.

Turning to the "Confucian" political economy that was, or may have been,
bequeathed to the Han, it soon becomes jarringly apparent that we are heading
into disputed territory. First, there is disagreement on the very existence and content of "Confucianism" in general, never mind as a doctrine of "political economy".[47] And second, even among scholars who claim to have discerned elements
of "Confucian" political economy, there is sometimes radical disagreement over
what those elements might be.

Part of the problem is that pre-Han "Confucianism" came in several varieties,
the principal ones being the version attributed to Confucius (ca. 551–479 BCE), a

later version attributed to Mencius (ca. 372–289 BCE) and a third version developed by Xun Qing (31 –? BCE). Not only were there differences in the ideas expounded by (or attributed to) the members of this "triumvirate", there are also serious questions over the meaning, and reliability, of passages that are key to the construction of interpretative positions. The latter consideration applies with particular force to Confucius's *Analects*.

In sharp contrast to the "Legalists'" contempt for antiquity, Confucius claimed to take the (Western) Zhou as his avowed model.[48] His ideal was a state ordered by ritual (or "rites") which "encompassed all forms of symbolic action from the most austere to the most mundane, ranging from the grand sacrifices of the imperial cult to the small courtesies (such as bowing) that transpired between people at a chance meeting".[49] Within such a state, the ruler is "economical in expenditure", "generous in providing for the needs of the people", employs people in the service of the state (as corvée labour) "only in due season" (not at critical times in the agricultural cycle) and limits the rate of personal taxation to 10%,[50] all with the objective of rendering the people orderly, deferential and loyal. At one level, the objectives and the means of achieving them are not so different from those of the Legalists, making it both curious and unsatisfactory that adherence to the three policies of low taxation, limitations on corvée labour and the provision of "welfare" should later become standard litmus tests for the detection of "Confucianism". Where there is a difference is with the greater emphasis placed on "rites" rather than punishments and profit-based incentives as a means of achieving the objectives, which just about exhausts the *differentia specifica* of Confucius's "political economy" as reviewed thus far.

Significant differences *would* emerge if, as some scholars have contended, Confucius endorsed the principle of "*laissez-faire*" and supported equality in the distribution of income or wealth.[51]

"For the exact statement of the *laissez faire* policy", Chen Huanzhang claimed that "we find a general economic principle given by Confucius himself [as translated by Chen], 'Follow what is the profit of the people, and profit them' [*Analects* 20.2]": a statement which happily (for Chen) "is most general and comprehensive and needs no particular explanation".[52] For a more disinterested investigator, however, "particular explanation" is *precisely* what it needs.

By choosing to use "profit" in his translation, Chen invites the reading that Confucius was (rather clumsily) exhorting the ruler to facilitate the people's unimpeded quest for *financial* profit because this is what they, the people, consider "profitable". But suppose, as given in two other translations, we use "benefit"[53] or "advantage"[54] in place of "profit". To benefit or advantage the people on the basis of what really *is* "beneficial" or "advantageous" to them is by no means necessarily equivalent to sanctioning their unrestrained pursuit of financial profit; it depends on where we think – or, in this context, where *Confucius* thinks – their "true" benefit or advantage lies.[55] To support the "*laissez-faire*" reading, we require clear evidence of Confucius's belief that their "true" benefit or advantage *did* lie in the unrestrained pursuit of financial profit.[56] That evidence is wanting.

The "equality" interpretation[57] is no less problematical. It hinges on the substitution of "inequality" for "inequity" and "equality" for "equity" in the following passage (using Annping Chin's recent translation):

> I have heard that the head of a state and a head of an hereditary family should not worry about poverty but should worry about inequity in the distribution of wealth. They should not worry about a lack of population but should worry about discontentment and unrest. When there is equity in the distribution of wealth, there will not be poverty. When there is concordance, there will not be a lack of population. When the people are content, there will not be any threat of [the state or the family] being toppled.
>
> (*Analects* 16.1)

The notion of an *equitable* distribution – of a distribution considered "fair" in terms of some particular set of values – is at least consistent with Confucius's ideal of a Zhou state with its clearly demarcated social hierarchy,[58] whereas an *equalitarian* distribution would be utterly incompatible with such an ideal. Thus, to the extent that the discussion in *Analects* 16.1 (itself of dubious provenance[59]) really did pertain to the distribution of wealth and income (which is by no means clear[60]); and if it really did allude to "equality" rather than "equity" (which is also unclear); then, the reference could only have been to equality within a given *stratum* of the hierarchy, nothing more.

The political economy of Confucius, so far as it can be discerned from the *Analects*, did not amount to very much. With Mencius, we find not only the statement and amplification of what were to become standard "Confucian" tropes – the importance of rites, promoting the ruler as "a father and mother" to the people (the "little children"), reducing demands on the people by limiting taxation and corvée labour,[61] aiding the helpless and destitute, distributing grain in times of drought and famine[62] – but also a more clearly articulated "political economy" of (agricultural) production, distribution and exchange.

The most striking of Mencius's proposals was the implementation of the *jing* system (see above, p. 8), which would be promoted by a "clear-sighted" ruler who wished his people to have "constant means of support" (adequate subsistence for their families). Once possessed of those means, the people would develop "constant hearts" (contentment with their lives), and their gratitude would be such that they would follow the ruler "like little children" who love him, and their other superiors, to the point that they would "die for them".[63] The proposal is represented by Mencius as a return to the policy of King Wen of the Western Zhou, thereby acquiring (and doubtless intended to acquire) added lustre through this venerable association.

With people having received instruction on agricultural methods from the perspicacious ruler and his *junzi*,[64] they would be left to cultivate the land that had been allocated to them, and the state's land at the centre of the *jing*, thereby providing for their own needs *and those of the state*. However, in recognition of the likelihood that people would be unable to satisfy all their (basic) material requirements from the produce of their own labour, Mencius acknowledged the necessity of exchange:

> If people cannot trade the surplus of the fruits of their labours to satisfy one another's needs, then the farmer will be left with surplus grain and the woman with surplus cloth. If things are exchanged, you can feed the carpenter and the carriage-maker.[65]

But what if there is no carpenter or carriage-maker in the vicinity of the *jing*? It is at this point that merchants enter Mencius's story and, with them, alleged evidence of *his* support for "*laissez-faire*".[66]

Despite a degree of ambivalence towards the probity of merchants,[67] Mencius does sanction a low-tax regime with the purpose of facilitating their activities. Thus:

> In the market-place, if goods are exempted when premises are taxed, and premises are exempted when the ground is taxed, then the traders throughout the Empire will be only too pleased to store their goods in your market-place. If there is inspection but no duty at the border stations, then the travellers throughout the Empire will be only too pleased to go by way of your roads.[68]

However, although Mencius may well have advocated unrestricted *mercantile* activity, that must be placed in the context of a state in which, ideally, around 90% of the population[69] was envisaged as having no geographical mobility at all:

> Neither in burying the dead, nor in changing his abode, *does a man go beyond the confines of his village*. If those who hold land within each *jing* befriend one another both at home and abroad, help each other to keep watch, and succour each other in illness, they will live in love and harmony.[70]

This life of "love and harmony" will *not* involve scurrying after profitable opportunities wherever they may lie. Indeed, Mencius's attitude to profit-seeking was distinctly reserved,[71] suggesting that the allowance for mercantile profit-seeking was an exception, not the rule. At any rate, it seems evident that he was *not* supporting or proposing a "*laissez-faire*" policy for the economy as a whole.

While there are differences between "Mencian Confucianism" and "Legalism" over some policy means (especially, implementing the *jing* system rather than using financial rewards and penalties to encourage agriculture) and ends (different priorities for state expenditure[72]), there are also similarities: both seek a docile and obedient population from which the resources for state expenditure are appropriated; both recognise the danger of over-burdening the people; both emphasise the importance of "primary" activities; and both are suspicious of the private individual's quest for profit. More succinctly, both are systems of *control* over the production, distribution and consumption of a state's wealth. With Xunzi's "Confucianism", to which I now turn, the proposed degree and detailed nature of control were to reach an extreme.

At one level, when Xunzi dutifully rehearses the "Confucian" tropes, it may seem that he has nothing original to offer. Thus:

> Make clear ritual and *yi* [rightness] so as to guide the people. Make yourself loyal and trustworthy so as to make the people care for you. Elevate the worthy and employ the capable so as to order the people in ranks. Make gifts of positions, emblems, and other rewards in order to make the people exert themselves. Make the people's works accord with the times and lighten their burdens, in order to harmonise them. Nurture and raise them, as though caring for a new-born.[73]

But these emollient sentiments belie Xunzi's view of the "little children" as being positively evil: they pose a malign threat to the very existence of society in the absence of enforced discipline and control.

The problem stems from human nature: "People's nature is bad . . ."[74] [it] is such that they are born with a fondness for profit".[75] Moreover, there is no point in hoping that human nature can change; as Xunzi asserted in a way reminiscent of the *Shangjun shu*:[76] "Having desires and lacking desires fall under two different kinds, namely being alive and being dead".[77] But therein lies the fundamental social problem, because if "there are no limits or degrees" to desire and profit-seeking behaviour, "wrangling" and "disorder" will follow. As Xunzi warns apocalyptically, the outcome would be one in which the "strong harm the weak and take from them. The many would tyrannise the few . . . [and] all under Heaven [would] arrive at unruliness and chaos and perish".[78]

Fortunately, with a rhetorical flourish that would appeal to "Confucian" admirers of antiquity, a solution is at hand if only the ruler emulates the policies of "former kings":

> The former kings hated such chaos, and so they established rituals and *yi* [rightness] in order to divide things among people, to nurture their desires, and to satisfy their seeking. They caused desires never to exhaust material goods, and material goods never to be depleted by desires, so that the two support each other and prosper. This is how ritual arose.[79]

Desires were "trained" so that people only *expected* a level of personal consumption (a stipulated bundle of "material goods") that the ruler *knew* to be achievable on the basis of the state's "production possibilities" (the physical output it was *actually* capable of producing in the exact quantities required).

To complicate matters, the kings are again enlisted in support of a hierarchical social structure in which "trained desires" depend on social rank:

> the former kings established ritual . . . in order to divide the people up and cause there to be the rankings of noble and base, the distinction between old and young, and the divisions between wise and stupid and capable and incapable. All these cause each person to carry out his proper task and each

to attain his proper place. After that, they [the kings] cause the amount and abundance of their salaries to reach the proper balance.[80]

Although the required computational skills might pose a challenge even for the wisest of "former kings", the basic idea is unchanged: the ruler ensures that *expected* material consumption for every person, in every rank, is equal to *actual* material output.

The state's role in achieving the desired outcome is specified by Xunzi in forensic detail. First, among the people, "no one obtains a livelihood through luck. He [the 'true king'] elevates the worthy and employs the capable, and no ranks and positions are left unattended".[81] Second, the state will determine the content of the "consumption bundle" that will be fixed for each social rank, with the bundle including items such as clothing, size of dwelling and vessels and trappings used in mourning and sacrifice.[82] Third, the state appoints directors of "fields", "artisans", "markets", "public works", "resources" and sundry other areas, who determine what is produced (for the consumption of ranked individuals and the state), who it is produced by, how it is produced (in pursuit of "efficiency and high quality")[83] and how it is distributed.

The level of detail given by Xunzi for the *modus operandi* of a centrally planned system is without parallel in ancient Chinese literature. But there are also areas of similarity with other positions. Ultimately, the aim of Xunzi's proposals, not unlike the aim of everyone else's, was to ensure that the ruling class can occupy their posts "in safety", that "the common people will comply with orders and peacefully and happily dwell in their villages"[84] in normal circumstances and that they will fight and die in the service of their state and ruler if called upon to do so. There are also similarities over the means to those ends: providing for material needs, dispensing "welfare"[85] and avoiding an excessive burden from taxation and corvée labour. Likewise, there was nothing original about Xunzi's wish to "encourage agriculture" and reduce "the number of craftsmen and merchants",[86] although here we encounter a different type of similarity: the problem of dealing with merchants.

Although Xunzi wished to reduce the number of merchants and regarded their profit-seeking as a drain on the state's resources, he evidently realised, like others before him, that they performed the necessary function of circulating wealth. So, although there are fewer of them, some must ply their trade even in a "well-ordered state", the difference being that they will be "honest, and without deception".[87] Exactly *how* they are transformed from their formerly dishonest and deceitful selves is not spelt out, although Xunzi's "legalist" belief in the utility of harsh punishments may hold the answer: "Those who in their talents and conduct go against the times should die without pardon".[88]

To the extent that it is now possible to form any idea of a *distinctive* "Confucian" political economy in the pre-Han period, its connection with Confucius himself would be in the name and, more substantially, his endorsement of (Western Zhou) rites as a means of structuring behaviour. Beyond that, Mencius and Xunzi broadly agreed with each other, and with "Legalists", on the singular importance of "primary" activities, although they differed over the means by which they should be fostered: profit-based incentives and the elimination of attractive alternatives for "Legalists", the *jing* system for Mencius and the centrally planned allocation of labour for Xunzi. Where they *all* agreed, Confucius included, was on the treatment of "the people": they should be provided with "welfare" and not overburdened by the state's demand on resources. Indeed, such are the similarities between the supposedly different "schools" that it is tempting to place them *all* in a category such as "pre-Han traditionalists", with an allowance for various "sub-groups" to accommodate particular shades of difference (on the means of encouraging "primary" activities, for example), while recognising their shared ambitions: an over-whelmingly "agricultural" society under the direction of a central state (paternal or otherwise) with a rigid social hierarchy and a docile and obedient population.

One further similarity, of a negative variety, was an attitude to *unrestrained* profit-seeking behaviour that ranged from caution (Mencius) to unqualified opposition (Xunzi and the "Legalists"). As a related point, there is no compelling evidence that *any* "pre-Han traditionalist" conceived of, advocated or even *might* have advocated a *laissez-faire* economic system in which individuals are given free rein to use such resources as they may own (their labour, land and "capital") in pursuit of their *own* private benefit (profit), wherever they believe that benefit may lie. For Xunzi and pre-Han Legalists, it is evident that such a system would be total anathema, while for (other) pre-Han "Confucians", any doubt should be dispelled by reflecting on whether a dutiful "father and mother" would allow "little children" full latitude to pursue whatever *they*, the children, considered beneficial and enjoyable, with no parental guidance or restraint. What, then, are we to make of the outbreak of *laissez-faire* activity, policy and thought that is alleged to have occurred in the early Han?[89]

The first question is whether there *was* an increase in *laissez-faire* activity (private, non-state activity, directed by the pursuit of profit). Judging from Sima Qian's account,[90] this was indeed the case from the founding of the Han to the reign of Emperor Wu, particularly in the areas of trading, farming, handicrafts, money-lending, iron-smelting, salt-extraction and coinage.[91] But *why* had this happened?

A leading contender for a "doctrinal" explanation is the influence of "Huang-Lao" (or plain "Daoist") thought in the early Han which, supposedly, favoured a "theory of *laissez faire* government"[92] and *laissez-faire* economic policies.[93] However, apart from there being no surviving record of any document from this period in which an *economic* doctrine of *laissez-faire* is adumbrated, or advocated,[94] its purported association with "Huang-Lao" (or "Daoist") thought appears to rest on the conception of the latter as a doctrine of *state non-intervention*. But as Cao Can, the "Daoist" Prime Minister under Emperor Hui, reportedly explained his policy: "Now if Your Majesty would be content to sit quietly upon the throne, *while I and the other officials guard our posts and endeavour to carry out the laws without error*, would that not be sufficient?"[95] Similarly, as expressed in what is, for some scholars,[96] a classic "Huang-Lao" text:

> The ruler's techniques [consist of] establishing non-active management and carrying out wordless instructions. . . . [He] relies on his underlings . . .

Therefore, though his mind knows the norms, his savants transmit the discourses of the Way; though his mouth can speak, his entourage proclaim his words.[97]

And in the same vein: "Non-action does not mean [that the ruler] froze and was inert but that nothing any longer emanated from the ruler personally".[98] This doctrine of (affected) non-involvement *by the ruler* is not equivalent to a policy of non-interference *by the state*.[99]

It is impossible to *disprove* the possibility that *laissez-faire* ideas may have been "in the air" at some time in the early Han, but rather than pinning an explanation on evidence that is impossible to substantiate, there is, I suggest, a more straightforward alternative: that the spread of private, profit-seeking activity was the result *not* of "doctrinal" inspiration, but of the weakness of a Han state that had succeeded to an empire ravaged by warfare. Simply put, the early Han was *incapable* of constraining the "profit-seekers".

As described by Sima Qian, when "the Han arose . . . the great towns and famous cities were deserted and in ruins"; there was "much hard work and little wealth"; and "laws and prohibitions" on trading were not enforced.[100] Even at the time of Emperor Wu's accession, some 60 years after the Han's founding, "the net of the law was slack", thus allowing people "to use their wealth to exploit others", "accumulate large fortunes" and devote themselves to the pursuit of private "reward and gain".[101] In the main, these were developments that the state was powerless to control or prevent, not ones that it sought actively to encourage.

One possible exception is the Han's position on private coinage,[102] beginning with Gaozu's injunction that the people be "*ordered* . . . to mint new coins":[103] an order that the people seem to have followed with gusto, resulting in a practice that was to continue until the reign of Emperor Wu. However, the undoubted reality of private coinage is not, in itself, evidence of a consciously formulated *policy* of *laissez-faire*, applied to coinage as a matter of doctrinal preference. According to Sima Qian, Gaozu issued his order because the currency had become "heavy": its supply was inadequate to meet a demand that was increasing following the introduction of a poll tax (*suan*) in 203 BCE that was *levied in cash*.[104] Ordering private coinage may therefore be seen as a pragmatic, *non-doctrinaire* solution to a problem, one that would shift the cost of coinage to the public at a time when the state was woefully short of resources.[105] Moreover, the continuance of the practice seems to have had as much to do with the state's inability to stop it as anything else.[106] As evidence of a considered policy of *laissez-faire*, private coinage is not a compelling example.

Taking stock, although there is evidence of an increase in *laissez-faire* activity in the early Han, there is no evidence that this was the result of decisions to implement a consciously formulated *doctrine* of *laissez-faire*, either of a "stand-alone" variety (unrelated to any other "school of thought"), or as something curiously associated with "Huang-Lao" thought, with which it would have no obvious affinity. Rather, the *laissez-faire* "turn" may be seen as a consequence of the early Han state's impotence to control events and, in the case of currency, by pragmatic financial exigency. With precious few exceptions, the policies adopted in the early Han were not inspired by *any* "school of thought", and certainly not by a *particular* "school", but may be better seen as desperate attempts to raise revenue and resources in desperate times.[107]

Whether circumstances had changed by Emperor Wu's reign is a contentious matter. Certainly, policies and ideas from this period are commonly represented as emanating from particular "schools", with the clash of "doctrine" portrayed as reaching its crescendo in the *Yantie lun* (*Discourses on Salt and Iron*), as the Wu-supporting "Legalists" battled it out with the opposing "Confucians". As I propose to demonstrate, however, anyone yearning for such clear lines of demarcation is likely to be disappointed.

The specific areas of criticism that were articulated by Wu's purportedly "Confucian" critics[108] included the following: the spread of private profit-seeking that allegedly occurred under his reign; the increase in "secondary" (non-essential) and decline in "primary" activities; the spread of luxury; and the increase in poverty and inequality. In fact, there is nothing distinctively "Confucian" about *any* of these concerns; at least, there is none that might not have been expressed by a pre-Han "Legalist". So, let us consider concrete reforms and policies that were advocated by these "Confucians" to see if this holds the key to a separate "doctrinal" identity.

One of their catchier refrains, ironically with an impeccable "Legalist" pedigree,[109] was that the central state should desist from "competing with the people", and to that end, they proposed the abolition of institutions and measures that had been introduced in Emperor Wu's reign, including the state monopolies in salt, iron, coinage and alcohol, the offices for the equalisation of goods by transportation (*junshu*), the equable transport system for tribute and the balanced standard system (*pingshun*) under which the state would take control of the distribution and sale of most commodities. By returning these activities to "the people", they argued, poverty would be alleviated, and government officials would cease to behave as profit-seeking, luxury-indulging "*xiao ren*" (little people, in a derogatory sense) and would instead become virtuous role models, thereby luring the people away from unwholesome pursuits and attitudes. All very "Confucian", one might think, except that *this* "Confucianism" is either a devious imposter or a new species of a "Confucian" genus that had evolved, or mutated, into a stark contradiction of its former self.

The abolition of state-run monopolies and "systems" might seem a truly "demotic" policy to the extent that "the people" would receive financial benefits that had previously accrued to the state (and the state's officials): it would be *they* who were now in control of minting coins, smelting iron, extracting salt, and of buying, storing, selling and distributing commodities, and it is *they*, not the state, to whom any financial rewards would accrue. However, to countenance a *general* policy of private, profit-seeking activity, which is what the policy of "abolition" amounts to, runs counter to earlier "Confucianism" (and "Legalism") in *any* of its variants, and the policy's "Confucian" credentials are called further into question by the possibility that "privatisation" would benefit only a small fraction of "the people" to the considerable detriment of "the many".

The features of a "privatised" state to which the "Confucians" were urging a return had been recorded in sombre detail by Sima Qian, based on his appraisal of early Han experience: people used their wealth "to exploit others and to accumulate large fortunes"; merchants and traders "were busy accumulating wealth and forcing the poor into their hire, transporting goods back and forth in hundreds of carts, buying up surplus commodities and hoarding them in the villages" (an "underhanded means" to make profit); those "who were engaged in smelting iron and extracting salt from sea water" were "exploiting the poor" and "did nothing to help the distress of the nation"; and merchants were "taking advantage of the frequent changes in the currency . . . in order to make a profit".[110] With no reason to expect any other outcome – it was not as if the *Yantie lun* "Confucians" were advocating measures to constrain monopolistic practices – the beneficiaries of "privatisation" were likely to be a small kleptocracy of merchants, traders and manufacturers, whose guardian angels turn out to include those – the "Confucians" – from whom they might have expected a very different reception.

It follows that *these* latter-day "Confucians" had indeed created a separate "doctrinal" identity: one that was *anti*-"Confucian" by pre-Han standards in its support for unrestrained profit-seeking and, arguably, in relaunching itself as a party of *the rich* while masquerading as the party of "the people".[111] But, to further muddy the waters, there were other Han "Confucians" who, before and after the *Yantie lun*, took a quite different position on Wu's policies, particularly on coinage and aspects of the "balanced standard", thus rendering "Confucian" political economy in the Han an even more indistinct entity.

The case against private coinage had been made to Emperor Wen by Jia Yi – a scholar- cum-minister with leaning towards a "Mencian" variety of "Confucianism"[112] – who argued that the absence of effective state control had resulted in people being enticed away from agriculture, price-instability and (by implication) impediments to exchange from a lack of trust in the legal status of coins. Likewise, Gong Yu (123–43 BCE), who became Grand Secretary in the reign of Yuandi (48–33 BCE) at a time when "Confucianism was adopted as the guiding principle of government",[113] argued that the drift of people away from agriculture to coinage was not only undesirable in itself (by damaging "primary" activity) but also resulted in people's hearts becoming "restless and vacillating" as they imbued the desire for personal gain, with a general increase in "crime and depravity" as the lamentable consequence. As for the "balanced standard" system, Sang Hongyang's *junshu* policy (which formed part of the system) is associated by Ban Gu with the "ever-level granaries" policy of Geng Shouchang:[114] policies that are *commended* by Ban Gu for their venerable "Confucian" origin[115] and their benefit to the people.

By this stage, describing policies as "Confucian", or the individuals associated with them as "Confucian" in virtue of the association, has become an enterprise beset with difficulty: different policies were advocated by different "Confucians", self-proclaimed "Confucians" in one period would have been castigated as apostates in another (as with the *Yantie lun* "Confucians") and many "Confucian" policies and objectives were not even uniquely "Confucian".

Analogous problems arise with the identification of "Legalist" political economy, and especially with the attempt to claim its renaissance during the reign of

Emperor Wu. To begin with, there is not one of the more "controversial" policies enforced under Wu that could not claim "Confucian" support, or could not be presented as consistent, or not *inconsistent*, with "Confucian" values. In the case of the state monopoly of coinage, the policy was endorsed explicitly by Jia Yi and Gong Yu,[116] and it was also defended in the *Yantie lun* by Sang Hongyang, cast in the role of a "Legalist", on the grounds that it would promote virtuous behaviour:[117] an argument that (some) "Confucians" might be expected to applaud.

Similarly, the salt and iron monopolies and the balanced standard and equable marketing schemes were defended by Sang Hongyang using arguments of a distinctly "Confucian" (people-benefiting) hue: the policies provided revenue to "improve canals and sluices, promote various kinds of agriculture, extend farm and pasture lands, and develop national reservations";[118] they facilitated "the circulation of amassed wealth and the regulation of the consumption according to the urgency of the need";[119] they reined in "the overbearing and aggressive in the pursuit of their covetous [profit-seeking] practices";[120] and they served "to relieve the needs of the people in emergencies",[121] thus providing "a recourse against flood and drought".[122] Granted, the policies may have been portrayed in a deceptively favourable light, but the very fact that such a plausible defence could be mounted at all points to the difficulty in distinguishing between self-evidently "Legalist" and "Confucian" positions, especially at a time when, on the reading offered here, the *Yantie lun* "Confucians" were surreptitiously promoting the interests of "the overbearing and aggressive".

It would seem that the choice of *policies* offers no persuasive reason to identify political economy under Emperor Wu as distinctively "Legalist": the same policies could be, and were, supported by putative "Confucians" *and* "Legalists"; supposedly "Legalist" policies could be rationalised in "Confucian" terms; and some "Confucian" criticisms emanated from those whose "Confucianism" was deeply suspect (at least by pre-Han standards). It might be argued, however, that the "Legalism" of the policies derives more from their (alleged) *origins*, and specifically from their association with Guan Zhong (minister in the state of Qi in the seventh century BCE).[123] Yet, even granting the association, and the further possibility that Sang Hongyang and other of Wu's ministers were inspired by Guanzi "doctrine",[124] it by no means follows as a matter of principle that policies would be radically distinct from, and incompatible with, positions taken by non-"Legalists"; and it certainly did not follow as a matter of fact. Are there, perhaps, other criteria by which Emperor Wu's "Legalist" political economy may be identified? According to Homer Dubs, there are:

His widespread military expeditions were un-Confucian. His heavy taxes and legal oppression of the people were un-Confucian . . . In many ways . . . he seems deliberately to have imitated the First Emperor of the Qin dynasty, who was a Legalist.[125]

Slightly to modify Dubs's assertions, we may take the first to be that the combined burden of Wu's policies on the people, necessitated by excessive spending commitments that were incurred, in part, by "widespread military expeditions", were both "un-Confucian" *and* "Legalist" in the tradition of the first Qin emperor, Shi Huangdi. However, to the extent that an excessive burden could be considered "un-Confucian", it was also "un-Legalist": neither "Confucians" *nor* "Legalists" saw any merit in a heavy burden for the same reason, that it would incur the wrath of "the people" and possibly threaten the state's very existence.[126] As for the military expeditions, it was not part of core "Legalist" doctrine that they should be pursued regardless of all other considerations, as exemplified by Li Si's advice to Shi Huangdi that Qin should desist from attacking the Xiongnu.[127] Placing excessive burdens on the people, for whatever reason, was a sign of bad governance, not of "Legalism" per se.

Turning to "legal oppression of the people" as a criterion for identifying the "Legalism" of Wu's political economy, it seems undeniable that harsh punishments were meted out by his officials to enforce particular policies, such as the levy on private wealth.[128] More generally, it could be argued that "Confucians" tended to favour rites rather than punishments to effect compliance with state policies. Thus, although it may be impossible to distinguish sharply between "Confucian" and "Legalist" political economy either in terms of individual policies, or the magnitude of their overall burden on the people, perhaps the means of their *implementation* may provide the basis for at least *some* distinction between them.

Even here, however, distinctions are not clear-cut. In the case of Xunzi, his favoured means of ensuring compliance with state directives was a combination of "ritual" *and punishment*, the latter to an extent that blurs any clear distinction with "Legalism". Moreover, if we were to hark back to recorded practice in the Western Zhou – the regime that Confucius is said to have taken as his "model" – we would find ample testimony to the importance accorded to punishments, as with King Cheng's recommendation of execution for cases of drunkenness.[129] The threat and use of punishment in the implementation of policy may be taken as a sign of "Legalism", but reliance on "Legalist" methods – the promulgation and enforcement of laws – was by no means confined to any single "school" or "doctrine".

The conclusion to which I am led is that the attempt to associate Han political economy with particular "schools of thought" (be they "Legalist", "Confucian" or "*laissez-faire*") is an exercise of questionable value, whether we focus on the reign of Emperor Wu or on Han experience more generally. Leaving aside "*laissez-faire*" thought which, on the argument presented here, is of little relevance to understanding the political economy in the Western Han,[130] we find that similar ideas and policies were advocated by putatively different "schools", and that different policies were supported by members of the same "school". For (most) "Confucians" *and* "Legalists" (if that is how we choose to label them), the shared aim was to impose systems of *control* over the production, consumption and distribution of wealth, with the objectives of providing for the state's needs, ensuring social stability and the hegemony of the "ruling class" and cultivating obedience and loyalty among the masses. To those ends, it was generally agreed that the state should encourage "primary" and discourage "secondary" activities; provide for the material needs of the people, particularly in times of crisis; and minimise the burden from taxation, corvée labour and whatever other measures the state used to appropriate resources. Granted, there were differences between policies in terms of *means*, with "Legalists" relying more on punishments, market-intervention and profit-incentives, and "Confucians" stressing the importance of rites. But some of these differences, particularly over the use of punishments, only involved matters of degree, while others, notably market-interventions, were not such as to prevent policies from attracting broader acceptance, an extreme instance being Wang Mang's incorporation of ordinances for the "six controls" within his aggressively "Confucian" system of governance.[131]

In sum, the political economy of the Han encompassed a variety of ideas and policies with the overriding aim of *controlling* "economic" activity, but the attempt to force this material into distinct categories, and to suggest direct influences and associations between ideas, policies and "schools", is to impose sharp distinctions and create well-defined entities that simply did not exist. The story of Han political economy may be better understood as a flux of ideas and policies, advocated by, and associated with, individuals and groups with their own fluid and multifaceted characteristics. As a matter of personal judgement, however, it seems to me that what united political economy in the Han is far more significant than the schisms that have been said to divide it, although it will become clear in the following chapters that these remain contested issues.

Notes

1 Loewe (2006), p. xii.
2 Loewe (1986), p. 103.
3 Beck (1986), p. 369.
4 Ibid., p. 373.
5 The historical reality of distinct "schools" of thought in (pre-)Han times is a contentious issue to which I return in the following section.
6 Dong is reported to have been an Erudite in the reign of Emperor Jing (157–141 BCE). He went on to hold high office under Jing's son, Emperor Wu.
7 Sima Qian followed his father, Sima Tan, to become *Taishi* (Grand Scribe, or Grand Historian) during the reign of Emperor Wu. He was the author of the *Shiji* (*Records of the Grand Historian/Scribe*), one of the two major primary sources on which our knowledge of the (Former) Han Dynasty is based (the other being the *Han shu*, or *Book of Han*).
8 Sang was appointed as a palace attendant at the age of 13, reputedly because of his skill at mental arithmetic. At Emperor Wu's behest, he was put in control of the ministry of agriculture – the most important "economic" position – in 110 BCE and came to assume the title of "Lord Grand Secretary" in the reign of Emperor Zhaodi (87–74 BCE), when he was implicated in a seditious plot and executed.
9 As recorded in the *Han shu*, "Capable and Good and Literary Scholars were recommended [to the imperial court, the government set to] enquire about what the people suffered from or were distressed by, [and] the [abolition of] salt and iron [monopolies] was discussed". In Dubs (1938–55), vol. II, p. 175.
10 Guan Zhong was a minister in the state of Qi under the rule of Duke Huan (r. 685–643 BCE). According to Sima Qian's account in the *Shiji*, "Duke Huan of Qi, following the advice of his minister Guan Zhong, initiated a system of buying up goods when the price was low and selling when it was high, and of exploiting the resources of

the mountains and seas, until he had the other feudal lords paying court to him and, with what had up until then been the little and out-of-the-way state of Qi, had won for himself the title of dictator" (*Shiji* 30, *Han* II, p. 84). The book that bears his name – *Guanzi* (*Master Guan*) – contains chapters that were "written by different writers spanning two or three centuries of time [late third to first century BCE] and often representing quite different points of view" (Rickett 1998, p. 6). The surviving version of *Guanzi* was edited by Liu Xiang circa 26 BCE.

11 Shang Yang, or the Lord of Shang as he became known, held high office in the pre-imperial state of Qin under Duke Xiao (361–338 BCE). He was credited, and often reviled, for introducing far-reaching reforms including the abolition of the *jing* ("well-field") land system (see below, p. 8) and the creation of a centralised, strong and punitive state in which the energies of the people would be channelled into the two activities of agriculture and warfare. The book that bears his name – the *Shangjun shu* (*Book of the Lord Shang*) – is "a compilation of paragraphs, of different styles, some of which are older than the others; the older ones contain probably the mutilated remnants of the original book that has been lost" (Duyvendak 1928, p. 86).

12 Han Fei was born into the ruling family of the state of Han and reputedly studied under the "Confucian" philosopher, Xunzi (312–? BCE). It has been said that he was "not the inventor of Legalism, but its perfecter, having left us the final and the most readable exposition of its theories [in the book *Han Feize*]" (Watson 2003a, p. 4).

13 The policy was commended to the first emperor of Qin by Li Si (ca. 280–208 BCE), the Commandant of Justice, on the grounds that it would "make the common people ignorant and see to it that no one in the empire used the past to criticise the present" (Sima Qian, *Shiji* 87, *Qin*, p. 185).

14 Although they do not discuss developments in Wang Mang's Xin (New) Dynasty; and they omit discussion of the "price equalisation" and "balanced standard" measures that were adopted in the reign of Emperor Wu, arguably with the aim, *inter alia*, of replenishing the state's coffers.

15 Swann (1950), p. 294.

16 Jia Yi (200–169 BCE) is represented by Sima Qian as a "Confucian" (*Shiji* 6), although some of his favoured policies – instituting a de facto government monopoly on coinage and driving people into agricultural employment – also fit a "Legalist" stereotype.

17 Chao Cuo (d. 154 BCE) is described by Sima Qian as a severe exponent of "Legalism" whose erudition earned him the nickname "Wisdom Bag" (*Shiji* 101, *Han* I, p. 463).

18 Sima Qian, *Shiji* 30, *Han* II, p. 82.

19 Ibid.

20 Ibid., my emphasis.

21 *Shiji* 110, "The Account of the Xiongnu". *Han* II, p. 129.

22 Ibid., p. 136.

23 Ibid., p. 139.

24 Yü Ying-Shih (1986), p. 387.

25 See above, p. 5 n.16.

26 See above, p. 5 n.17.

27 *Han shu* 24, in Swann (1950), pp. 162–164.

28 Ibid., pp. 144–145, 180–181.

29 *Han shu* 24, in Swann (1950), pp. 182–183.

30 *Han shu*, in Dubs (1938–55), vol. III, p. 287.

31 As pointed out by Dubs, "'the Kings fields' comes (or may come) from the *Odes*, as quoted in *Mencius* (V.A.4), 'There is no territory under Heaven which is not the king's'. Wang Mang took the title of King, hence applied this saying to himself" (Dubs 1938–55, vol. III, p. 286 n.8.10).

32 Rather than describing the protagonists of the *Yantie lun* as "Confucians" and "Legalists", one scholar has proposed using "modernist" and "reformist" on the grounds that

the former antinomies "had hardly emerged as discrete, defined unities during the first two centuries BCE. Moreover, the issues on which Han statesmen differed were by no means identical with those which subsequently became criteria for distinguishing Legalist and Confucian thought" (Loewe 1986, p. 104).

33 Young (1996), p. 144.

34 In particular: "Society obviously must have farmers before it can eat; foresters, fishermen, miners, etc. before it can make use of natural resources; craftsmen before it can have manufactured goods; and merchants before they can be distributed. But once these exist, what need is there for government directives, mobilisations of labour, or periodic assemblies? Each man has only to be left to utilise his own abilities and exert his strength to obtain what he wishes. Thus, when a commodity is very cheap, it invites a rise in price; when it is very expensive, it invites a reduction. When each person works away at his own occupation and delights in his own business then, like water flowing downward, goods will naturally flow forth ceaselessly day and night without being summoned, and the people will produce commodities without having been asked" (*Shiji* 129, "The Biographies of the Money Makers", *Han* II p. 434). This passage clearly makes a link between price signals and resulting output variations from gain-seeking independent producers. But there is no further *analysis* of the phenomena that have been described, such as we find, for example, in the writings of Adam Smith. Hence the anachronism of crediting Sima Qian with the statement of a "theory" or an elaboration of "principles": a common but regrettable misrepresentation that may speak more to the contemporary aims of its perpetrators.

35 At this juncture I omit consideration of Guan Zhong (ca. 723–645 BCE). Although he is commonly portrayed as a "Legalist", his association with, and possible influence on, "Legalist" doctrine only becomes visible during the reign of Emperor Wu (see below, p. 23 n.124).

36 *Han Feize*, "The Way of the Ruler", in Watson, B. (tr., ed.) (2003a), pp. 17–18.

37 *Shangjun shu* [*Book of Lord Shang*] 4.17, p. 144.

38 *Han Feize*, "The Five Vermin", in Watson, B. (tr., ed.) (2003a), p. 118.

39 A "backstop" proposal for agriculture was to make it illegal for people to change their place of residence without authorisation (the *hukou* system): "If people are not allowed to change their abode unauthorisedly, then stupid and irregular farmers will have no means of subsistence and will certainly turn to agriculture" (*Shangjun shu* [*Book of Lord Shang*] 1.2, p. 96).

40 Ibid. 1.2, 1.3, 5.26.

41 *Shang shu* (*The Most Venerable Book*, or *Classic of History/Documents*), "The Counsels of Yu the Great", p. 18.

42 *Han Feize* is emphatic that the ruler "must never allow his ministers to dole out charity on their own", for fear that the people may come to direct their gratitude, and loyalty, to anyone other than him ("The Eight Villainies", in Watson, B. tr., ed. 2003a, p. 47).

43 These would be the only source of reserves, with the state having appropriated private stocks by means including the sale of official positions and honorary ranks in exchange for grain (*Shangjun shu* [*Book of Lord Shang*], 3.13, p. 131).

44 Ibid. 1.2, p. 94.

45 Additionally, the aim should be a trade surplus with other states: "Orderly government brings strength, but disorder brings weakness; when there is strength, products are imported, but when there is weakness, products are exported. Therefore a state that imports products is strong and one that exports products is weak" (*Shangjun shu* [*Book of Lord Shang*], 5.20, p. 154).

46 Ibid. 1.2, p. 97.

47 According to Nylan (2001, p. 3), the "stable entity that later scholars have called Confucianism has never really existed". Cf. Loewe (1986), pp. 652–653. One response to such criticism has been to present "Confucianism" as "a capacious, somewhat baggy

term, rather like 'Christianity' or 'Marxism'", with "Confucians" identified as those who regard Confucius as "the pre-eminent sage of human history" who provided the "authoritative and canonical guide to creating a good society and a just and effective government" (Queen and Major 2016, p. 13).

48　*Analects* 3.14, cf. 8.20.
49　Major et al. (2010), p. 124.
50　Respectively, *Analects* 1.5, 5.16 and 6.4, 1.5, 12.9.
51　Fortunately, how one might set about reconciling these two positions is a question that is needless to pursue.
52　Chen (1911), pp. 175–176. Cf. Hu (1988), pp. 45–46. "*Laissez-faire*", "free-economy" and "liberal economy" interpretations of Confucius are also advanced by Ma Tao [1998] (2014), Spengler (1964) and Chang (1987); they have been opposed by Wu Baosan [1991] (2014) and Tang Renwu [1996] (2014).
53　Dawson (1993), p. 82.
54　Waley (1938), p. 221. Also Chin (2014), p. 325.
55　Arthur Waley suggested the following as exemplifying the "advantage" that Confucius may have been thinking of: "if he promotes agriculture instead of distributing doles and largesses" ([1938] 2000, p. 221 n.1). However, as with Chen's reading, Waley's is guesswork, which reinforces the point that *Analects* 20.2, taken in isolation, is silent on the precise nature of the "benefits" or "advantages" in question.
56　Ideally, we also require such evidence to be less dubious than *Analects* 20.2, which has been regarded by Waley as having "no intrinsic connection" with the rest of the *Analects* ([1938] 2000, p. 15) and by Chin as an "interloper" (2014, p. 323).
57　This being the "generally accepted" interpretation in China, according to Hu Jichuang (1988, p. 49 n.19).
58　With the ruler at the apex, "common people" at the base and, in ascending order, scholars, gentlemen (*junzi*) and ministers, and feudal lords ("princes"), in between.
59　Waley ([1938] 2000, p. 15) considered it to be a late interpolation to the text. See also Chin (2014), p. 269.
60　The "distribution" in James Legge's translation referred to the allocation of people to specific geographical locations (1861, p. 25).
61　Mencius adds the caveat that there are limits to lightening the people's burdens, because state expenditure must be sufficient to provide for city walls, ancestral temples, sacrificial rites and diplomacy ("gifts and banquets"). *Mencius* 6.B.10.
62　As with the "legalists", Mencius suggests that it is the responsibility of the ruler to acquire, store and distribute grain for the benefit of the people. *Mencius* 1.A.3.
63　Ibid. 1.B.12.
64　See ibid. 1.A.3, 1.A.5, 1.B.4, 6.B.7.
65　Ibid. 3.B.4.
66　See Esson M. Gale (1931), "Historical Background to the Debate".
67　As suggested by the story of the "despicable fellow" who sought "to secure for himself all the profit that was in the market. The people all thought him despicable, and, as a result, they taxed him. The taxing of traders began with this despicable fellow" (*Mencius* 2.B.10).
68　Ibid. 2.A.5. Cf. 1.A.7.
69　A rough estimate of the agricultural population around this time (Loewe 1986, p. 150).
70　*Mencius* 3.A.3, my emphasis.
71　According to *Mencius* 1.A.1, "If your majesty says, 'How can I profit my state?' and the Counsellors say, 'How can I profit my family?' and the Gentlemen and Commoners say, 'How can I profit my person?' then those above and those below will be vying with each other for profit and the state will be imperilled'". The sense of this passage is that profit-seeking in general is an existential threat to a state's stability (cf. 6.B.4). Mencius also remarked that seeking wealth and profit is antithetical to benevolence and morality (6.B.4, 7.A.25). All things considered, it seems improbable that he would have countenanced profit-seeking in anything other than exceptional cases.

72 Particularly, the importance of military expenditure for legalists as against expenditure on ancestral temples, sacrificial rites and diplomacy ("gifts and banquets") for Mencius.

73 *Xunzi*, "A Debate on Military Affairs", in Hutton (tr., ed.) (2014), pp. 159–160.

74 Or "evil" in Watson's translation (2003b, p. 161).

75 *Xunzi*, "Human Nature Is Bad", in Hutton (tr., ed.) (2014), p. 248.

76 See above, p. 11.

77 *Xunzi*, "Correct Naming", in Hutton (tr., ed.) (2014), p. 243.

78 Ibid. "Human Nature Is Bad", p. 252.

79 Ibid. "Discourse on Ritual", p. 201.

80 Ibid. "On Honour and Disgrace", p. 30.

81 Ibid., "The Rule of a True King", p. 73. According to Watson's translation, each person "shall be assigned to his appropriate position without oversight" (2003b, pp. 44–45).

82 In Hutton (tr., ed.) (2014), p. 73.

83 According to Watson's translation (2003b, p. 51).

84 *Xunzi*, "The Rule of a True King", in Hutton (tr., ed.) (2014), p. 78.

85 In Xunzi's case, to the "five incapacitated groups" of the "dumb, deaf, cripples, missing an arm or a leg, or dwarfed" (Watson 2003b, p. 36 n.3).

86 *Xunzi*, "Enriching the State", in Hutton (tr., ed.) (2014), pp. 85, 95; "The Way to Be a Lord", ibid. p. 123.

87 Ibid., "The True King and the Hegemon", p. 116.

88 Ibid., "The Rule of a True King", p. 68.

89 "During the early years of the Han, the government in most respects tended to follow a *laissez-faire* policy in economic matters" (Rickett 1998, pp. 348–349). This thesis is developed at length in Glahn (2016).

90 Given in *Shiji* 129 and 30.

91 Robbing, killing and prostitution could be added to this list (*Shiji* 129, *Han* II, pp. 441–144).

92 Watson, *Han* I, p. 364 n.1.

93 Glahn (2016), pp. 85–86.

94 Sima Qian's sketch of *laissez-faire* activity (see above, p. 10 n.34) came later.

95 *Shiji* 54, *Han* I, p. 366, my emphasis.

96 But not all: see Major et al. (2010), p. 32.

97 *Huainanzi, Zhu shu* ("The Ruler's Techniques") 9.1.

98 Ibid. 9.23.

99 As expressed by Rickett (1998, p. 21), the "Huang-Lao" ruler "becomes a Daoist sage, ruling through non-assertiveness (*wu wei*) and practicing various quietist techniques, *while the work of his administration is performed by his ministers and bureaucracy*" (my emphasis). Cf. Loewe (2006), pp. 11–12.

100 *Shiji* 18, *Han* I p. 428 and *Shiji* 30, *Han* II, p. 61.

101 *Shiji* 30, *Han* II, pp. 63, 67.

102 As argued by Glahn (2016, p. 107).

103 *Shiji* 30, *Han* II, p. 61, my emphasis.

104 Dubs (1938–55), vol. I, p. 93 n.1.

105 Similar reasoning may apply to Emperor Wen's encouragement of private coinage in 175 BCE (see *Shiji* 30, *Han* II, p. 62). Wen's objective was to replace a circulating medium that had become "light" (over-supplied). Placing the cost of new coinage on the public may have appealed to a ruler who was lauded by Sima Qian for limiting state expenditure (*Shiji* 10, *Han* I, p. 305).

106 Unsuccessful attempts were made to prevent private coinage in 186 BCE, 144 BCE, 120 BCE and 115 BCE.

107 The closest to a "doctrinaire" policy might be the law "disesteeming" merchants enacted in 199 BCE by Emperor Gaozu, although this could claim support from "Confucianism" *and* "Legalism". At the other end of the spectrum, perhaps the least

"doctrinaire" and most desperate *ad hoc* policy was the sale of merit ranks, applied in 191 BCE under Emperor Hui and adopted frequently as a financial expedient thereafter.

108 Described as those who "venerate Confucius . . . [as] intellectual progenitor, and intone lauds in praise of his virtue, as being unsurpassed from high antiquity down to the present time" (*Yantie lun,* 11.a, where the numeral denotes the chapter and the letter indicates the passage).

109 It can be found in the *Shangjun shu* (see above, p. 12). Postdating Shang Yang, but predating the *Yantie lun,* it may also be found in writings attributed to Dong Zhongshu. See Queen and Major (2016), *Chunqiu fanlu* ("Luxuriant Gems of the Spring and Autumn"), 27.3, p. 272; and Dong Zhongshu's "Reply to the Third Instruction from Emperor Wu", *Han shu* 56, ibid., p. 642.

110 All quotations in this paragraph are from *Shiji* 30. Sang Hongyang recalls a similarly bleak account of the activities of merchants and traders in the *Yantie lun* (6.c, 9.b).

111 Cf. "The scholars who are shown as arguing so passionately for the discontinuance of the monopolies were actually promoting the interests of the great merchants and powerful families when they reproached the government for competing with the people for profit" (Sadao [1969] (1986), p. 605).

112 As indicated by his implicit approval of the *jing* system. *Shiji* 6, *Qin*, p. 82.

113 Dubs (1938–55), vol. II, p. 279.

114 Proposed in 54 BCE during the reign of Emperor Xuandi (74–48 BCE). The policy was that "frontier provinces be ordered to erect granaries so that at times when grain was cheap it might be bought at an increased price [for storage by government] in order to benefit the farmers; and that at times when grain was expensive [stored grain] might be sold at a decreased price [to benefit the people]. [To such granaries] was given the name of *Chang ping* 'ever-level [price]' granaries. The people found them advantageous" (*Han shu* 24. In Swann 1950, pp. 195–196).

115 As attested by their conformity with ideas that can be found in *The Book of Changes* (*I Ching*), *The Book of Documents* (*Shang shu*) and the *Mencius*, according to Ban Gu.

116 See immediately above.

117 It was claimed that the policy would reduce "dishonesty", "double dealing" and the "hope for wrongful gain". *Yantie lun* 4.e.

118 Ibid. 8.b.

119 Ibid. 1.i.

120 Ibid. 5.a, cf. 5.c, 5.d, 9.b, 14.e.

121 Ibid. 7.c, 12.b, 14.b.

122 Ibid. 2.a.

123 See above, p. 3 n.10.

124 Advanced in what have been described as the "Ratios of Exchange" or "Pseudo-Guanzi" chapters (68–85) of the *Guanzi*. According to Glahn (2016, p. 120), these chapters contain "the theoretical principles underlying the command economy they [Sang Hongyang et al.] inaugurated". Not to quibble over their elevation to the status of "theoretical principles", the chapters do contain *arguments* in support of state monopolies and state intervention in markets with the aim of equalising prices and regulating supplies (particularly of grain) and (of course) providing resources for the state. They also contain arguments in favour of restraining state expenditure, providing "welfare", reducing "nonessential" activities in favour of agriculture and eliminating profit-seeking activities by big traders and rich families, who stood charged of taking advantage of "the people". It should be evident that non-"Legalists" could find much they would agree with.

125 Dubs (1938–55), vol. II, pp. 347–348.

126 See above, pp. 12–14, 17. Precisely this argument had been put to Emperor Wen by the "Legalist" Chao Cuo (*Han shu* 24 in Swann 1950, pp. 159–164). The same position was stated repeatedly in the *Guanzi*; see, for example, XVII, 52 "*Qi Chen Qi*

Zhu" ("Seven Ministers and Seven Rulers"), p. 207; XXXIII, 80 "*Qing Zhong Jia*" ("*Qing Zhong* Economic Policies: Part A", p. 460; and XXI, 68, "*Chen Cheng Ma*" ("Planned Fiscal Management"), p. 361.

127 As recorded by Sima Qian, Li Si remonstrated to Shi Huangdi as follows: "Even if we were to seize control of the Xiongnu lands, they would bring us no profit, and even if we were to win over their people, we could never administer and keep control of them . . . Therefore we would only be wearing out the strength of China in an attempt to have our way with the Xiongnu. Surely this is not a wise policy!" (*Shiji* 112, *Han* II, p. 194).

128 See *Shiji* 30, *Han* II, pp. 76–77.

129 *Shang shu*, "The Pronouncement on Drinking [A]". Palmer (2014), p. 119.

130 The arguable exception being the *Yantie lun* "Confucians'" *implicit* support for a more *laissez-faire* policy.

131 "It was commanded that the imperial government should (1) dispense liquors, (2) sell salt and (3) iron implements, (4) cast cash, and that all who picked or took the various things from (5) famous mountains or great marshes were to be taxed. It was also ordered (6) that the offices [in charge of] the market-places should collect [things when they are] cheap and sell them [when they are] dear" (*Han shu*. In Dubs 1938–55, vol. III, p. 300). Although not identical, these measures were clearly similar to policies enacted under Emperor Wu.

References

Beck, B.J.M. (1986) "The Fall of Han". In Twitchett and Loewe (eds.), *The Cambridge History of China*. Cambridge: Cambridge University Press.

Chang, J.L.Y. (1987) "History of Chinese Economic Thought: Overview and Recent Works". *History of Political Economy*, 19:3, pp. 481–502.

Chen, H. (1911) *The Economic Principles of Confucius and His School*. New York: Columbia University Press.

Chin, A. (tr., ed.) (2014) *The Analects*. New York: Penguin.

Dawson, R. (tr., ed.) (1993) *The Analects*. Oxford: Oxford University Press.

Dubs, H.H. (tr., ed.) (1938–1955) *The History of the Former Han Dynasty*. Vols. 1–3. Baltimore: Waverly Press.

Duyvendak, J. (tr., ed.) (1928) *Book of the Lord Shang* ("*Shangjun shu*"). London: Arthur Probsthain.

Gale, E.M. (1931) *Discourses on Salt and Iron: A Debate on State Control of Commerce and Industry in Ancient China*. Leyden: Brill.

Glahn, R. von (2016) *The Economic History of China*. Cambridge: Cambridge University Press.

Hu, J. (1988) *A Concise History of Chinese Economic Thought*. Beijing: Foreign Languages Press.

Hutton, E.L. (tr., ed.) (2014) *Xunzi: The Complete Text*. Princeton, NJ: Princeton University Press.

Legge, J. (tr.) (1861) *The Chinese Classics*. Vol. 1. Hong Kong: The London Missionary Society.

Loewe, M. (1986) "The Former Han Dynasty". In Twitchett and Loewe (eds.), *The Cambridge History of China*. Cambridge: Cambridge University Press.

Loewe, M. (2006) *The Government of the Qin and Han Empires*. Indianapolis: Hackett.

Ma, T. [1998] (2014) "Confucian Thought on the Free Economy". In Cheng, Peach and Wang (eds.), *The History of Ancient Chinese Economic Thought*. London: Routledge.

Major, J.S., Queen, S.A., Meyer, A.S. and Roth, H.D. (trs., eds.) (2010) *The Huainanzi*. New York: Columbia University Press.

Nylan, M. (2001) *The Five "Confucian" Classics*. New Haven: Yale University Press.

Palmer, M. (tr., ed.) (2014) *Shang Shu ("The Most Venerable Book")*. London: Penguin.

Queen, S.A. and Major, J.S. (trs., eds.) (2016) *Luxuriant Gems of the Spring and Autumn ("Chungqiu fanlu")*. New York: Columbia University Press.

Rickett, W.A. (tr., ed.) (1998) *Guanzi*. Princeton, NJ: Princeton University Press.

Sadao, N. [1969] (1986) "The Economic and Social History of Former Han". In D. Twitchett and M. Loewe (eds.). *Sima Qian Shiji ("Records of the Grand Historian")*.

Spengler, J.J. (1964) "Sima Qian, Unsuccessful Exponent of Laissez Faire". *Southern Economic Journal*, 30:3.

Swann, N.L. (tr., ed.) (1950) *Food and Money in Ancient China* [*Han shu* 24 and 91]. Princeton, NJ: Princeton University Press.

Tang, R. [1996] (2014) "A Comparison between Confucian and Daoist Economic Philosophies in the Pre-Qin Era". In Cheng, L. Peach, T. and Wang, F. (eds.), *The History of Ancient Chinese Economic Thought*. London: Routledge.

Twitchett, D. and Loewe, M. (eds.) (1986) *The Cambridge History of China*. Cambridge: Cambridge University Press.

Waley, A. (tr.) [1938] (2000) *The Analects*. London: Alfred A. Knopf.

Watson, B. (tr., ed.) (1993) Sima Qian: *Records of the Grand Historian* in 3 volumes (*Qin*, *Han* I and *Han* II). New York: Columbia University Press.

Watson, B. (tr., ed.) (2003a) *Han Feizi: Basic Writings*. New York: Columbia University Press.

Watson, B. (tr., ed.) (2003b) *Xunzi: Basic Writings*. New York: Columbia University Press.

Wu, B. [1991] (2014) "On the Major Fields and Significance of the Study of the History of Ancient Chinese Economic Thought". In Cheng, Peach and Wang (eds.), *The History of Ancient Chinese Economic Thought*. London: Routledge.

Young, L. (1996) "The Tao of Markets: Sima Qian and the Invisible Hand". *Pacific Economic Review*, 1.

Yü, Y.-S. (1986) "Han Foreign Relations". In Twitchett and Loewe (eds.), *The Cambridge History of China*. Cambridge: Cambridge University Press.

2 From contention to unification

Transformation of economic thought in the Han Dynasty and its heritage

Cheng Lin and Zhang Shen[*]

Introduction

Chinese economic thought[1] took shape in the pre-Qin period and continued to develop in the Qin Dynasty (221–207 BCE) and Han Dynasty (202–220 BCE). Scholars have paid the greatest attention, and awarded the greatest accolades, to Chinese economic thought in the pre-Qin period. Before New China (1949), many monographs on economic thought in the pre-Qin period were published, and they continued to appear even in the 1990s (Wu, 1996). The first work on history of Chinese economic thought written by a Chinese scholar and published in the West, *The Economic Principles of Confucius and His School* (Chen, 1911), focused mainly on pre-Qin thought. In terms of research quantity, research on economic thought in the pre-Qin period accounts for a large proportion both in early modern times (1849–1949) and in the contemporary era (1949–).[2] In respect of evaluation, Tang Qingzeng[3] believed that pre-Qin economic thought was "the most splendid and promising discipline in China", which laid the foundation for Chinese economic thought up to modern times.[4] Hu Jichuang[5] claimed that the pre-Qin period had drawn the outline of the development of traditional Chinese economic thought, guided economic policies in successive dynasties and, overall, had "exerted a huge influence beyond imagination".[6] Similarly, Wu Baosan[7] observed that "in addition to economic philosophy and policy insight, the economic thought of pre-Qin writers contained some brilliant examples of economic analysis".[8]

In comparison, Chinese scholars have shown less enthusiasm for, and have thought less highly of, economic thought in the Han Dynasty. The number of research findings on dynastic history and figures in the Han is significantly fewer compared with studies of the pre-Qin period.[9] As Wu Baosan remarked, "research on dynastic history and economic thought has always been restricted to the pre-Qin Dynasty and early modern times",[10] and it was not until the 1960s that research monographs on later periods first appeared in Taiwan (Han, 1969), and then, in the 1990s, in mainland China (History of Economic Thought Study Group, Institute of Economics, Shanghai Academy of Social Sciences, 1989; Xie, 1989; Wang et al., 1991). Some scholars, represented by Gan Naiguang,[11] held that Chinese economic thought ended in the Qin Dynasty, and that the few outstanding representatives of economic thought in later times "could not get away from the pathway of pre-Qin thought".[12] In contrast, other scholars, notably Tang Qingzeng, asserted that much progress was made in economic thought during the Han Dynasty,[13] although he failed to provide specific examples.

Turning to the period after the foundation of the People's Republic, a more favourable reception was given to economic thought in the Han. Hu Jichuang pointed out that economic thought after the pre-Qin period was enriched and developed in terms of specific content, although most reformers utilised and applied only small parts of pre-Qin thought,[14] and dealt with some problems in a way inferior to that in earlier times.[15] Zhao Jing[16] argued that "both the Qin and Han Dynasties and the pre-Qin period produced the most active and brilliant thoughts in ancient China", but from the period of Emperor Yuan of Han (74–33 BCE), Chinese economic thought changed from being progressive to being "conservative".[17] In the 1990s, Wu Baosan argued that the lack of attention paid to the post-Qin period was not so much a reflection of its lack of interest but rather stemmed from the fact that the discipline of the history of Chinese economic thought was only in its "start-up" period.[18] Ye Shichang[19] also considered that the period from the pre-Qin times to the Western Han Dynasty was rich in thought, developing by leaps and bounds and having great effects on later generations.[20] Nevertheless, there remains a paucity of systematic research on economic thought in the Han Dynasty, even to the present day.

We take the view that the Han Dynasty was a transitional period in the evolution of Chinese economic thought, quite different from the pre-Qin period and with profound effects on later generations. Among the questions deserving of further scholarly attention are: what was the process of the transformation of economic thought in the Han Dynasty, and what were its concrete manifestations? What foundation did the Han Dynasty lay for economic thought and economic policy, and how did it influence later generations? And which fields of economic thought were developed in the Han, and what were the differences with pre-Han thought? This chapter seeks to address those questions.

The paper proceeds as follows. First, we discuss the path of transformation of economic thought in the Qin and Han dynasties. Next, we extract and expound four characteristics of economic thought in the Han Dynasty: its guiding principles, principal objects of enquiry, applications of economic thought and new developments. Finally, we evaluate the historical influence of economic thought in the Han Dynasty.

Paths of transformation of economic thought in the Qin and Han Dynasties

We suggest that the "transformation path" of economic thought in the Han was from "contention of a hundred schools of thought"[21] to "grand unification". "Contention of a hundred schools of thought" refers to the active, open and critical atmosphere in the pre-Qin period,[22] when a variety of ideas and schools of thought were developed; it also refers to different opinions on issues such as justice and benefit, consumption, finance, governance, and the relationship between agriculture, industry and commerce, between and even within those contending schools of thought. However, in the Qin and Han Dynasties, different schools of thought began actively or passively to contribute to the trend of "one school of thought becoming dominant", and then the "grand unification" took shape.[23] In this chapter, the "grand unification" in the field of economic thought can be defined as the creation of a set of comparatively unified economic principles, issues and policies. This "grand unification" was gradually formed and established over four stages, to which we now turn.

The first stage began with the foundation of the Qin Dynasty (221–207 BCE). The establishment of the Qin enabled China for the first time to evolve from decentralisation and separateness to centralisation of authority. The maintenance and consolidation of the newly unified country became the primary goal of the ruling class. In the field related to economic thought, the Qin Dynasty took two important measures. First, it issued the *Burning Book Decree*,[24] adopted ideological and cultural autocracy, resolutely eliminated the phenomenon that "people appreciate what they learn in private, but criticise the system established by the imperial court"[25] and advocated Legalism alone.[26] The existence of this last measure was not only because the pre-imperial state of Qin had flourished in virtue of laws made by the Legalist Shang Yang early in the Warring States period, but also because during the latter part of that period Lü Buwei (292–235 BCE), Prime Minister of the state of Qin, had realised the importance of ideological unification: each of the schools of thought had its own beliefs, but "if a state is governed depending on the opinions of all, then the state will soon perish"; therefore, "if the whole nation works in union, national peace and stability will be achieved".[27] Second, it established a single geographical entity over which governance was exercised by the central power: "the State of Qin pursued the system of prefectures and counties, and unified laws nationwide, with the supreme legislative power belonging to the emperor".[28] After the collapse of Qin, some of its systems were adopted by the Han, and the pursuit by Qin of unification and centralism laid a foundation for Han's later development.

The second stage began with the first Han emperor, Gaozu (r. 202–195 BCE). In the early days of the Han Dynasty, so-called Huang-Lao thought[29] was adopted and implemented, involving a significant reduction of state intervention in the economy. This shift in approach was necessitated by at least two considerations. First, it was believed that a more "hands-off" approach would facilitate a reprieve from the economic depression of "farmers losing cultivated land and mostly suffering from famine".[30] Second, since the Qin Dynasty had perished because of its tyrannical imposition of enormous burdens on the people (such as heavy taxation and corvée labour), the new ruling class sought to pacify the "common people" by reducing its demands. This attitude is exemplified in the book *Xin Yu*, written by Lu Jia,[31] which exhorted the rich to embrace a more frugal lifestyle, reduce their demands for "forced labour and tributes" and promote the "fundamental" activities of farming and sericulture; as for rulers, Lu advised they should adopt the position that "the best Daoism is inaction [*wu wei*]".[32] It should be noted that ideas from different schools of thought in this period had mixed with each other so that, for example, the *Xin Yu* contained both Daoist principles and the typical Confucian view[33] that "state governance should focus on morality, and behaviour should be humane and righteous".[34] In fact, pure contention of schools of thought was no longer the primary focus of attention for the ideologists; all schools of thought focused more on maintaining the stability and unification of the empire. Thus, Jia Yi,[35] who was considered as a Confucian,[36] advocated a state monopoly on minting currency,[37] which was more of a Legalist position. And Chao Cuo, who had a mastery of both Confucianism and Legalism, was greatly appreciated by the "Daoist" Emperor Wen (r. 180–157 BCE), to whom he proposed the way of governance of "allowing people to be engaged in farming and sericulture, reducing taxes and levies, and increasing savings".[38] Thus, the thoughts of Emperor Huang and Laozi, which were blended with elements of Confucianism, became the second candidate for "dominant school of thought" following the Legalism of the Qin.

The third stage began with the period of Emperor Wu of Han (r. 141–87 BCE). By this time, the external circumstances had changed yet again. Domestically, land annexation had aggravated economic and political contradictions, and the expansion of the merchant class also posed a threat to the agricultural economy. In addition, the unity of the empire was under threat from rebellious feudal states. Abroad, the expansion of territory and external wars were resulting in a heavy financial burden. Haung-Lau non-interventionism was no longer compatible with present and pressing needs.

It was at this time, and in response to changing circumstances, that two outstanding intellectuals of the Former Han, Dong Zhongshu[39] and Sima Qian,[40] made their contributions. Dong Zhongshu's version of Confucianism incorporated the "divine rights of emperors", the use of rites and morality to maintain social order[41] and the construction of a system of governance based on "conforming to Heaven's will", "educating the people" and "making laws".[42] In the economic field, he proposed placing limitations on land ownership, abolishing the state's salt and iron monopolies and the reduction of taxes, levies and demands for corvée labour.[43] He also proposed that all schools of thought other than Confucianism should be banned.[44] Thus, he had not only principles for governing a state but also corresponding polices. As for Sima Qian, his aim was to seek objective clues on historical development.[45] He maintained that "humans are born to have desires" and that "people are always busily seeking profits";[46] and he advocated a governance that accorded with "human nature", even though that could result in economic inequalities.[47] As interesting and valuable as Sima Qian's ideas were, however, it was Dong Zhongshu who was to have the greater influence on economic thought and policy, although it was to be several generations before this came to pass.

The fourth stage coincides with the reign of Emperor Zhao (87–74 BCE) and centres on the rejection of the economic policies promoted by Sang Hongyang (180–152 BCE). Those policies had been implemented during the reign of Emperor Wu as strategies to solve financial problems, but it was not until the debate held in 81 BCE, subsequently written up as the *Discourses on Salt and Iron* (*Yantie lun*), that the policies were subjected to searching critical analysis. Sang's political views originated in Legalism, and his economic views were influenced by ideas contained in *Guanzi*[48] and the opinions of wealthy traders.[49] He promoted state monopolies in the production and sale of salt, iron implements and alcohol, as well as the equitable distribution[50] and price equalisation systems which, at least in the short term, achieved the objectives of "grain accumulation in granaries, armies maintained and famine refugees relieved"[51] "without levying more taxes on common people".[52] However, the demands on resources from Emperor Wu's policies were such that, by the end of his reign, there were reported to be "nearly empty granaries across the country and a halved population".[53] The backlash against Sang Hongyang was soon to follow.

As named in the *Yantie lun*, the critics of Sang Hongyang's policies were "Xian Liang" and "Wen Xue",[54] denoted in English translations as (Confucian) Literati and Worthies. They valued only benevolence and righteousness and opposed any interference by the government; hence they criticised all Sang's economic policies, especially the monopolies. Although Xian Liang and Wen Xue are represented as having won the debate, the outcome was more confused: at the moral level, the position of the Confucians prevailed, while at a practical level many of Sang Hongyang's policies continued to be favoured by the government.

In summary, the transformation from "contention of a hundred schools of thought" to the "grand unification" in the Han Dynasty led ultimately to a dominant school of thought, or orthodoxy, that was a synthesis of views from various sources, including Legalism, Daoism, Confucianism and the merchant class. The synthesis thus formed provided a basic framework consistent with mainstream social values and the state governance system that was designed and utilised to provide guidance for regime consolidation and development. The characteristics of the framework are considered further in the following section.

Characteristics of economic thought in the Han Dynasty

Guiding principles

"Guiding principles" are akin to "generally acknowledged truths" regarding economic issues, which provide guidelines on action and judgments on economic activities in a wide range of fields. In the past, scholars delineated three such principles with "three main doctrines of feudalist orthodox economic thought",[55] and this chapter will build on those insights.

Emphasis on collective interest rather than individual interest

Economic thought in the pre-Qin period exhibited both individualistic and collectivist characteristics.[56] Individual interest was the concern of, for example, Yang Zhu ("it is wrong for an individual to sacrifice his own benefits for national benefits")[57] and Shen Dao[58] (if the emperor does not "force someone to do what he does not want to do, then there will no man who cannot be employed").[59] In contrast, a more collectivist interest is suggested by the following saying attributed to Confucius:

> I have heard that the possessors of states or noble families do not worry about under-population, but worry about the people being unevenly distributed; do not worry about poverty, but worry about discontent. For when there is equitable distribution there is no poverty, and when there is harmony there is no under-population, and when there is contentment there will be no upheavals.[60]

Some governance and financial management thought also belongs in the "collectivist" category,[61] as with Shang Yang's doctrine that "farming can bring benefits",[62] which was intended to encourage people to devote themselves to agriculture, thus benefiting the state. Policies for national economic intervention in the *Guanzi* belong in the same category.

As a notable exception in the Western Han period, Sima Qian could be considered as more of an "individualist". Thus, according to his *Shanyin* thought:

> the highest type of ruler accepts the nature of the people, the next best leads the people to what is beneficial, the next gives them moral instruction, the next forces them to be orderly, and the very worst kind enters into competition with them.[63]

However, it was "collectivist" thought that was dominant during the Han Dynasty. The "three principles and five virtues"[64] put forward by Dong Zhongshu may have discussed the relationships between different individuals, but the aim was to safeguard social morality and order. Meanwhile, some collective economic ideas were implemented, as with Sang Hongyang's policies mentioned above, which are typically collectivist as they focus on the interests of the state. Also, in discussions of agricultural problems, thinkers focused more on the whole peasant *class* rather than individuals.

"Benevolence and righteousness outweighing benefit"

Views on the relative importance of benevolence, righteousness and benefit were a focus of discussion in the pre-Qin period. Unlike Confucius, who is represented as someone who valued "benevolence and righteousness" over "benefit" (personal gain), Mencius did not completely abandon "benefit" and could even make it a priority in some cases.[65] Meanwhile, there were thinkers who advocated combinations of benevolence, righteousness *and* benefit, such as "benevolence and righteousness is benefit" and "loving each other and benefiting each other", as Mozi did.[66] However, Dong Zhongshu pushed the principle of justice outweighing benefit to an extreme, as in "one does anything for upholding justice instead of pursuing personal interest".[67] And the critics of Sang Hongyang in the *Discourses on Salt and Iron* took a similar position:

the Son of Heaven should not speak about *much and little*, the feudal lords should not talk about *advantage and detriment*, ministers about *gain and loss*, but they should cultivate benevolence and righteousness, to set an example to the people, and extend wide their virtuous conduct to gain the people's confidence. Then will nearby folk lovingly flock to them and distant peoples joyfully submit to their authority.[68]

"Emphasising *ben* and restraining *mo*"

In the pre-Qin period, the thought of "emphasising *ben*" (agriculture and sericulture) was commonplace, reflecting the widely held belief that agriculture is the foundation of the state. But no consensus was reached on "restraining *mo*" (the so-called secondary activities of manufacturing and commerce). It was during the Warring States period that the thought of "restraining *mo*" became more prominent. With respect to handicraft industry, Li Kui[69] argued, "if it is not banned by the government, then it will lead to a poor country".[70] Shang Yang asserted, "those who can devote themselves to agriculture and abandon commerce will get rich",[71] thus endorsing the view that only farming could bring material benefits. Later, Han Fei expanded the scope of *mo* to include handicrafts, commerce and wandering scholars and condemned all such activities. More importantly, he was the first to put forward the slogan "agriculture is *ben*, handicrafts and commerce are *mo*".[72] However, this view had not become part of the orthodoxy in the pre-Qin period, and the affirmation of the role of handicraft and commerce coexisted with ideas about restraining handicrafts and commerce in the early Han Dynasty. For example, Jia Yi called for "driving the common people to return to farmlands and be engaged in farming"[73] on the basis of "viewing agriculture as *ben* and handicraft and commerce as *mo*".[74] Later, however, Sang Hongyang designed a series of financial management policies using commercial techniques, such as the equitable distribution and price equalisation systems mentioned above. In the salt and iron meeting, Literati and Worthies greatly consolidated the principle of emphasising agriculture and restraining commerce, insisting that food, clothing and farming were all that was needed to "enrich a country and secure people",[75] while handicraft and commerce might harm agriculture. Finally, those advocating restraints on handicraft and commerce were triumphant over Sang Hongyang, marking an important turning point in mainstream ideology in dealing with the relationship between agriculture, handicrafts and commerce. Thereafter, most thinkers in ancient China held the viewpoint of emphasising agriculture and restraining handicrafts and commerce. Even after industry and commerce became developed in early modern times, most people continued to adhere to that viewpoint.[76]

At the same time, dissenting voices continued to be heard. Wang Fu[77] proposed "keeping a balance between agriculture, handicrafts and commerce" and objected to agriculture overweighing commerce; for him, "of all industries, useful goods are *ben* while rare and cunning goods are *mo*".[78] According to Wang, some handicrafts must be considered *ben* if the outputs count as "useful goods". This amounted to one of the first recorded defences of handicrafts in ancient Chinese economic thought.

Emphasis on frugality and accumulation

In the pre-Qin period, many thinkers supported frugality as against extravagance but disagreed on standards of frugality.[79] One notable exception is the chapter *Chi Mi* ("On Extravagance") in *Guanzi*, in which "extravagance" is advocated as a means of stimulating economic activity and increasing employment. Therefore, in respect of extravagance and thrift, it could be said that early Chinese economic thought was somewhat diversified. However, from the time of the Qin and Han Dynasties onward, "opposing extravagance and advocating frugality" became an established principle for promoting economic development.

Reducing inequality

Although most pre-Qin scholars tended to advocate an equitable treatment in distribution, involving a reduction in inequality, there were some notable exceptions. Thus, Xunzi held that inequalities of wealth and status were essential to the maintenance of an ordered, stable society,[80] and Han Fei believed that inequality was merely the inevitable result of differences in the propensities to extravagance and hard work between individuals.[81] For most writers, however, narrowing the gap between rich and poor was regarded as not only morally desirable but also conducive to social and economic stability.

Principal objects of enquiry

Economic thought in ancient China was mainly addressed and related to the following areas: justice and benefit; *ben* and *mo*; currency and finance; land; governance; commercial trade; price and value; (division of) labour; production, consumption, circulation and distribution; population; and miscellaneous other areas, including philosophical concerns. In Figure 2.1, we indicate the relative importance of the different subject areas both within and between different periods.

Figure 2.1 shows that the pre-Qin period witnessed a large and roughly equal number of discussions on all themes. In the Qin and Han Dynasties, there were some changes in the attention of scholars: they paid less attention to issues of justice and benefit, price and value, (division of) labour and circulation; and they began to concern themselves more with issues of land and currency. With respect to finance and governance, roughly the same attention was paid in both periods. Thereafter, land, currency, finance and governance became the objects of attention over successive dynasties. Even in the Ming and Qing Dynasties, with the development of capitalist industry and commerce, great attention continued to be paid to those same four areas.

The marked increase of interest in land and currency issues in the Qin and Han Dynasties is striking. Although the pre-Qin period witnessed changes in agrarian

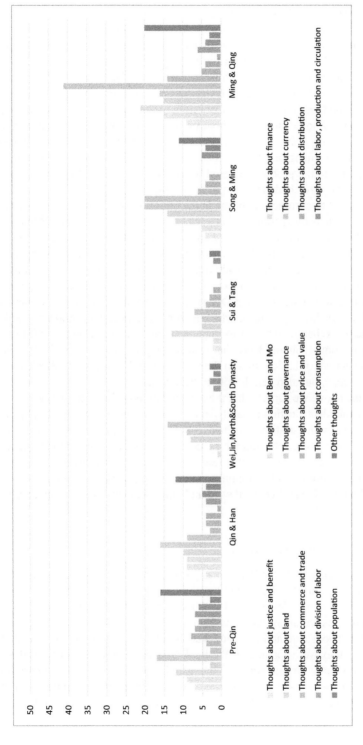

Figure 2.1 Classified statistics of economic thought in Ancient China by content and quantity[82]

Sources: Hu Jichuang (1998a–c) and Zhao Jing (ed.) (1991–1998).

institutions and relationships,[83] these found relatively little expression in the realm of ideas. Such ideas as were expressed at this time included "all lands under the Heaven are owned by the emperor",[84] Mencius's *jing*-field thought and Shang Yang's policy of "abolishing the *jing*-field system and removing the footpaths between fields",[85] which involved the transition from public to private ownership. In addition, there was some discussion of population density with respect to land area.[86] In the Qin and Han Dynasties, however, the attention paid to land issues increased, in particular to the question of land allocation. So, for example, we have Dong Zhongshu's ideas about limiting private land and restraining land annexation; Wang Mang's "King's land system" and his support of the *jing* system; and Zhong Changtong's ideas about "officially-owned land", each representing a response to the problems caused by the demand to own land on the part of the rich and the wretched condition of the peasantry.[87]

With respect to currency, attention in the pre-Qin period focused on theoretical principles, such as the distinction between "light" and "heavy" coins.[88] In the Qin and Han Dynasties, attention focused more on monetary policies and the stability of the monetary system, as with Jia Yi's advocacy of monopoly in mintage, Sang Hongyang's and Jia Shan's ideas about currency unification and their opposition to private coinage, Yu Gong's theory of abolishing currency and Wang Mang's currency reform.[89] After the Han Dynasty, scholarly discussion of currency centred mainly on three questions: whether to replace coin with grain and silk as the media of exchange, whether to implement coin depreciation and whether the central government should have the exclusive right to coin money.[90] Therefore, the establishment of basic issues in the Qin and Han Dynasties involved not only the rough scope, but also details within the scope.

From the above we can see that the consolidation of dynastic rule was accompanied by the identification of land and currency systems as necessary objects of enquiry along with questions of finance and economic governance. At the same time, economic philosophy and ethics, consumption, division of labour and even *ben* and *mo* received significantly less attention in later dynasties, not so much because they were considered unimportant, but because the positions taken had come to be regarded as "received wisdom": there was considered little more to be said on these topics.

Application of economic thought

A further development in the Han Dynasty was the application of economic thought in the formulation of policy. This development has been widely recognised.[91] Interestingly, a similar development took place in Europe, hence the description of Rome as the "executor" of thoughts from ancient Greece.[92]

Thoughts about land and currency were among the first to be implemented as policies, but they were not the last. The book *Guanzi* contained not only the thought of "state monopoly in salt and iron" but also the "Light and Heavy" theory (*qing zhong zhi fa*), which systematically explored exchange value (comparison relations between currency and all other goods, grain and all other goods and currency and grain), advocated state monopoly of important natural resources and developed a complete theoretical system.[93] All these ideas were used to frame practical policies. Sang Hongyang held that "if people are prohibited to freely exploit and utilise resources such as mountains and seas, they will not have chances of fighting each other for benefits".[94] So, in the case of salt, the government organised people to produce and provided them with tools; it then purchased the salt, which was transported and sold by officials at a higher price, thus creating a monopoly in circulation. As for iron, the state created a monopoly both for mining and casting (using conscripted labour) and for distribution (either through sale or hire).[95] Sang Hongyang also applied the "Light and Heavy" theory in the equitable distribution and price equalisation systems. These applications of *Guanzi* thought by Sang Hongyang were later adopted by Wang Mang in his "six measures of economic control",[96] and were also followed by reformers in later times, as with Wang Anshi's equitable distribution system.[97]

The transition from ideas to policies is also evident in other areas. For example, early in the Han Dynasty, Emperor Gaozu "issued an order forbidding merchants to wear silk or ride in carriages, and increased the taxes that they were obliged to pay in order to hamper and humiliate them",[98] the aim being to discourage "secondary" activities and promote agriculture. Likewise, the salt and iron monopolies further restricted the scope for (private) enterprise, and similar measures were commonly adopted in later dynasties.[99]

Development of economic thought

Economic thought in the Han Dynasty developed as follows. First, there were debates about *laissez-faire*[100] versus government intervention. In the pre-Qin period, the issue of national and economic governance was discussed by thinkers with varying viewpoints, but without direct confrontation.[101] In the Qin and Han Dynasties, many thoughts developed under the discussion framework of *laissez-faire* or government intervention: the thought advocating free economy had a definite viewpoint and policy proposal at that time, such as "When he acts with non-assertion there is nothing ungoverned"[102] and "giving people peace and security".[103] The thought objecting to "scrambling for benefit against the common people"[104] was also developed. For example, Dong Zhongshu censured the privileged class for "having enjoyed major benefits but not letting go of minor ones".[105] Later, "scrambling for benefit against the common people" became a main argument of "Xian Liang" and "Wen Xue" in criticising Sang Hongyang. It appears that the thought of *laissez-faire* in the Han Dynasty had included the connotation requiring government to minimise interference in economic activity, on the basis of which a complete theory of economic governance was developed, as with Sima Qian's "*Shanyin* (Following Natural Tendency) Thought". Thus, having affirmed people's natural instinct to pursue riches, Sima Qian added,

> Each man has only to be left to utilise his own abilities and exert his strength to obtain what he wishes. . . . When each person works away at his own

occupation and delights in his own business then, like water flowing downward, goods will naturally flow forth . . . and the people will produce commodities without having been asked.[106]

He had therefore prepared a solid theoretical foundation for *laissez-faire* thought.[107]

Thought advocating state intervention also underwent great development, with the "Light and Heavy" theory as the theoretical core. This kind of thought also existed in the pre-Qin period. For example, Shan Qi,[108] when expounding currency–commodity relations, advanced the concepts of light and heavy, small and large and zi and mu;[109] and Fan Li[110] and Li Kui proposed grain stabilisation by sale and purchase measures. However, these thoughts were not as rich and systematic as the treatment in *Guanzi*, where it is clear that they provide the basis for a range of interventionist measures with the aim of increasing state revenues. Indeed some scholars maintain that the "Light and Heavy" doctrine was developed in direct opposition to *Shanyin* thought.[111]

Ideas were also developed during the Han in response to new practical problems. Such was the case with land management policy at the frontiers, where large numbers of troops were garrisoned to repel nomadic incursions. Policies were put forward to recruit farmers, or deploy troops, to reclaim state-owned land so as to achieve the twin objectives of developing agricultural production and strengthening frontier defences.[112] The *Chao Cuo, Book of Han* and the *Treatise on Food and Money* recorded various ideas relating to the garrisoning which became models for later generations who faced similar problems.

The Ever-normal Granary is another example of new thought in the Han Dynasty. As mentioned above, the idea of applying supply–demand relationships and law of price to regulating the price of grain had occurred in the pre-Qin period, as with Fan Li's "*Ping Di*" and Li Kui's "*Ping Tiao*". The ideas behind the Ever-normal Granaries were similar in terms of basic principles, but the emphasis differed. Fan Li held that, "in terms of grain price, when it is 20 coins per Dou, farmers' interests will be hurt; if it is 90 coins per Dou, businessmen will be weakened",[113] so he wanted to design a system to keep price at a normal level and protect both agriculture and commerce. Li Kui proposed that government should purchase surplus grain in bumper harvest years and sell in lean years, so as to protect the people "and encourage farmers to work harder".[114] However, the core idea behind Geng Shouchang's Ever-normal Granary was "increasing purchase of grain when it is cheap" and "decreasing purchase of grain when it is expensive",[115] both to stabilise the grain price and regulate grain supply[116] In fact, it was only in the Eastern Han Dynasty that the Ever-normal Granary became an institutional reality.

Ideas concerning water transport are another example. Water transport played an important role in national finance and material supply as being the main way to transport tribute in ancient times. Since the Qin and Han Dynasties, China established the integrated water transport system for the first time and developed a complete set of methods in canal digging, maintenance and management in tribute collection and distribution. Although not expounded formally in scholars' writings, ideas relating to the system were recorded in many decrees and annals of local history.[117]

Conclusion: historical influence of economic thought in the Han Dynasty

The importance of economic thought in the Han Dynasty is not simply a matter of its originality; it is at least as much a reflection of the influence it came to exert on later generations. The "grand unification" of economic thought in the Han was the starting point for later Chinese economic thought. As we have shown, the "grand unification" was the outcome of a tortuous process from "contention of different thoughts" to "one school emerging as the dominant school of thought" which absorbed, remodelled, developed and applied a synthesis of pre-Qin thought. The body of thought that emerged emphasised collectivism over individualism, justice over benefit and agriculture over commerce; it also opposed extravagance, advocated frugality and emphasised equitable distribution. The unified system highlighted issues of land, currency, finance and governance as basic topics, turned many thoughts discussed in the pre-Qin period into policies, deepened original thoughts and developed new ideas.

However, economic thought inherited from the Han Dynasty did have certain negative consequences. Once it had become accepted as the privileged economic discourse or "paradigm", it placed limits on the scope of economic analysis and became a barrier to the development of new economic thought. It was not until the late Qing Dynasty, when China witnessed "great social changes unprecedented over the past 3,000 years",[118] that the conditions were created for revolutionary changes in the subject area.

Notes

* The authors wish to thank the China National Social Science Foundation for funding the project "On the Status and Value of Traditional Chinese Economic Thought" (17AJL006), from which this paper originated.
1 "Economic thought" in this chapter refers to people's thinking on economic issues which is expressed in writings, biography and economic policy, the latter regarded by us as the institutionalisation of thought.
2 Economic thought of scholars in pre-Qin times is a focus of research in monographs on history of economic thought in modern China. See Ye Shichang (2003), pp. 1–7 and Cheng Lin (2004), pp. 139–148. In modern times, 322 papers on history of economic thought in ancient China have been published, including 187 on the pre-Qin to Western Han period, accounting for 56.3% of the total. See Cheng Lin and Bi Yanfeng (2008), pp. 26–38. In respect of research on individuals, there are 88 articles on figures including Confucius, Mencius, Mozi, Zhuangzi, Shang Yang and Li Kui, accounting for 28.6% of the total, second only to the number of articles on the thought of persons in modern times. See Zhu Hongxiang and Sun Wei (2009), pp. 30–33. For research topics in modern times, see Zhang Yaguang (2009), pp. 16–23.
3 Tang Qingzeng (1902–1972) studied at the Universities of Michigan and Harvard and was Professor at Fudan University after 1949.
4 Tang Qingzeng (1936), p. 8.
5 Hu Jichuang (1903–1993), a scholar of economics and the history of economic thought. He studied at LSE and held positions at Shanghai University of Finance and Economics. He was also President of the Association of History of Chinese Economic Thought and is regarded as the founder of the discipline of the history of Chinese

economic thought. His major works include *History of Chinese Economic Thought* vols. 1–3 (Shanghai: People's Publishing House, 1962, 1978, 1981).

6 Hu Jichuang (1998a), p. 508.

7 Wu Baosan (1905–1999) studied at Harvard University. He held positions including Director of the Institute of Economics in the Chinese Academy of Social Sciences and Vice-President and Honorary President of the Association of the History of Chinese Economic Thought. His edition of *National Income of China in 1933* (Beijing: Zhong Hua Book Company, 1947) was the first academic work of its type.

8 Wu Baosan (1996), p. 21.

9 Only 94 relevant papers on the Western Han Dynasty to the eve of the Opium War were published in modern times, about half of those on the pre-Qin period. See Cheng Lin and Bi Yanfeng (2008), pp. 26–38. Only 41 articles on individuals were published, accounting for 13.3% of total of such articles published in modern times and less than half of those on the pre-Qin period. See Zhu Hongxiang and Sun Wei (2009), pp. 30–33.

10 Wu Shenyuan (1984), pp. 26–29.

11 Gan Naiguang (1897–1956), scholar and diplomat. His work *History of Economic Thought in the Pre-Qin Period* (Shanghai: Commercial Press, 1926) is regarded as the first systemic research on history of Chinese economic thought. See Ye Tan (2013), pp. 131–141.

12 Gan Naiguang (1926), pp. 7–8.

13 Tang Qingzeng (1936), p. 8.

14 Hu Jichuang (1998b), p. 508.

15 Hu Jichuang. Ibid., p. 497.

16 Zhao Jing (1912–2007), Professor of Economics at Beijing University and President of the Association of History of Chinese Economic Thought. Major works include *History of Chinese Economic Thought in Modern Times* vols. 1–3, co-authored with Yi Menghong (Beijing: The Chinese Publishing House, 1964, 1965, 1966); and *History of Modern Chinese Economic Thought* vols. 1–4 (Beijing: Beijing University Press, 1991–1998). These works are regarded as among the three path-breaking works in the history of Chinese economic thought field, the others being the publications of Hu Jichuang and Ye Shichang.

17 "Conservative" here means lacking in criticism, creativity and diversity. See Zhao Jing (1991), p. 660.

18 Wu (1990), pp. 64–67.

19 Ye Shichang (1929–), Professor of Economics at Fudan University and Director of the Association of History of Chinese Economic Thought. Major works include *A Concise History of Chinese Economic Thought* vols. 1–3 (Shanghai: Shanghai People's Publishing House, 1978–1993) and *A General Financial History of China* (Beijing: China Finance Publishing House, 2002).

20 Ye (2003), p. 118.

21 "A hundred schools of thought" is the expression used to indicate a multiplicity of schools and is not intended literally. The principal schools include the Confucian, the Legalist, the Daoist, Mo Di and his school, the Agriculturalist school, as well as ideas associated with particular individuals such as Bai Gui, Shan Qi and Fan Li.

22 Zhao Jing (1991), pp. 642–647.

23 Another expression is "feudalist orthodox economic thought". See ibid., pp. 664–673.

24 A government decree in the Qin Dynasty suggested by the then-chancellor Li Si (284–208 BCE), which called for the incineration of all books except *Records of the Qin Dynasty* and reference books such as medical books and agronomic books. Li Si also called for the extermination of Confucian scholars.

25 "The Burning Book Decree", ibid.

26 Legalists believed that the essence of human nature was to seek personal benefit and avoid harm. They favoured a bureaucratic system of governance in which behaviour was strictly controlled and channelled for the benefit of the State by a rigid framework of laws backed by severe punishments.

27 As Lü Buwei put it, "Lao Dan values softness, Confucius advocates benevolence, Mo Di advocates austerity, Yin Xi advocates peace and quiet, Lie Zi advocates emptiness, Chen Pian advocates equality, Yang Sheng advocates self, Sun Bin advocates power, Wang Liao advocates taking the first-mover advantage, while Ni Liang advocates taking the second-mover advantage; therefore, if each sticks to his own opinions, it is difficult to govern a state". *On Insight and Governance of Mister Lü's Spring and Autumn Annals.*

28 "Basic Annals of the First Emperor of Qin", *Shiji* 6.

29 Huang-Lao thought is one of the Daoist schools, purportedly established by Huang Di (also called the Yellow Emperor) and Laozi (the fabled author of the *Daodejing*).

30 "Treatise on Food and Money", *Han shu (Book of Han)* (I).

31 Lu Jia (ca. 240–170 BCE), ideologue, statesman and diplomat during the Western Han period. "Annals of Emperor Gaozu", *Han shu (Book of Han)*.

32 Lu Jia believed, "The explanations that farming and sericulture are about traveling in mountains and seas to fish pearls, hunt animals, mine jade and enjoy springs, so as to please their ears and eyes and satisfy their desires for luxury, is wrong". This indicates to some extent his emphasis on basic agriculture. The sentence is quoted from Lu Jia's *Xin Yu.*

33 The most basic characteristic of the Confucian school is that they prioritised ethics and advocated the administration of the nation by '*Li*' (moral conventions or "rites").

34 Some scholars insist that Lu Jia *was* a Confucian. See Ma Tao (2002), pp. 14–19.

35 Jia Yi (200–168 BCE), statesman during the Western Han period.

36 Hou (1957), p. 66.

37 "Treatise on Food and Money", *Han shu (Book of Han)* (II).

38 "Treatise on Food and Money", *Han shu (Book of Han)* (I).

39 Dong Zhongshu (179–104 BCE) was an ideologue, statesman and philosopher during the Western Han.

40 Sima Qian (145–90 BCE), historian and author of the *Shiji (Records of the Grand Historian)*.

41 Dong claimed that "benevolence refers to love for people, not love for self; while justice and righteousness refers to making oneself upright, not making people upright". See "The Standard of Selflessness and Right", *Chunqiu fanlu "Luxuriant Dew of the Spring and Autumn"*.

42 "Thus, the emperor should act on the orders of the Heaven to obey destiny, humanise all peoples to form humanity, make proper laws and distinguish the upper class from the lower one to kill desires. If all the three can be done, it will be a great achievement". See "Dong Zhongshu", *Han shu (Book of Han)*.

43 "Treatise on Food and Money", *Han shu (Book of Han)* (I).

44 See Sun Jingtan (1993), pp. 102–112. Guan Huailun (1994), pp. 13–18. Zhuang Chunbo (2000), pp. 59–71.

45 Hu (1998b), p. 547.

46 "The Biographies of the Money-makers", *Shiji* 129.

47 For example, Sima Qian believed that it was natural that the poor were driven by the rich, and he did not deny the saying that "all the common people will behave humbly before those whose wealth is ten times more than theirs, be fearful of those whose wealth is a hundred times more than theirs, be enslaved to those whose wealth is a thousand times more than theirs, and become slaves of those whose wealth is ten thousand times more than theirs; this is a common sense". See "The Biographies of the Money-makers", *Shiji* 129.

48 That is, the book *Guanzi,* not the historical figure. This chapter will refer several times to one section of *Guanzi, Light and Heavy. Guanzi* is controversial in terms of the time of completion. Hu Jichuang thought that completion was in the Warring States period, but more scholars favour a Han Dynasty dating. Guo Moruo claimed in his *Corrections and Supplements to Guan Zi* that all articles in the *Light and Heavy* section were completed in the Emperor Wen and Jing periods; Luo Genze's

Research and Exploration of Thinkers in Pre-Qin Period: Origin of Guan Zi argued that it was completed at the time of Emperors Wu and Zhao in the Western Han; Ma Feibai held that it was completed in the Xin Dynasty ruled by Wang Mang (*New Annotations to the Light and Heavy in Guan Zi*); while Shi Shiqi et al. favour a Western Han dating, but believe that evidence is wanting for a more precise attribution. See Shi Shiqi and Chen Weimin (1982), pp. 299–318. Meanwhile, Rickett suggests that the last seven chapters of the *Light and Heavy* section may be somewhat later than the others, for which an early or middle Han dating is given. See Rickett, W.A. (1988), p. 357.

49 Hu (1998b), p. 76.
50 Equitable distribution refers to the system whereby tributes – other than those that were valuable and necessary to the capital city – were not to be sent to the capital but should be converted into cheap and available local products customarily bought by the merchants of other districts. The local officer in charge of the system might then transport the products to a district where their prices were high and resell them there. All the disadvantages of direct transportation of the tribute to the capital were thus avoided while the officer of the system would finally acquire considerable profit. The aim of price equalisation systems was to stabilise the prices of commodities in the capital city. To achieve that aim, the operation had command over a tremendous quantity of commodities, the means of transportation and a great number of labourers. When the price of a commodity rose, the operation would flood the market with the same commodity, already in hand, at a lower price. When the price of a commodity fell, the operation would buy it. See Hu Jichuang (2009), pp. 269–270.
51 Li Geng, *Discourses on Salt and Iron*.
52 "The Treatise on the Balanced Standard", *Shiji* 30.
53 "Annals of Emperor Zhao", *Han shu* (*Book of Han*).
54 Xian Liang is an honourable title officially granted to those selected and recommended by a local government as men of good behaviour and ability, and Wen Xue is an ordinary title for an established scholar. Both groups are Confucians.
55 The three orthodox economic thoughts are "benevolence and righteousness outweighing benefit", "agriculture overweighing commerce and handicrafts" and "emphasising frugality and accumulation while rejecting extravagance". See Zhao Jing (1991), p. 671 and Zhu Yong (1999), pp. 151–154.
56 Here "emphasis on individual interest" means that the individual interest is prioritised over the collective, whereas "emphasis on collective interest" means that the collective interest may be furthered regardless of the interests of particular individuals.
57 "Yang Zhu", *Collection of Works of Liezi*.
58 Shen Dao (390–315 BCE), considered to be one of the founders of Legalism.
59 "Conforming to Law and Nature", *Shenzi,*.
60 "Shu Er" (Chapter 7), *The Analects of Confucius,*.
61 Zhong (2013), pp. 126–137.
62 "Weakening People", *The Book of Lord Shang*.
63 "The Biographies of the Money-makers", *Shiji* 129.
64 "Three principles" include the King being superior his officials, a father being superior to his son and husband being superior to his wife. "Five virtues" include benevolence, righteousness, propriety, wisdom and honesty.
65 On the comparison of importance between benefits and rites, Mencius said that "when getting food is of primary importance and observation of rites of minor importance, after weighing the relative importance of each, why not give preference to getting food?" (*Mencius, Gao Zi* II, Book 6B). See also Hu Jichuang (1998a), p. 230.]
66 *Mozi* (*Master Mo*), "Fa Yi" ("Standards and Rules", Chapter 4) and "Geng Zhu" (Chapter 46).
67 "Treatise on Dong Zhongshu", *Han shu* (*Book of Han*).

68 "Basic Topics", *Discourses on Salt and Iron.*
69 Li Kui (455–395 BCE), statesman and Legalist scholar during the Warring States period.
70 *Of Governance, a Collection of Historical Events and Stories.*
71 "Yi Yan", *The Book of Lord Shang.*
72 Han Fei believed that "the reason why granaries are full is that farming is regarded as the dominant profession, but now those engaged in non-essential professions such as textile, embroidery and carving are rich". See *Han Feizi*, "Of Rulers".
73 "Treatise on Food and Money", *Book of Han* (I).
74 "The Biographies of the Money-makers", *Shiji* 129.
75 "On Commercial Policies", *Discourses on Salt and Iron,.*
76 Tan (1985), pp. 113–119.
77 Wang Fu (85–163 CE), publicist, writer and ideologue in the Eastern Han period.
78 *Centring on the Fundamental, Qianfu's Theory.*
79 Zhao Jing (1991), p. 679.
80 "Governance Rules and Systems", *Xunzi.*
81 "The Most Famous Schools", *Han Feizi,.*
82 In respect of the statistical approach, economic thought as defined by the above-mentioned classification is included, but no allowance is made for the perceived "richness" or "merit" of a contribution. Hence, the statistics mainly indicate the trend of discussion and concerns of economic thought in different periods, with no adjustment for "quality", however that might be defined.
83 See Wang Fang (2005).
84 "Lesser Court Hymns", *The Book of Songs.*
85 "History of State of Zhou (II)", *Zizhi Tongjian.*
86 For example, Shang Yang found that the Qin State was "a vast territory with a sparse population" while the neighbouring state was "a small territory with a surplus population". He therefore suggested that Qin should attract people from its neighbouring state.
87 Tao (2000), pp. 14–15.
88 "In ancient times, when meeting natural disaster, government always made statistics of properties and goods and weighed value of currency so as to provide the victims with better disaster relief. If the common people complain of light coins but heavy goods and large coins are therefore cast, then small coins ("zi") are circulated together with large ones ("mu") to benefit the common people. If they complain of heavy coins but light goods and thus small coins are cast in large quantity for circulation, and at the same time large coins are not abolished, so large coins ("mu") are circulated together with small ones ("zi"). In this way, regardless of small or large coins, the common people will not feel they suffer losses". See "State of Zhou (B)", *History and Affairs of Warring States.*
89 Wang Mang implemented four currency reforms in 8, 9, 10 and 14 CE. The main idea of the first three reforms was to change the monetary standard in order to make money of small value replace big value coins, or "light" money to replace the "heavy". The last reform was to amend the earlier measures.
90 Zhang Jiaxiang (ed.) (2001), p. 10.
91 See, for example, Tang Qingzeng (1936), p. 8.
92 See Haney (1949), p. 73 and Bell (1953), p. 45.
93 Ye (1965), pp. 56–61.
94 *Discourses on Salt and Iron*, "Preventing Farmland Affairs",
95 Zhou (1981), p. 110.
96 The government monopoly of salt, iron and alcohol; change of the monetary standard; state control of mountain and water resources; and government-operated money-lending.
97 Wang Anshi (1021–1086 CE), celebrated scholar and statesman of the Northern Song Dynasty. The principle of his equitable distribution system was the same as Sang's although the practical details were a little different.

98 *Shiji* 30, "The Treatise on the Balanced Standard".
99 Ma Bohuang (ed.) (1993), pp. 508–511, 515.
100 *"Laissez-faire"* refers in this chapter to propositions that oppose the interference of the government and advocate more a liberal economic policy.
101 But some scholars pointed out that two kinds of macro-economy management principles had been formed in the Warring States period, one of which is the principle emphasising centralisation represented by Shang Yang, and the other is the principle of *laissez-faire* advocating benevolent governance represented by Mencius. He Liancheng (1991), pp. 113–124.
102 *Daodejing.*
103 "Annals of Emperor Zhao", *Han shu* (*Book of Han*).
104 "Scrambling for benefit against the common people" refers to two phenomena, the first that government rakes in market gains by right of privilege, the second that government directly participates in economic affairs. See Zhong Xiangcai (2005), pp. 96–105.
105 "Dong Zhongshu", *Han shu* (*Book of Han*).
106 "The Biographies of the Money-makers", *Shiji* 129.
107 Leslie Young (1996) held that Adam Smith's "Invisible Hand" and Sima Qian's *Shanyin* Thought share a common philosophical foundation as a general and spontaneous natural order, and that they both arrived at a similar position in opposing government intervention. According to Young, however, Sima Qian's viewpoint was richer since he linked the "invisible hand" explicitly to the price mechanism. For a quite different opinion see Chiu and Yeh (1999), pp. 79–84.
108 Shan Qi was a statesman in the Spring and Autumn Period who probably lived in the first half of the sixth century BCE.
109 See above p. 10 n. 88.
110 Fan Li (536–448 BCE), statesman and businessman during the Spring and Autumn Period.
111 Chen (1997), p. 300.
112 Ma Bohuang (ed.) (1993), p. 129.
113 "Biographies of the Money-makers", *Shiji* 129,.
114 "Treatise on Food and Money" (I), *Han shu* (*Book of Han*).
115 Ibid.
116 For more detailed analysis, see Hu Jichuang (1998b), p. 130.
117 Guo (2009), pp. 48–52.
118 Li Hongzhang. [1872] (2008), p. 107.

References

Bell, John Fred (1953). *A History of Economic Thought*. New York: The Ronald Press Company.
Chen Huan-Chang (1911). *The Economic Principles of Confucius and His School*. New York: Columbia University.
Chen Shigai (1997). *Thoughts in Ancient China and Modern Business Management*. Dalian: Dongbei University of Finance and Economics Press.
Cheng Lin (2004). "Research on History of Chinese Economic Thought in the 20th Century: A Survey Mainly on Academic Works". *Research in Chinese Economic History*, (4).
Cheng Lin and Bi Yanfeng (2008). "The Academic Achievements and Historical Position of History of Chinese Economic Thought in the Preliminary Period". *Journal of Finance and Economics*, (10).
Chiu, Y.-S. and Yeh, R.S. (1999). "Adam Smith versus Sima Qian: Comment on the Tao of Markets". *Pacific Economic Review*, 4(1).

Gan Naiguang (1926). *History of Economic Thought in the Pre-Qin Period*. Shanghai: Commercial Press.

Guan Huailun (1994). "Emperor Wu of Han 'Banning a Hundred Schools of Thought and Respecting Only Confucianism' Actually Happened: Upon Discussion with Comrade Sun Jingtan". *Social Sciences in Nanjing*, (6).

Guo Yang (2009). *Departure and Integration of Publicness and Marketability: Economic Exploration of the Thought of Water Transport System in Ancient China*. Shanghai: Shanghai People's Publishing House.

Han Fuzhi (1969). *Economic Thought in the Western and Eastern Han Dynasties*. Taibei: The Commercial Press, Ltd.

Haney, Lewis H. (1949). *History of Economic Thought*, Fourth and Enlarged Edition. New York: The Macmillan Company.

He Liancheng (1991). "Economic Management Thoughts in Ancient China and Macro-Economy Management in China". *Economist*, (6).

History of Economic Thought Study Group, Institute of Economics, Shanghai Academy of Social Sciences (1989). *History of Economic Thought in the Qin and Han Dynasties*. Beijing: Beijing Publishing House.

Hou Wailu (1957). *The General History of Chinese Thought*, Vol. 2. Beijing: People's Publishing House.

Hu Jichuang (1998a). *History of Chinese Economic Thought (I)*. Shanghai: Shanghai University of Finance and Economics Press.

Hu Jichuang (1998b). *History of Chinese Economic Thought (II)*. Shanghai: Shanghai University of Finance and Economics Press.

Hu Jichuang (1998c). *History of Chinese Economic Thought (III)*. Shanghai: Shanghai University of Finance and Economics Press.

Hu Jichuang (2009). *A Concise History of Chinese Economic Thought*. Beijing: Foreign Languages Press.

Li Hongzhang [1872]. "Reconsideration of Unadvisable Cancellation of Manufacturing Ships". In Gu, T. and Dai, Y. (eds.) (2008) *Li Hongzhang's Complete Works*, Vol. 5. Hefei: Anhui Publishing Group.

Ma Bohuang (ed.). (1993). *History of Chinese Thought on Economic Policy*. Yunnan: Yunnan People's Publishing House.

Ma Tao (2002). "On Economic Thought of Lu Jia and Their Effects on Economic Policies in the Early Han Dynasty". *World Economic Papers*, (3).

Rickett, W.A. (tr. ed.) (1988). *Guanzi*. Princeton, NJ: Princeton University Press.

Shi Shiqi and Chen Weimin (1982). "Preliminary Exploration of the Light and Heavy Theory in Guanzi". In Wu, B. and Chen, Z. (eds.) *Collection of Theses on the History of Economic Thought*. Beijing: Peking University Press.

Sun Jingtan (1993). "The Non-Existent 'Banning a Hundred Schools of Thought and Respecting Only Confucianism' by Emperor Wu of Han: A Basic Error in Reflection on Confucianism in Modern and Contemporary China". *Social Sciences in Nanjing*, (6).

Tan Min (1985). "Historical Evolution of the Thought of the Agricultural Foundation". *Quarterly Journal of Shanghai Academy of Social Sciences*, (4).

Tang Qingzeng (1936). *History of Chinese Economic Thought (I)*. Beijing: Commercial Press.

Tao Yitao (2000). *Review of Economic Thought in Ancient China*. Beijing: China Economic Publishing House.

Wang Fang (2005). *The Relationship between the Ownership and the Use Rights of Rural Land in Ancient China: A Historical Study on Evolution of Institutional Thoughts*. Shanghai: Fudan University Press.

Wang Naicong, Zhang Hua and Zheng Zhenhua (1991). *Brief History of Economic Thought in the Pre-Qin Period and the Western and Eastern Han Dynasties*. Beijing: China Ocean Press.

Wu Baosan (1990). "Prospect of Research on History of Chinese Economic Thought". *Economic Research Journal*, (4).

Wu Baosan (1996). *History of Economic Thought in the Pre-Qin Period*. Beijing: China Social Sciences Press.

Wu Shenyuan (1984). "Review of Research on History of Chinese Economic Thought". *Journal of Fudan University (Social Sciences)*, (5).

Xie Tianyou (1989). *History of Economic Policies and Thoughts in the Qin and Han Dynasties: And on the Theory of Natural Economy*. Shanghai: East China Normal University Press.

Ye Shichang (1965). "On the *Light and Heavy, Guan Zi*". *Economic Research Journal*, (1).

Ye Shichang (2003). *History of Economic Thought in Ancient China*. Shanghai: Fudan University Press.

Ye Tan (2013). "An Investigation of Academic History of Chinese Economics: Discussion on the Origin, Development and Advantages of the Discipline of the History of Chinese Economic Thought". *Research in Chinese Economic History*, (12).

Young, Leslie (1996). "The Tao of Markets: Sima Qian and the Invisible Hand". *Pacific Economic Review*, 1(2).

Zhang Jiaxiang (ed.) (2001). *History of Monetary Thought of China (I)*. Hubei: Hubei People's Press.

Zhang Yaguang (2009). "The Development of the Discipline of History of Chinese Economic Thought over the 60 Years after the Foundation of the PRC". *Journal of Guizhou University of Finance and Economics*, (6).

Zhao Jing (1986). *Dogmatic Economic Thought in Ancient China*. Beijing: People's Publishing House.

Zhao Jing (ed.) (1991–1998). *History of Chinese Economic Thought (I–IV)*. Beijing: Peking University Press.

Zhong Xiangcai (2005). "On Thoughts Objecting to 'Scrambling for Benefit against the Common People' in the History of China". *Journal of Social Sciences*, (3).

Zhong Xiangcai (2013). "A Possible Pedigree of History of Economic Thought". *Journal of Social Sciences*, (9).

Zhou Bodi (1981). *The Fiscal History of China*. Shanghai: Shanghai People's Publishing House.

Zhu Hongxiang and Sun Wei (2009). "On Research on History of Chinese Economic Thought in the First Half of the 20th Century: A Survey based on Academic Papers". *Journal of Hubei University of Economics*, (4).

Zhu Yong (1999). "On the Content of Chinese Orthodox Economic Thoughts and Their Correlation". *Academic Journal of Zhongzhou*, (6).

Zhuang Chunbo (2000). "Research and Investigation into Emperor Wu of Han 'Banning a Hundred Schools of Thought and Respecting Only Confucianism'". *Confucius Studies*, (4).

3 Dong Zhongshu and Confucian economic thought as state ideology in the Western Han Dynasty

Zhong Xiangcai

In the Western Han Dynasty, the government implemented the policy of "reject-ing the other schools of thought and respecting only Confucianism" (罢黜百家, 独尊儒术), making Confucianism the official state ideology. This was a signifi-cant event in the history of Chinese economic thought. Though Confucianism had great social influence in the pre-Qin period, it was only one of several schools of thought. Not only were Confucius and Mencius sometimes not welcomed when they went out to preach their doctrines, but there was also the alleged "burning of books and burying of Confucian scholars" (焚书坑儒) by Emperor Qin Shihuang. The dramatic reversal of the position of Confucianism in the Western Han Dynasty is closely related to significant changes in Confucian economic thought itself on subjects including the Great Unity social ideal, the land system and industrial and commercial policy. Dong Zhongshu[1] played a very significant role in this change and a study of his economic thought will help us to understand the key points in the transformation.

The Great Unity

Liji, or the *Book of Rites*, possibly compiled at some point(s) between the end of the Warring States period and the early Han, first put forwarded the notion of "the Great Unity".[2] Thus:

> When the Grand course was pursued, a public and common spirit ruled all under the sky; they chose men of talents, virtue, and ability; their words were sincere, and what they cultivated was harmony. Thus men did not love their parents only, nor treat as children only their own sons. A competent provision was secured for the aged till their death, employment for the able-bodied, and the means of growing up to the young. They showed kindness and compas-sion to widows, orphans, childless men, and those who were disabled by disease, so that they were all sufficiently maintained. Males had their proper work, and females had their homes. (They accumulated) articles (of value), disliking that they should be thrown away upon the ground, but not wishing to keep them for their own gratification. (They laboured) with their strength, disliking that it should not be exerted, but not exerting it (only) with a view to

their own advantage. In this way (selfish) schemes were repressed and found no development. Robbers, filchers, and rebellious traitors did not show themselves, and hence the outer doors remained open, and were not shut. This was (the period of) what we call the Grand Union ["Great Unity"].[3]

There were many previous discussions along the lines of "Great Unity". For example, Mozi advocated "identification with the superior". In his opinion, before the state came into being, "the disorder in the human world could be compared to that among birds and beasts".[4] Therefore, "[Heaven] chose the virtuous, sagacious, and wise in the world and crowned him emperor [Son of Heaven]".[5] Once there was an emperor, other leaders could be selected from the top down and the people would all identify themselves with the Son of Heaven,[6] resulting in a unification of standards[7] and the achievement of good governance. These ideas are similar in spirit to choosing "men of talents, virtue and ability" in the "Great Unity".

Confucianism focused on the harmony of society: "to bring comfort to the old, to be of good faith, and to cherish the young".[8] Mencius pointed that

> old men without wives, old women without husbands, old people without children, young children without fathers – all these four types of people are most destitute and have no one to turn to for help. When King Wen put benevolent measures into effect, he always gave them first consideration.[9]

When Mencius proclaimed the excellence of the *jingtian* (or "*jing*"/well-field) system,[10] he said it can ensure that "those who belong to the same nine squares all render friendly offices to one another in their going out and coming in, aid one another in keeping watch, and sustain one another in sickness".[11] To achieve such good governance, an unavoidable question is how to have a virtuous and able ruler. There were various theories of human nature in the pre-Qin period. Confucius classified people (men) into two categories: gentlemen and petty persons. The differences between them were reflected in several ways. For example, "there are three things of which the superior man stands in awe. He stands in awe of the ordinances of Heaven. He stands in awe of great men. He stands in awe of the words of sages";[12] "the mind of the superior man is conversant with righteousness; the mind of the mean man is conversant with gain";[13] "the object of the superior man is truth. Food is not his object"; and "the superior man is anxious lest he should not get truth; he is not anxious lest poverty should come upon him".[14] About human nature, Confucius thought: "by nature, men are nearly alike; by practice, they come to be wide apart".[15] He also said: "There are only the wise of the highest class, and the stupid of the lowest class, who cannot be changed".[16]

Mencius believed that in the beginning, human nature is kind: "The tendency of man's nature to good is like the tendency of water to flow downwards".[17] Different environments result in different behaviour. For people to become gentlemen (*junzi*) depends on their unflagging efforts to follow the Way (*Dao*) of benevolence and righteousness (morality). As Mencius argued, "for the mouth to desire sweet tastes, the eye to desire beautiful colours, the ear to desire pleasant sounds, the nose to desire fragrant odours, and the four limbs to desire ease and rest – these things are natural"; but for gentlemen there is higher pursuit of life, because they have a special mission given by Heaven.[18]

Why is the gentleman different from ordinary people? Because he stands in awe of Heaven, has stronger self-discipline and is dedicated to the pursuit of benevolence and righteousness. For ordinary people, however, it is not only impossible but also unrequired of them to follow that elevated path. Mencius stressed:

> Heaven's plan in the production of mankind is this: that they who are first informed should instruct those who are later in being informed, and they who first apprehend principles should instruct those who are slower to do so. I am one of Heaven's people who have first apprehended; I will take these principles and instruct the people in them. If I do not instruct them, who will do so?[19]

There was much attention on such training and education in the pre-Qin Confucian literature.

The assumption about humanity proposed by the Confucian school in the pre-Qin period was objective and real. It provided a vision of the ideal personality, but without denying that humanity has its limitations. Hence, the so-called gentleman or real man was only a target of personal improvement. To reach that stage could require a lifetime and might not be achieved even by rulers. Therefore, it was not only beneficial but also necessary to scrutinise and even criticise the behaviour of rulers. The pre-Qin Confucian school revered the Mandate of Heaven; they placed both the monarch and the people under the divine majesty of Heaven and argued that the ruler, above all others, needed to be self-disciplined and virtuous. However, such assumptions about humanity were not consistent with the ideal of the Great Unity proposed by the Confucian scholars in the times of Qin and Han. Dong Zhongshu took up the responsibility to resolve this contradiction.

Dong Zhongshu classified humanity into three grades – the wise man, the average man and the petty man – and claimed that the political hierarchy in society was in conformity with the Mandate of Heaven. In his opinion,

> the emperor is appointed by the Mandate of Heaven. Therefore, the one who is called "Son of Heaven" should regard heaven as father and serve heaven with filial piety. Vassals should sincerely respect the Son of Heaven whom they serve. *Daifu* (the senior official) should be loyal and honest, making his goodness even larger than the righteousness held by ordinary men so he can instruct them. *Shi* (general officials) should supply services and the ordinary people are unwise and confused. . . . In this way, things comply with their names, and their names comply with heaven. Heaven and people become united as one. They are the same so share the same reason, interact to benefit each other, and agree with and thus accept each other, which is called the way of morality.[20]

In this structure, the supreme ruler, the "Son of Heaven", stands above the people; the humanity of his kind is perfect, while his responsibilities are to rule the country and instruct the people; for him alone, perfection meant that self-improvement and self-restraint were no longer required. Just as Dong Zhongshu said,

> the one who is greatly respected and made emperor by heaven must have done something that could not be done by the power of man, which is the sign of his appointment. The people under heaven submit to him with one heart as they submit to their parents, so the auspicious omen from heaven is invited by his sincerity.[21]

And:

> The humanity of the people created by heaven contains goodness, but the people cannot fulfil it, so heaven sets up the emperor to guide them, which is the Mandate of Heaven. The people are endowed by heaven with a nature that cannot fulfil goodness by itself and are educated by the emperor to cultivate their nature. The emperor bears the Mandate of Heaven and takes the responsibility for cultivating the nature of the people.[22]

Dong Zhongshu stressed that the above-mentioned differences within humanity, and the structure of governance, would never change; as he put it, "the fundamental principle comes from heaven, and so as long as heaven does not change, so too the fundamental principle will not change".[23]

In Dong Zhongshu's theory of the "divine rights of emperors", the wise men who were rulers, and the social elites, were invested from birth with extraordinary wisdom. Such a slight but important modification of the conceptualisation of humanity not only made the ideal of Great Unity, described in the *Book of Rites*, a possibility, but also provided support for state intervention from the perspectives of political philosophy and economic methodology. Individuals in society are now divided into two broad categories, those who are saints and those whose moral transformation is incomplete. Those in the latter class – the *xiao ren* or "little people", who form the bulk of society – are naturally subject to rule by *xian* (men of quality). By extension, the economy can and should be autocratic and centralised, guided by the decisions of a wise and altruistic policy-maker. Moreover, because it *is* so guided, the best possible outcome is *necessarily* secured for all: a legal system is not required to guarantee an individual's rights and responsibilities, and competition between individuals is unnecessary to the achievement of personal welfare (as determined by the ruler).

Dong Zhongshu had not only condensed the theoretical basis of the Confucian "Great Unity" but also created the conditions for the development of a holistic economic methodology. As mentioned above, because of their experience-based and unadorned view of human nature, pre-Qin Confucian scholars were cautious about economic intervention from government. According to Confucius, the gentleman "is economical in expenditure and displays love of others"; as he explained, "when the person in authority makes more beneficial to the people the things from which they naturally derive benefit; – is not this being beneficent without great expenditure?"[24] Similarly, when asked by King Hui to suggest ways of profiting the state of Liang, Mencius retorted, "What is the point of mentioning the word 'profit'?"[25] The government should not be doing things for the purpose of making profit; rather, it should be concerned with the economic interest of the people. So Mencius proposed that the ruler should ensure that people have "constant means of support" (meaning that they should be assured of their subsistence)[26] and, to that end, "make the taxes on them light".[27] Further:

> In the market-place, if goods are exempted when premises are taxed, and premises are exempted when the ground is taxed, then the traders throughout the Empire will be only too pleased to store their goods in your market-place. If there is inspection but no duty at the border stations, then the travellers throughout the Empire will be only too pleased to go by way of your roads.[28]

In these views we can see clearly the *laissez-faire* dimension to Confucian thought.

In contrast, Legalists advocated state intervention. Shang Yang argued: "The important thing in undertaking the administration of a country is to make the rich poor, and the poor rich. If that is effective, the country will be strong".[29] From his point of view, it is necessary to manage the economy to achieve the goal of a "strong state"; as he emphasised,

> if the profit disappears through one outlet only, the state will have no equal; if it disappear through two outlets, the state will have only half the profit; but if the profit disappears through ten outlets, the state will not be preserved.[30]

Pre-Qin Legalists, including Guan Zhong of the Qi State in the Spring and Autumn Period, and Shang Yang and Han Fei in the Warring States period, consistently supported state intervention and control of the economy. Their economic thought had traits of holism. That is, from a consideration of the overall interests of the country, they advocated the central allocation of wealth and resources in order to achieve rapid economic development. To an extent, this holistic approach did achieve results. Indeed, it was by following the Legalist strategy that Qin eventually succeeded in defeating its rivals and establishing a unified state.

In the Confucian economic thought of the pre-Qin period, especially from this quotation of the Confucius – "the superior man is affable, but not adulatory; the mean man is adulatory, but not affable"[31] – we can say that they tended be more individualistic and were wary of the risks of holism. Therefore, the "Great Unity" that appeared in *Liji* is likely to be a product of the political development in the end of the Warring States period or during the Qin and Han Dynasties. But it still had internal contradictions. This contradiction was solved by Dong Zhongshu's introduction of theology into the theory of human nature. In his view, the highest governor was the recipient of the Mandate of Heaven and had no defects. It was therefore safe and wise that he should control the economy. This opened the gate for holistic economic thought to be pervasive in the economic methodology of ancient China, applying to both Legalism and Confucianism.

Production and distribution

From "one of the many schools of thought" to becoming the state ideology – "the sole respected thought" – under Emperor Wu of the Western Han Dynasty, there were some key developments within the evolutionary process. In terms of economic thought, some of Dong Zhongshu's ideas were inherited from predecessors, while others were departures from popular Confucian thought. His ideas on distribution and his position on land annexation are examples of the former and latter, respectively.

On distribution, Confucius had a famous quote:

> I have heard the saying: He is not concerned lest his people should be poor, but only lest what they have should be ill-apportioned. He is not concerned lest they be few, but only lest they should be divided against one another. And indeed, if all is well apportioned, there will be no poverty; if they are not divided against one another, there will be no lack of men. . . . And where there is contentment there will be no upheavals.[32]

Here we must pay attention to "well-apportioned", which implies *not* that wealth should be distributed *equally*, but that it should be distributed according to social rank: something that was explained very clearly by Dong Zhongshu and, later (in the Southern Song), by Zhuxi.[33]

The notion of "perfect virtue" (仁) is at the core of Confucius's thought, and it is the principle by which he proposed to adjust people's economic relationships. To Confucius, "to subdue one's self and return to propriety, is perfect virtue".[34] The "propriety" here refers to the social institutions of the Western Zhou, which was a strict hierarchical society where wealth (mainly land) was distributed according to a person's social class. So, the value advocated by Confucius was not *equality* of income and wealth but rather an *equitable* distribution according to his standard of equity/fairness.

Confucian ideas about distribution were developed further during the Warring States period by Xun Kuang (Xunzi). Xunzi realised that the unequal distribution of wealth and income originated from the scarcity of economic resources. As he remarked:

> Human beings are born with desires; when desires are not gratified, they strive for satisfaction; if there are no limits or degrees to their seeking, there will be conflicts and chaos. Ancient sage-kings hated chaos and therefore they established ritual principles to differentiate between people so as to have their desires adapted to their status and their proper desires satisfied, lest their desires not be satisfied for shortage of resources nor resources exhausted by indulgence of their desires.[35]

The "differentiation" mentioned by Xunzi has three meanings: in terms of social relations, in terms of social classes and in terms of people's occupations in society. These are the principles involved in determining the distribution of social wealth.

For Xunzi, "differentiation" is crucial: "a wise king should differentiate between people", otherwise there will be "conflicts" and "chaos"[36] Therefore, the king "should not think it is not too much" for him to possess all the income of the country, and a solder or common person "should not think it is too little" for them to receive a petty income.[37] These arrangements are all in accordance with rules of "propriety".

It can be seen that the pre-Qin Confucian scholars were not thinking of distribution in terms of efficiency and incentives, unlike the Legalists. However, Xunzi's emphasis on the king's rights in decision-making, and his hierarchical views on distribution, do shown signs of the integration of Confucianism and Legalism. As one scholar has argued,

> with the social transformation at the end of the Warring States Period, the newly differentiated social strata gradually became fixed, and the ideas of Xunzi thus naturally appeared and were used for the consolidation of the interests of the new class.[38]

Dong Zhongshu's views fitted the demands of Western Han rulers just as well:

> Confucius said: "Do not worry about poverty, worry about inequality". Therefore where there is abundance and excess, there is shortage and deficiency. Great wealth gives rise to haughtiness; great poverty gives rise to desperation. Desperation gives rise to thievery; haughtiness gives rise to violence. These are the emotional propensities of the majority of human beings. The sage establishes rules based on the emotions of the majority of human beings and observes from whence disorder arises. This is why the sage regulates the Way of Humanity by distinguishing superior and inferior. He ensures that the wealthy have sufficient means to reveal their nobility and [are not enriched] to the point of haughtiness. He ensures that the poor have sufficient means to nourish their lives and are not [impoverished] to the point of desperation.[39]

So, according to Dong, what rulers should "worry about" is the *extent* of inequality, not its very existence.

Restricting land annexation was another major contribution in Dong Zhongshu's economic thought. This is a classic example of promoting Confucian economic thought from the realm of pure ideas to national policy, and it had profound implications for Chinese economic thought for more than one thousand years.

Pre-Qin Confucian scholars also discussed land issues. Mencius designed his plan of livelihood like this:

> Let mulberry trees be planted about the homesteads with their five *mu*, and persons of fifty years may be clothed with silk. In keeping fowls, pigs, dogs, and swine, let not their times of breeding be neglected, and persons of seventy years may eat flesh. Let there not be taken away the time that is proper for the cultivation of the farm with its hundred *mu*, and the family of several

mouths that is supported by it shall not suffer from hunger. Let careful attention be paid to education in schools, inculcating in it especially the filial and fraternal duties, and grey-haired men will not be seen upon the roads carrying burdens on their backs or on their heads. It never has been that the ruler of a State, where such results were seen – persons of seventy wearing silk and eating flesh, and the black-haired people suffering neither from hunger nor cold – did not attain to the royal dignity.[40]

Mencius also stressed the importance of clearly demarcated boundaries:

Now, the first thing towards a benevolent government must be to lay down the boundaries. If the boundaries be not defined correctly, the division of the land into squares will not be equal, and the produce available for salaries will not be evenly distributed. On this account, oppressive rulers and impure ministers are sure to neglect this defining of the boundaries. When the boundaries have been defined correctly, the division of the fields and the regulation of allowances may be determined by you, sitting at your ease.[41]

In the Western Han Dynasty, new problems arose with social and economic development and the evolution of the relationship between city and countryside. For example, land concentration reduced the number of agricultural labourers and increased unemployment in the cities. Officials, including Jia Yi and Chao Cuo, were deeply worried and suggested paying more attention to grain production and storage, driving people from cities back to the land and restricting land annexation by merchants.

Dong Zhongshu's analysis was deeper and more focused. He thought that the problem of land annexation had started from Shang Yang's reforms in the state of Qin during the Warring States period.[42] Because land could be traded, the result was that "the rich have many acres of fertile land, and the poor have no place for living".[43] The former "lived wantonly and without restriction, vying with each other in luxury. In every city, there is someone who assumes the dignity of a King. Every mile one finds someone whose wealth rivals that of a Duke or Marquis". As for the poor:

corrupt officials repressed people arbitrarily. People had no means of subsistence and so escaped to the mountains and became thieves. The number of these people was so large that tens of thousands of them were sentenced to prison every year.[44]

Dong Zhongshu also criticised other economic policies such as the state monopoly on resources of the forests, the state control of the salt and iron industries, heavy taxation and excessive demands for corvée labour. His policy suggestions were as follows:

Although it would be difficult to act precipitately [in a return] to the *jingtian* land system (井田制) [the well-field system], it is proper to draw somewhere near to the old system. Let people's ownership of land be limited in order to sustain [the poor in] the insufficiency, and to block the road to monopoly. The [profit of both] salt and iron should go to the people where it belongs. Abolish [excessive uses of] enslavement [of men and women as a punishment for crime], and eliminate the prerogative of killing [servants and slaves] on one's own authority. Reduce poll taxes and other government levies . . . and lessen labour services.[45]

Dong Zhongshu's position reflected features of the Confucianism of his time. He attributed the problem of land annexation in the Western Han to Shang Yang's reforms in the Warring State period, and he praised the policies of low taxation and *laissez-faire* suggested by pre-Qin Confucians. Regarding the content of the Confucianism, in his "livelihood" proposal Mencius suggested government give farmers basic means of production and guarantee a minimum level of land holdings. Dong Zhongshu proposed an upper limit of land holdings.

We can also see that there are some similarities between Dong Zhongshu's and the economic thought of Legalists, particularly regarding the interventionist role of the central state.

The pre-Qin Confucian school paid close attention to agriculture and expressed sympathy with the suffering of the people. Dong Zhongshu's analysis also started with the depression of agriculture and was supported by references to earlier Confucians, but his value orientation and policy advice were very different from those of his predecessors. First, in the area of production and circulation, pre-Qin Confucianism was inclined to decentralisation and diversity, whereas Dong Zhongshu showed a preference for centralised state power and uniformity.

Second, in the economic arguments of the pre-Qin Confucians, the role of the government was mostly passive, with the pursuit of wealth and profit being left to the people's own devices. But in Dong Zhongshu's theory, the intervention function of the government was strengthened to the extent that the limit of land occupation was clearly defined and carried into practice.

Third, pre-Qin Confucians typically considered social and economic problems at the level of the individual, whereas Dong Zhongshu's analysis was more focused on issues – such as wealth polarisation and social conflicts – involving social aggregates. This was also true of his proposal to restrict land annexation, in which the objects of analysis changed from individuals to collectives. What this suggests is Dong Zhongshu's conscious or unconscious acceptance of a holistic methodology.

The proposition of restricting land annexation had a profound impact on the development of economic thought in ancient China and on the institutional evolution of the Chinese economy and society. In the later Western Han, Shi Dan,[46] Konguang[47] and He Wu[48] followed Dong Zhongshu in repeatedly emphasising the importance of restricting the private ownership of land (and slaves). In the Eastern Han, Xun Yue[49] and Zhong Changtong[50] also followed this idea of restricting land ownership. In practice, the *Wangtian* system implemented by Wang Mang, the *Zhantian* system (占田制) formulated in the Western Jin Dynasty, and the *Juntian* system (均田制) put into practice from the Northern Wei Dynasty to the Tang Dynasty, all implemented policies of restricting the upper limit for land ownership. These ideas and policies were derived from Dong Zhongshu.

Market institutions

As mentioned earlier, in explaining the restriction of land annexation, Dong Zhongshu expressed his dissatisfaction with the monopolistic policies originating in the pre-Qin period on the state control of forest resources and the salt and iron industries, and a similar position was to be taken by the Confucian representatives in the *Discourses on Salt and Iron* (*Yantie lun*). The stance of the Confucian school in the Western Han Dynasty was opposed to people like Sang Hongyang on the issues of state intervention in circulation and market activity.

In analysing the cause of the widening gap between the rich and the poor, Dong Zhongshu appealed to ideas about natural evolution in his criticism of powerful and rich families' competition for profit with the people. Thus:

> Nature gives means to all living creatures. He gives some strong teeth but does not allow them horns, he give some wings but only two legs. Thus if you have the big you should not get the small. In ancient times, people who received salaries were prohibited from taking part in commercial activities because they did not need the additional income. Such institutional arrangements are based on the natural law that "if you get the big, you should not get the small". It is because that law is not obeyed that poor people experience starvation and cold; the rich use their power to compete for profit with ordinary people, making it impossible for the latter to secure a better livelihood.

Hence, Dong proposed:

> families that enjoy salaries live on those salaries alone and do not compete for work with ordinary people, so that the profit can be evenly distributed, and normal people can enjoy an adequate living. This is the law of nature and the way of ancient times. The Son of Heaven ought to establish institutions in accordance with ancient tradition and the literati ought to constrain their activities accordingly.[51]

In the history of Chinese economic thought, the problem of the rich and powerful "competing for profit with ordinary people" was debated repeatedly. Dong Zhongshu was the first person to address the problem. His position was, to an extent, a development of pre-Qin Confucian views. But there were also other influences, particularly of Legalist thought.

According to one scholar, "when Dong Zhongshu expressed his point, the policies of state-run industrial and commercial business carried out by Emperor Wu had not begun. So his suggestion was clearly not against the policy of state-run business policy"; further, after the policies of state-run industrial and commercial business were put into practice, according to Dong Zhongshu's thought it would be a case of the state competing for work and for profit with ordinary people. He would certainly oppose those policies.[52]

However, such an inference needs to answer two questions. First, if Dong Zhongshu took such a stand after the implementation of policies like the state monopoly of salt and iron and equitable distribution and price equalisation, would it still be possible for Confucian economic thought to acquire its position as "the sole respected school"? Second, how do we explain that the measures imposed by Wang Mang, a self-declared Confucian, should have included government regulations on market exchange and commodity circulation that were even harsher than those proposed by Sang Hongyang?

To address this puzzle, we have to escape from the view that Confucianism and *laissez-faire* economic policy were indissolubly linked. Going back to the Confucian idea of the "Great Unity", the highest authority ought to be possessed by worthy and able persons whose ideal is to bring justice to all. But whether such people actually exist is treated as an unknown by the pre-Qin Confucians, so casting doubt on the possibility of attaining the "Great Unity" ideal. However, Dong Zhongshu's theory of the "divine rights of the emperor" made that possibility a reality. Since the personality of the Son of Heaven is perfect, he can naturally control the economy for the good of all. Moreover, to the extent that problems arise in consequence of government intervention, the fault must lie in the execution of the ruler's plan by officials, since the plan itself is, necessarily, faultless. Therefore, even if Dong Zhongshu *had* expressed his views after the introduction of the salt and iron state monopolies, he would neither be convicted for his words nor forced to change his views, because his criticisms would be directed against those inferior beings who were implementing policy, not the policy itself or its originator. Thus, according to Dong's revised Confucianism, interventionist economic policy was no longer to be regarded as anathema.

Letting the feasibility of an economic system depend upon the political need and moral motivation of the decision-maker is one characteristic of a holistic methodology of economics. Dong Zhongshu's theory of restricting land annexation and his criticism of "competing for profit with ordinary people" lacked feasibility, because he substituted political power and morality for economic rules. This was the inevitable result of the gradual inclination towards a holistic methodology of Confucian economic thought in the Western Han.

Confucianism has the characteristics of idealism, while government intervention has the characteristics of holism. The combination of the two makes the risk posed by holism even worse. Sang Hongyang managed the policy of the state monopoly of the salt and iron industries and presided over the equitable distribution and price equalisation systems. The negative impacts of these measures in impeding the normal development of a market economy were apparent, and one or more policies were repealed many times due to their drawbacks. However, after Wang Mang grasped power, those policies were implemented once again. From his perspective,

> salt has the priority of foods and delicious viands. Wine is the senior of the "hundred" medicines, the delight of felicitous gatherings. Iron is a fundamental in farming. Celebrated mountains and great marshes are the storehouses for rich and abundant resources. [The seven markets which equalise prices] and [the system of credit and loans] are [means by] which the "hundred clans" procure equalisation [of prices, and to which] they look in order to supply their wants. Cash and cast cloth money are made from copper, prepared for use of the people, by which what they have is exchanged for what they have not.
> [. . .]
> The six are such that families enregistered as common people cannot [be allowed to] manufacture in their own homes (or without license in shops). [For them] they must necessarily look to the markets. Even though things are several times as expensive [as they should be], there is no option but to buy. Overbearing [wealthy] people and rich merchants then menace the poor and the weak. Former Holy [Rulers] knew it was this way. For these reasons [the six categories of products] were controlled.

The aim of continuing these policies is also "to equalise all people and restrain annexation".[53]

By this time, the distinction between Confucianist and Legalist policies on industry and commerce had completely disappeared; for both camps, the aim was to pursue national interest and an ideal social and economic order. As one scholar has remarked,

> there was a Chinese historical turning point between the Western Han and the Eastern Han. In the former, politicians thought that society can be controlled by human strength and every unjust institution ought to be corrected with human strength. It is the so-called changing disorder to order.[54]

Moreover, "the failure of Wang Mang was not a failure of Wang Mang himself. It was a common failure of advocates of social reform ever since the pre-Qin period. Wang Mang was just a collector of earlier views".[55] Here the "common failure of advocates of social reform" sharply revealed the historical fate of the methodological holism embraced by both Legalists in pre-Qin times and Confucians in the Western Han Dynasty.

However, the methodological holism that came to be adopted and modified by the Confucianism of the Western Han did meet the needs of a great centralised and authoritarian system, and it is therefore not surprising that Dong Zhongshu attracted the attention of Emperor Wudi. Dong's message was clear:

Today, students learn from different teachers, people discuss different theories, what they say and mean therefore are quite different. This is why the ruler has no way to unify the people and systems change frequently. Meanwhile people do not know what they ought to respect. I think it is necessary to prohibit all the various schools except the Confucian. Do not allow them to develop. Heresy will be eliminated thereby, discipline can be enforced, law can be clear, and all people will know that they must obey.[56]

His suggestion was accepted. As Liang Qichao observed, the Qin and Han Dynasties were established after war, at times when the emphasis was, or should have been, on reconstruction.

> However, it is most unfortunate that the main power behind the reconstruction was not scholars but emperors. An Emperor takes the country as his own, so he certainly wants to unify the way people think. If there are a variety of theories in society, people will think differently. To unify their way of thinking there is nothing better than to unify academic thought. Therefore, an authoritarian dynasty always forbids people to speak and think freely. The period between Qin and Han dynasty was one of complete authoritarian systems, the ruler as constructor seeking unity rather than diversity, sanctioning only one school of thought rather than allowing the coexistence of many. Such outcomes were inevitable.[57]

Yet, the "sole respected" Confucianism was not the same as it had been in the pre-Qin period. As Huang Junjie observed:

> the most reliable expressions of the original Confucian doctrine is in books of Confucius and Mencius. They lived in the Spring and Autumn and the Warring State periods, before China became a unified empire. At that earlier time, their thought was relatively unaffected by political authorities. Indeed, they often strove to check and balance political authority by the power of morality. As Confucius said, "a great minister is one who serves his prince according to what is right, and when he finds he cannot do so, he retires". Similarly, Mencius said, "a prince who is to accomplish great deeds will certainly have ministers whom he does not call to go to him". These words show that pre-Qin Confucians placed more importance on morality (or *Dao*) than power[; . . .] but when the Qin and Han empires emerged, Confucian scholars began to face pressure from authoritarian regimes and had to adjust their positions.[58]

Huang went on to remark that after the Second World War in the twentieth century, there were two versions of Confucianism in Taiwan: one was "official Confucianism" which supports the official political agenda, and the other was "common Confucianism" which emphasises national cultural identity rather than the political identity. Such a phenomenon "is actually a modern replication of common practices in the history of Chinese Confucianism".[59]

Conclusion

In terms of the development of Chinese history and thought, the elevation Confucianism to "the sole respected school" reinforced the dominance of holistic methodology, with profound consequences. Liang Qichao argued that to

> allow one school to be the absolute judge of people's conscience and excluding all other schools is what we call dictatorship of academia. As it is dictatorship, there will be no discussion about whether it is good or not. Even if it is extremely good, it hinders the progress of learning[; and the] decline of the Chinese academia actually started with the unification of Confucianism.[60]

Liang continued:

> Evolution interacts with competition, which means there will be no evolution without competition. The reason that Chinese politics does not evolve is because of the autocracy of the monarch; the reason that Chinese academia does not progress is because of the autocracy of the Confucians. Such misfortune all began during the Qin and Han dynasties. Thus, the era of Qin and Han was truly one of the most critical points in the thousands of years of Chinese history.[61]

This painful reflection of Liang Qichao's is very valuable and should really make us think more deeply.

Notes

1 Dong Zhongshu (195–104 BCE), born in what is now Guangchuan, Hebei province. His responses to the imperial request for enlightenment on "the essentials of the great Way and the ultimate truths of its highest principles" were praised by Emperor Wu (汉武帝), under whom he held three government positions successively (江都王相、中大夫、胶西王相). He was still consulted on important government policies after his retirement.
2 Hou Wailou (1959), p. 11.
3 *Li Ji* (*Book of Rites*) "*Li Yun*" ("The Conveyance of Rites") (礼记·礼运).
4 *Mozi* (*The Book of Master Mo*) "Shang Tong Shang" (墨子·尚同上) ("Exalting Unity I").
5 Ibid.
6 Ibid.
7 Ibid., "Shang Tong Zhong" (墨子·尚同中) ("Exalting Unity II").
8 *Lun Yu* (*Analects*), "Gong Ye Zhang" (论语·公冶长) (Chapter 6).
9 *Mengzi* (*Mencius*), "Liang Hui Wang Xia" (孟子·梁惠王下) (Book 1B).
10 *Jingtian* (the well-field) system was a land system of ancient China according to some historical documents. But there is no conclusive evidence to prove that it ever existed.
11 *Mengzi* (*Mencius*), "Teng Wen Gong Shang" (孟子·滕文公上) (Book 3A).
12 *Lun Yu* (*Analects*), "Ji Shi" (论语·季氏) (Chapter 16).

13 Ibid., "Li Ren" (论语·里仁) (Chapter 4).
14 Ibid., "Wei Ling Gong" (论语·卫灵公) (Chapter 15).
15 Ibid., "Yang Huo" (论语·阳货) (Chapter 17).
16 Ibid.
17 *Mengzi* (Mencius), "Gao Zi Shang" (孟子·告子上) (Book 6A).
18 Ibid., "Jin Xin Shang" (孟子·尽心上) (Book 7A).
19 Ibid., "Wan Zhang Shang" (孟子·万章上) (Book 5A).
20 *Chunqiu fanlu* (*Luxuriant Gems of the Spring and Autumn*), "Shen Cha Ming Hao" (春秋繁露·深察名号) ("Deeply Examine Names and Designations", Chapter 35).
21 *Han shu* (*Book of Han*), "Biography of Dong Zhongshu" (汉书·董仲舒传).
22 *Chunqiu fanlu* (*Luxuriant Gems of the Spring and Autumn*), "Shen Cha Ming Hao" (春秋繁露·深察名号) ("Deeply Examine Names and Designations", Chapter 35).
23 *Han shu* (*Book of Han*), "Biography of Dong Zhongshu" (汉书·董仲舒传).
24 *Lun Yu* (*Analects*) "Yao Yue" (论语·尧曰) (Chapter 20).
25 *Mengzi* (*Mencius*) "Liang Hui Wang Shang" (孟子·梁惠王上) (Book 1A).
26 Ibid., "Teng Wen Gong Shang" (孟子·滕文公上) (Book 3A).
27 Ibid., "Jin Xin Shang" (孟子·尽心上) (Book 7A).
28 Ibid., "Gong Sun Chou Shang" (孟子·公孙丑上) (Book 2A).
29 *Shangjun shu*, "Shuo Min" (商君书·说民) ("Discussion about the People").
30 *Shangjun shu*, "Jin Ling" (商君书·靳令) ("Making Orders Strict").
31 *Lun Yu* (*Analects*) "Zi Lu" (论语·子路) (Chapter 13).
32 Ibid., "Ji Shi" (论语·季氏) (Chapter 16).
33 *Chunqiu fanlu* (*Luxuriant Gems of the Spring and Autumn*), "Zhi du" (春秋繁露·度制) ("Regulating Limits", Chapter 27); *Si Shu Ji Zhu*, "Lun Yu" (四书集注·论语).
34 *Lun Yu* (*Analects*), "Yan Yuan" (论语·颜渊) (Chapter 12).
35 *Xunzi* (*Master Xun*), "Li Lun Pian" (荀子·礼论篇) ("Discourse on Ritual", Chapter 19).
36 Ibid., "Fu Guo Pian" (荀子·富国篇) ("Enriching the State", Chapter 10).
37 Ibid., "Rong Ru Pian" (荀子·荣辱篇) ("On Honour and Disgrace", Chapter 4).
38 Guo Moruo (1954), p. 205.
39 *Chunqiu fanlu* (*Luxuriant Gems of the Spring and Autumn*), "Zhi du" (春秋繁露·度制) ("Regulating Limits", Chapter 27).
40 *Mengzi* (*Mencius*), "Liang Hui Wang Shang" (孟子·梁惠王上) (Book 1A).
41 Ibid., "Teng Wen Gong Shang" (孟子·滕文公上) (Book 3A).
42 The reform included the abolition of the original land system and allowance of private land ownership.
43 *Han shu* (*Book of Han*), "Shi Huo Zhi Shang" (汉书·食货志上) ("Treatise on Food and Money I").
44 Ibid.
45 Ibid.
46 Shi Dan (dates unknown), born in Shandong province. During the reign of Emperor Chengdi (33–7 BCE) (汉成帝) he held several senior government positions, and in the reign of Emperor Aidi (7–1 BCE) (汉哀帝) he advocated limited ownership of both land and slaves.
47 Kong Guang (65–5 BCE), a fourteenth-generation descendant of Confucius, born in Shandong province. In the late Western Han, he held various government positions, including Prime Minister. Like Shi Dan, he also followed Dong Zhongshu in advocating limits on the ownership of land and slaves.
48 He Wu (dates unknown), born in Sichuang province. In the late Western Han Dynasty he held ministerial positions, and he advocated limitations on the ownership of land and slaves.
50 Zhong Changtong (179–220 CE), born in Shandong province. He was a philosopher of the Eastern Han Dynasty and held a government position in the period of the Hanxian Emperor (汉献帝). He was the author of the book *Chang Yan* (昌言).
51 *Han shu* (*Book of Han*), "Biography of Dong Zhongshu" (汉书·董仲舒传).

52 Ye Shichang (2003), p. 151.
53 *Han shu (Book of Han)*, "Shi Huo Zhi Xia" (汉书·食货志下).
54 Lü (1992), p. 366.
55 Ibid., p. 84.
56 *Han shu (Book of Han)*, "Biography of Dong Zhongshu" (汉书·董仲舒传).
57 Liang Qichao (2006), p. 42.
58 Huang Junjie (2001), p. 290.
59 Ibid., p. 299.
60 Liang Qichao (2006), p. 57.
61 Ibid., p. 41.

References

Guo, M. (1954) *Book of Ten Criticisms*. Beijing: People Press.

Hou, W. (ed.) (1959) *Great Unity Ideals of All Ages in China*. Beijing: Science Press.

Huang, J. (2001) *Confucianism and Modern Taiwan*. Beijing: Chinese Academy of Social Sciences Press.

Liang, Q. (2006) *On General Trend of Change of Chinese Academic Thought*. Shanghai: Shanghai Ancient Books Press.

Lü, S. (1992) *A History of China*. Shanghai: East China Normal University Press.

Ye, S. (2003) *A History of Economic Thought in Ancient China*. Shanghai: Fudan University Press.

4 The monetary and fiscal system of the Western and Eastern Han Dynasties

Ma Tao and Li Wei

The Western Han and Eastern Han dynasties were important times for political, economic and cultural development in China and have left us with a rich cultural heritage. At the time of the Han, the centralised system of political authority that had been implemented under the Qin Dynasty was only in its early stages of development. In the formulation of that centralised system, the design of the economic system was of great significance as the prerequisite for ensuring the state's very survival. Focusing on the monetary and fiscal system of the Han Dynasties will help to better understand the evolution of early China's economic system and also provide us with a glimpse of the social, political and cultural realities at that time. It may also cast light on monetary and fiscal reforms in modern China.

The monetary system of the Han Dynasties

During the Western and Eastern Han Dynasties, the commodity economy was developing rapidly and currency became the common means of conducting transactions. Monetary thought at the time had an evident inclination towards a Nominal Theory of Money, the main feature of which is the treatment of currency as a measure of value, not as something with its own inherent value. By issuing excess currency, the government can create inflation in order to gather wealth from the society and relieve financial crises. Under the influence of Nominal Theory, gold, silver, copper coin and textiles performed currency functions successively in the Han Dynasties, but it was copper coin that was the main circulating medium. There was no normative standard-fractional money system and no limitation of money supply, which allowed the government to create inflation more or less at will.

Copper coin was to undergo a long and tortuous process of development. After ten changes in currency, it eventually formed the *Wu Zhu Qian* system in 113 BCE. In 205 BCE, military conflict resulted in a severe financial crisis for the nascent Western Han government, which carried out the first currency reform on the grounds, or pretext, that the *Ban Liang Qian* of the Qin Dynasty[1] was too heavy to use. It therefore replaced the *ban-liang* ("half-tael") 12-*shu* coin of the Qin with a 3-*shu* "elm-pod" coin, named *Yu Jia Ban Liang*.[2] Also, it not only extended the right of coinage to the people but also actually *ordered* them to mint the new currency.[3] This currency reform is the first time that the government tried to solve a financial crisis by reducing the weight of coins to increase the amount of currency. The government issued more currency by lowering its weight in order to stimulate market activity. This act increased the income of the government in the short term but caused serious consequences in the devaluation that ensued, with the price of one *shi* of rice rising from "1600 cash" (i.e. 1600 *Ban Liang Qian* of the Qin Dynasty) in 216 BCE to "ten thousand cash" (i.e. ten thousand *Yu Jia Ban Liang*). Meanwhile, the coins minted by the public were getting lighter and lighter, and the trend of the devaluation became increasingly serious.

After the Western Han had consolidated its rule, the government introduced measures to stabilise the currency. A prohibition on public minting was introduced in 186 BCE, and the *Ba Fen Qian* was put into circulation. The weight of *Ba Fen Qian* was only two-thirds of *Qin Ban Liang* and it was called *Ba Zhu Ban Liang*. Only four years later (182 BCE), the weight of copper coin was lowered once again as the government minted small coins shaped like elm seeds, named *Wu Fen Qian*,

Figure 4.1 Ban Liang Qian of the Qin Dynasty[4]

which weighed only one-fifth of *Qin Ban Liang*. Moreover, private coinage had not declined even though it had been officially prohibited.

After Emperor Wen of the Han Dynasty succeeded to the throne (r. 180–157 BCE), the quantity of coin in circulation was reduced in order to stabilise the value of the currency. Because of the increased quantity of 3-*shu* "elm-pod" coins, and their reduction in weight (through filing), it was ordered in 175 BCE that they should be replaced with *Si Zhu Qian* (4-*shu* coins) on which was engraved "*Ban Liang*". Meanwhile, the general public were permitted to mint coins and Deng Tong, a favoured minion of Emperor Wen, and Liu Bi, King of Wu, were allowed to produce their own *Si Zhu Qian*.

Jia Yi (200–168 BCE),[5] Jia Shan[6] and others had signed petitions to oppose Emperor Wen allowing private coinage, and this was the first debate about the right of coinage in Chinese history. Jia Shan took the "nominalist" position that a currency has no ("absolute") value itself, only exchange value as the medium of exchange. Also, because wealth and rank are the tools for the emperor to use in ruling the country, and money can be used to obtain wealth and rank, Jia Shan argued that the issue of currency should be controlled by the emperor alone: allowing private coinage would mean that ordinary people are sharing power with the emperor, so undermining his authority.

Jia Yi considered that there were three main disadvantages of private coinage. First, allowing private coinage would induce people to commit crimes. Second, without any unified standard of coinage, the monetary system would become more confused. Third, private coinage is lucrative, and this may induce people to give up farming to take on mining copper and minting coin. Like Jia Shan, Jia Yi concluded that the government should monopolise coinage. However, he believed that the means to achieve the objective was by creating a government monopoly over copper mining, which would not only stop private coinage but also bring seven additional advantages: there would be no forging of coins, no circulation of counterfeit coins, people would go back to farming and manufacturing, prices in the market would be stable, copper could be used to manufacture weapons or for rewards, the arbitrage opportunities of businessmen would be limited and the government could accumulate wealth to secure the empire's borders.

Emperor Wen believed that the priority was to revitalise the economy and that it was not the time to unify the coinage by a centralised authority. He therefore rejected the advice of Jia Shan and others. In order to guarantee the quality of coins, the government implemented the system of *Fa Ma Qian* and *Cheng Qian Heng*[7] to ensure that the issue of *Si Zhu Qian* was subject to explicit laws and strict management. The policy was a success and the trend of lowering the weight of coins was curbed. The high-quality coins stabilised the value of currency and brought unprecedented prosperity.

By the time that Emperor Wu (r. 141–87 BCE) succeeded to the throne, the country was strong and the economy was prospering. In 140 BCE, the government started minting a 3-*shu* coin, only to re-adopt the 4-*shu* coin some four years later.

There were frequent wars during the middle and late periods of Emperor Wu's reign, and the government turned to issuing new currency to provide for the

Figure 4.2 Coins in the early Western Han Dynasty[8]

Source: 1–3. Ban Liang in early Han; 4–5. Ba Zhu Ban Liang; 6–8. Si Zhu Qian; 9–11. Yu Jia Ban Liang; 12–13. San Zhu Qian

Figure 4.3 Round dragon coin

Figure 4.4 Square horse coin

Figure 4.5 Oval turtle coin

expenses of the state and to suppress those they regarded as idle and unscrupu-lous landlords. In 119 or 120 BCE, it issued high denomination currency made from deerskin and silver. The so-called leather notes, measuring one foot square with colourful decoration on the edges, were made of the skin of white deer from Shanglin Park (the imperial park), and each note was deemed to be worth 400,000 *Qian*.[9] The idea appears to have been that feudal lords would be obliged not only to present jade to the emperor but also to obtain the deerskin on which the jade was presented. However, the deerskin was not intended for general circulation, and the only way it could be purchased was directly in cash from the imperial treasury. The deerskin "money" was therefore not so much a monetary phenom-enon as a way by which the emperor could directly extract more wealth from the feudal lords.

The silver coins were made of silver–tin alloy with three different forms, including a round dragon coin, which weighed 4 *liang* and was worth 3000 *Qian*, a square horse coin which weighed 6 *liang* and was worth 500 *Qian* and an oval turtle coin which weighed 4 *liang* and was worth 300 *Qian*. The government had gained an enormous amount of income from the coinage because there was no legal regulation on the quality of the currency and the cost of minting was far less than the actual value. But this also led to large-scale private coinage. Therefore,

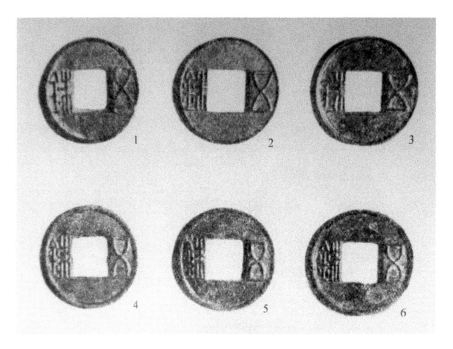

Figure 4.6 Wu Zhu Qian in West Han[10]

Source: 1–3. *Wu Zhu Qian* minted by prefectures; 4–6. *Chi Ze Qian* or *Wu Zhu Qian* minted in Shanglin Park

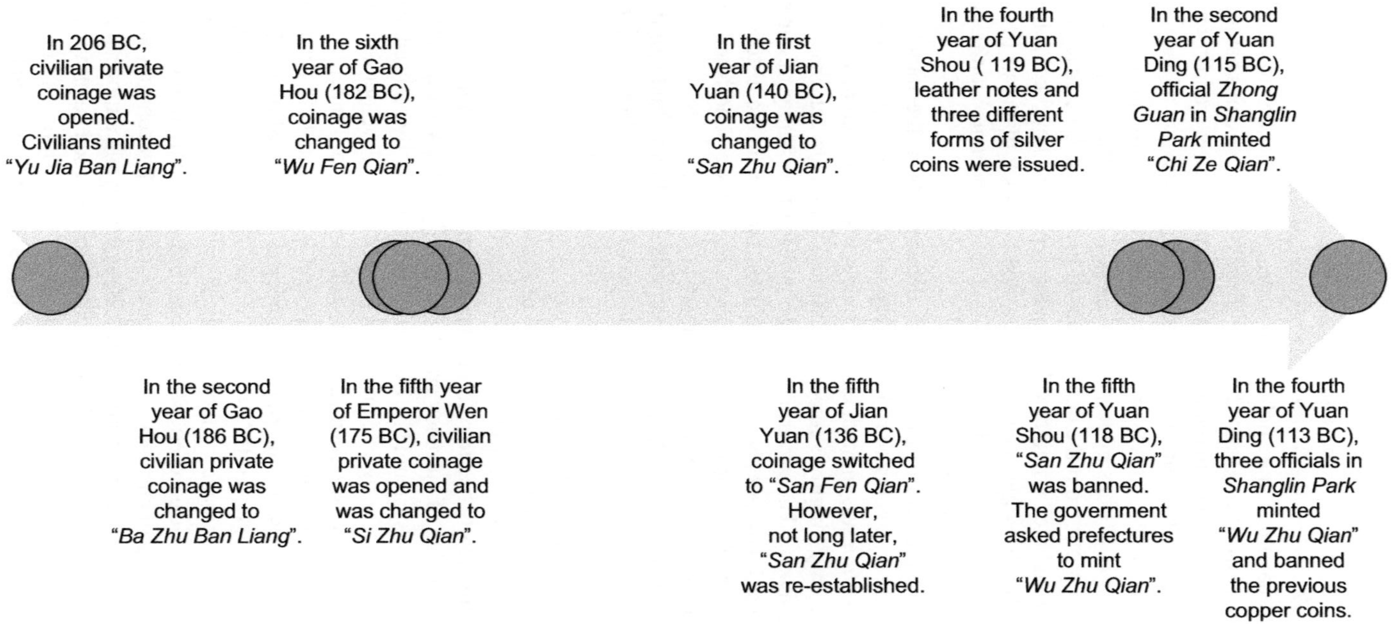

In 206 BC, civilian private coinage was opened. Civilians minted "Yu Jia Ban Liang".

In the sixth year of Gao Hou (182 BC), coinage was changed to "Wu Fen Qian".

In the first year of Jian Yuan (140 BC), coinage was changed to "San Zhu Qian".

In the fourth year of Yuan Shou (119 BC), leather notes and three different forms of silver coins were issued.

In the second year of Yuan Ding (115 BC), official Zhong Guan in Shanglin Park minted "Chi Ze Qian".

In the second year of Gao Hou (186 BC), civilian private coinage was changed to "Ba Zhu Ban Liang".

In the fifth year of Emperor Wen (175 BC), civilian private coinage was opened and was changed to "Si Zhu Qian".

In the fifth year of Jian Yuan (136 BC), coinage switched to "San Fen Qian". However, not long later, "San Zhu Qian" was re-established.

In the fifth year of Yuan Shou (118 BC), "San Zhu Qian" was banned. The government asked prefectures to mint "Wu Zhu Qian".

In the fourth year of Yuan Ding (113 BC), three officials in Shanglin Park minted "Wu Zhu Qian" and banned the previous copper coins.

Figure 4.7 Timeline of ten currency reforms

not long after their introduction, leather notes and silver coins were abolished. It is worth mentioning that the three different forms of silver coins are the earliest legal silver coins in Chinese history.

In 118 BCE, in a renewed attempt to stabilise the currency, the government banned *San Zhu Qian* (the 3-*shu* coins introduced in 120/119 BCE, which were considered to have become "light") and instructed prefectures to mint the 5-*shu Wu Zhu Qian*. Only three years later, with illegal minting of coins having occurred on a grand scale, officials in the imperial (Shanglin) park were instructed to mint new, red-rimmed 5-*shu* coins, with an official conversion rate of one new coin for five old ones. Moreover, it was ordered that all payments to the government must be made in new coin, thus giving rise to the possibility that the government may have sought to profit from the debasement of the 118 BCE currency by insisting on sums owed at "old" nominal values being repaid in "new" coin (i.e. at a premium of 500%). It would seem, however, that any such plan was thwarted: two years later the red-rimmed coins are reported to have become worthless and were withdrawn from circulation.

According to the reform of 113 BCE, departments in the imperial Shanglin Park were given the exclusive right and responsibility for issuing currency. A new 5-*shu Wu Zhu Qian* was minted, but this time it was produced to such an intricate standard that only "highly skilled professional criminals continued to produce counterfeit coins".[11] The government monopolised the issuing of currency from that time onward. *Wu Zhu Qian* played an important role in the history of Chinese currency. It circulated for more than 700 years and was abolished only in the fourth year of Wu De in the Tang Dynasty (621 CE).

For the purpose of strengthening the centralised authority and gaining revenue from minting, rulers have an obvious incentive to monopolise the right of coinage. Under the influence of Nominal Theory of Money, they also have a motive to gain wealth and transfer the burden of crises by lowering the weight of coins and issuing excessive currency. An overview of the ten currency reforms has shown that, except for the two reforms during the Jian Yuan period (140–135 BCE), the government frequently had to reform after gaining income from inflation in order to stabilise the value of currency and the price of goods. After the establishment of the *Wu Zhu Qian* system (113 BCE), the rulers gradually realised that a stable currency policy plays a significant role in the economic development of society.

In the sixth year of Shi Yuan (81 BCE), in the reign of Emperor Zhao (87–74 BCE), the *Yantie lun* ("Discourses on Salt and Iron") was held between a group of Confucian scholars, on one side, and imperial officers led by the Grand Secretary, Sang Hongyang (?–80 BCE), on the other. The scholars were opposed to the monopolisation of coinage by the centralised authority. In response, Sang Hongyang called on historical experience to demonstrate that only when the government controls the minting of currency would people have trust in currency and the stability of the currency system be guaranteed. Sang Hongyang's monetary thought is undoubtedly a high-level generalisation and summary based on previous ideas and experience. However, there is a one-sidedness to his position, in that he regarded the monopolisation of coinage as the *only* means to stabilise the value of currency.

After Emperor Yuan succeeded to the throne (r. 48–33 BCE), there were sharp social contradictions because of frequent natural disasters and the wide gap between the rich and the poor. The lives of the people were also affected by ongoing private coinage and violent price fluctuation. The middle and small landlords generally believed that the currency was the root cause of the problem and advocated abolishing currency and implementing barter. Gong Yu (127–44 BCE)[12] was one such landlord, who held that the circulation of currency had four main disadvantages. First, the minting of coins was labour consuming and diverted labour away from agricultural production. Second, the mining of copper would damage the ecological environment and cause natural disasters. Third, during the 70 years when *Wu Zhu Qian* were circulating, many people were convicted of private coinage. And fourth, the gap between the rich and poor had been widened and this would endanger social stability. However, it is not difficult to see that there is no necessary correlation between the disadvantages described by Gong Yu

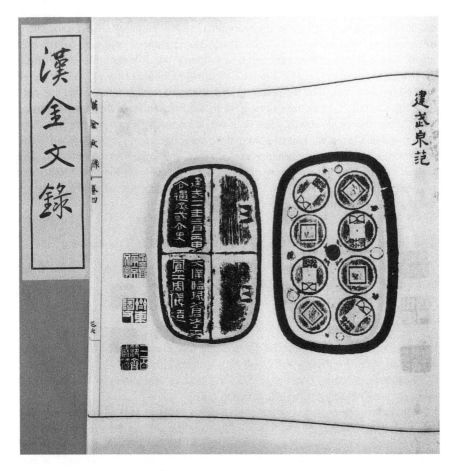

Figure 4.8 Jian Wu Quan fan[13]

and the circulation of currency. The proposal to abolish currency was not adopted, but its advocates remained undaunted.

In the first 15 years of the Eastern Han Dynasty (25–40 CE), the government did not engage in minting but used cloth, silk, gold and millet as currency. Thereafter, the government started to mint *Wu Zhu Qian*. After the re-establishment of the *Wu Zhu Qian* system, the commodity economy continued to develop and monetary conditions remained relatively stable, at least until the middle period of the Eastern Han.

As for gold, in the Han Dynasty it was mainly used to perform the functions of a store of value and a means of rewarding meritorious deeds, but had not been in circulation as high denomination currency. The forms of gold mainly included golden cake, gold shaped like a horseshoe and gold shaped like the toes of a kylin (a mythical hooved creature). Golden cake was round in shape and could be used only after cutting and weighing. There were two kinds of golden cakes, one larger, the other smaller. As to the other forms, they were developed in response to reports to the emperor from local officials about "auspicious signs". It was in order to harmonise with celestial phenomena that the emperor changed the shape of the gold to a horseshoe and a kylin's toes. The amount of gold used for rewards reached its maximum during the reign of Emperor Wu. For example, in 119 BCE the troops led by Wei Qing (?–106 BCE) and Huo Qubing (140–117 BCE)[14] were praised for their attack on the Xiongnu and rewarded with 500,000 catties of gold by Emperor Wu.[15] As to the use of gold in the Eastern Han, there is little to be learnt from historical records. However, we do know that extravagance was common and that a large amount of gold had flowed out through the Silk Road. Also, elaborate funerals became popular at that time, and golden ornaments and jade clothes sewn with gold wire were prized funerary objects for the rich. Finally, the introduction of Buddhism (67 CE) led to the increasing use of gold for casting figures of the Buddha.

The fiscal system of the Western and Eastern Han Dynasties

The fiscal system of Western and Eastern Han includes fiscal revenue, fiscal expenditure and fiscal management. We deal with these in turn.

Fiscal revenue

Statutory taxes in the Han may be divided into four classes: the poll tax (including *Kou Qian*, *Suan Fu*, *Hu Fu* and *Geng Fu*), land tax (including *He*, *Chu* and *Gao*), business tax (including *Guan Shui*, *Shi Zu* and taxes on mountains and lakes) and property tax (including vehicle and vessel tax).

Poll tax was the most important source of tax revenue in the Han Dynasty and was levied on minors and adults. *Kou Qian* was the poll tax for minors aged 7 to 14 and was set at 23 *Qian*. *Suan Fu* was the poll tax for adults aged 15 to 56 and it was 120 *Qian*. Although regulations stated that the tax should be paid in currency, both currency and goods were accepted in payment. In the Eastern Han, it became increasingly common to take goods when collecting tax. At the end of the Eastern Han, *Suan Fu*, *Kou Qian* and so on had converged gradually because of wars, and the payment of taxes imposed on households was changed from money to goods. In the Western Han, the government's tax revenue, *Suan Fu*, belonged to *Dasinong* (the minister of finance). The imperial tax revenue, *Kou Qian*, belonged to *Shaofu* (literally, "Royal Butler").

Hu Fu was a tax imposed on households of farmers and businessmen and was set at around 200 *Qian* per household. The revenue went to the local nobility. *Geng Fu* was a tax paid in currency in lieu of performing corvée labour. By the middle of the Western Han, it had evolved from an occasional to a regular tax.

In the Han Dynasty, land tax was part of the national fiscal revenue that went to the *Dasinong* (minister of finance). It was originally paid in goods, and later in goods and currency. The rate of land tax was subject to considerable variations in the early Western Han. In the first year of Emperor Jing's rule (156 BCE), the rate had been fixed at one-thirtieth of the produce, and this became the standard rate in both the Western and Eastern Han dynasties. Land tax included *He*, *Chu* and *Gao*. *He* is the general term for crops, and there were different crops – rice, grain, millet – in different areas. *Chu* and *Gao* refer to the stems and leaves of crops, respectively, and these were mostly used to make feedstuff. The unit for land tax was the *qing* (about 3.33 hectares). *He* was calculated on the size of the harvest. As for *Chu* and *Gao*, they were three *shi* (a unit of weight) and two *shi* per *qing*, respectively. In early Han, land tax was paid in produce, but with the development of the economy *Chu* and *Gao* were paid in goods and currency and the rate was decided locally. In the Eastern Han, land tax was also applied to textiles. In addition, land tax in the Han included *Jia Shui*, which was an income tax on farmers who were using lands lent to them by the government. The rate of the tax was also one-thirtieth. Strictly speaking, *Jia Shui* was the rent that farmers paid for using public land.

Guan Shui and *Shi Zu* were the main business taxes in the Han. *Guan Shui* was a type of transport tax or toll, paid by merchants at borders and ferry ports, while *Shi Zu* was a form of market tax. At that time, commercial activities in cities were carried out in designated areas. Settled market traders used houses, shops and yards provided by the government, for which they were required to pay a house tax and an income tax, known collectively as *Shi Zu*.

Taxes on mountains and lakes were targeted at craftsmen and businessmen who developed and traded in the products obtained from those natural resources (such as fish, wood, furs and so on). In the early and middle Western Han, the tax on the private provision of salt and iron fell into the same category. These taxes remained in place until the Eastern Han Dynasty. In the Western Han, business tax revenue was used to meet the expenses of the imperial family and sovereign. In the Eastern Han, national finance and imperial finance had merged, so the revenue went to the national treasury.

Property tax had been levied since the early Western Han, but the nature of the tax was subject to considerable change. Some property taxes were national, others were local; some forms existed in both the Western and Eastern Han, others were more ephemeral.

The reign of Emperor Wu was marked by frequent external wars. In order to solve the financial crisis, the government started to collect *Min Qian Shui* (a tax levied on assets at a rate of 2%), vehicle and vessel tax. These taxes were self-reported and the rates of vehicle and vessel tax were different among different people. After that, an act named *Gao Min Ling* was promulgated to prevent tax evasion by confiscating property. As recorded in *The History of the Han Dynasty*, *Gao Min Ling* led to the prosecution of the majority of middle- and upper-ranking families (in terms of wealth). The government confiscated vast sums of money, thousands of maids, several hundred hectares of lands and many houses. The system of *Gao Min Ling* was enforced for about 12 years and stopped only when national finances had improved considerably. Short-lived as it was, however, the long-term economic consequences were profound. Most wealthy families had gone bankrupt and fewer people engaged in mercantile activities, resulting in shortages of commodities and price fluctuations.

Shi Dai Shui was a form of interest tax, levied on the gains from loans of currency and grain. With the development of a commodity economy in the Western Han, the number of private lenders increased significantly and the rates they charged were often punishingly high: the *daily* interest rate in the Great Wall region is recorded as having reached 3%.[16] Towards the close of Emperor Jing's reign, the government imposed *Shi Dai Shui* in order to limit the activities of lenders and impose an upper limit on their gains. The collection of *Shi Dai Shui* was based on self-declaration; unfortunately, there is no surviving record of the rate at which it was imposed.

Income from corvée (or conscript) labour[17] *and the monopolies*

The activities performed by corvée labour in the Han mainly included the following. First, the building of city walls and roads at both the central and provincial levels, including roads between residential areas and counties. Second, the water conservancy projects, including local projects and national projects. Third, the transportation of wealth and goods at all levels of government. Fourth, the construction of imperial tombs and cemeteries.

A fifth use of conscript labour was in the state-owned industries. At the end of the Western Han, it is estimated that in the region of 1.5 million labourers were conscripted annually.[18] Although the use of these labourers did not bring book income for the government, it saved them the difference in cost from employing non-conscript labour, as well as the long-term benefits from the outputs to which they contributed. Some scholars believe that in the Western Han Dynasty, the burden of corvée labour calculated in currency was about four times the burden of taxation (excluding miscellaneous taxes).[19] Indeed, it would have been impossible to undertake some of the massive infrastructural projects in the Han *without* conscript labour

The government could also call on the revenue from its monopolies.[20] The most important were the monopolies of salt and iron, which provided the major source of revenue for the Han Dynasty, generating more than half of its annual total revenue.

It was in 117 BCE that the ministers responsible for salt and iron, Kong Jin[21] and Dongguo Xianyang,[22] proposed their monopoly scheme to Emperor Wu. The detail was as follows. The government would be responsible for recruiting salt producers and providing necessary equipment, while the producers themselves would take responsibility for all other aspects of production. The purchase and sale of salt would be monopolised by the government. The manufacture of ironware would also be monopolised by the government, and government officers would have responsibility for the manufacture and sale of ironware throughout the empire.

In 110 BCE, Sang Hongyang had been promoted to *Zhisu Duwei* with responsibility for finance. He also replaced Kong Jin and was in charge of the state-owned salt and iron industries. As part of his efforts to improve the management and operation of those industries, he set up 36 salt officers in 27 counties where salt was produced and 48 iron officers in 40 counties. The effects of implementing the monopolies were mentioned many times in the *Discourses on Salt and Iron (Yantie lun)*. The monopolies greatly increased the government's revenues, put a break on land purchases by merchants and manufacturers who had lost income from the institution of the monopolies, and lessened the threat to the central state from areas and individuals that had previously benefited from salt and iron revenues. However, it was alleged at the time that the efficiency of production in the monopolies was low, that prices were high, that the quality of outputs was variable, and that government officials at all levels were milking the enterprises for their own private benefit. Suffice it to say that debate over the advantages and disadvantages of the monopolies did not end with the "Discourses on Salt and Iron" of 81 BCE.

Fiscal expenditure

Expenditure on salaries of government officers

Monthly pay, or salary, was expressed in terms of quantities of grain, measured in *hu*, with the quantity depending on the official's rank. Officers also received benefits such as meal allowances. In the Western Han, the salary was usually paid in currency based on the monetary value of grain. In the Eastern Han, because of the decline of commodity economy, the salary was mainly paid half in currency and half in grain. Expenditure on salaries during the Han took up roughly half of total tax revenue.

Administrative expenditure

Administrative expenditure was huge and mostly involved payment for the transfer of messages and the filing of documents.

A complete postal network was established with responsibility for the transfer of mail and tribute and the board and lodging of its officers. As recorded in a bamboo book that was unearthed in Dunhuang, the expenditure for *Xuanquan Zhi* (the low-level post office) for two months in 23 BCE was more than 10,000 *Qian* and the funds were allocated by the county where the office was located.[23] By way of comparison, Gong Yu, the *Guanglu Dafu* in the reign of Emperor Yuan (48–33 BCE), who held a position ranked fifth of the 22 official ranks at that time, revealed that his monthly salary was 12,000 *Qian*.

There was also a strict filing system that officials were obliged to follow. Apart from regulations applied to subject matter, there were also exacting regulations governing the physical properties of documents, with the choice of wooden slips and book ropes that tied the slips together differing according to the type of document involved. Needless to say, the costs involved were considerable.

Military expenditure

Expenditure on defence and the military was no doubt the biggest item among the government fiscal expenditures of the Han Dynasty. It covered six areas: (1) funding the central army which protected the capital city; (2) local standing armies of 270,000 soldiers in total (not including frontier forces); (3) the frontier force, comprising of 600,000 troops under Emperor Wu (according to Sima Qian), subsequently falling to around 300,000 in the middle and late Western Han; (4) breeding of cavalry horses; (5) manufacture and maintenance of weapons; and (6) sundry miscellaneous items of expenditure (including transportation of food and equipment). Altogether, military expenditure was around 1.7 billion *Qian* annually.

Based on reports from the late Western Han, tax revenue per year was around 1.8 billion *Qian*, and the revenue from state-owned industries was approximately 4 billion *Qian*. Inclusive of other sources of revenue, the total annual take would have been not far short of 6 billion *Qian*. While this may have been sufficient in most years, any surge in military expenditure was likely to cause serious financial problems. As recorded in *The History of the Han Dynasty – The Biography of Zhao Chongguo*, in 61 BCE Emperor Xuan deployed 60,000 troops to put down the rebellion of *Qiangs* at a cost of 5 billion *Qian*. Thus, in the event of major military engagements, or serious natural disasters, the resources of the national treasury would be stretched thin.[24]

Other expenditure

In addition to the above, areas of expenditure included public services and infrastructure, imperial cemeteries and hardship payments.

Even though the government could mobilise large numbers of corvée labour, it still had to pay for food, equipment, raw materials and project design. As for imperial cemeteries, costs were borne by the national treasury (overseen by *Dasinong*)[25] and could be vast, depending on the extravagance of individual emperors. Finally, "hardship payments" included payments to the old and to refugees from war zones or areas of natural disaster who were given clothes, food and loans of grain in order to help them return to productive activities.

Fiscal management

National fiscal management evolved gradually over three phases during the Western and Eastern Han dynasties. In the first phase, from the early Han to the rule of Emperor Jing (157–141 BCE), the *Neishi* (the governor of capital) was responsible for managing the capital city following the precedent set under the Qin. In the second phase, from the time of Emperor Wu to the end of the Western Han (141 BCE–9 CE), *Dasinong* managed national finance, and *Shaofu* and *Shuiheng Duwei* were in charge of imperial finance, with *Shuiheng Duwei* also responsible for issuing currency. In the third phase, corresponding to the Eastern Han, *Dasinong* was put in charge of overall finance, a development that had come about as follows.

In the middle and late Western Han, the national treasury was experiencing financial crisis while the funds of the imperial treasury were abundant. In response, money from the imperial treasury would be allocated to *Dasinong* to solve urgent problems. As a result of the de facto interdependence between the two treasuries, Emperor Guangwu (r. 25–57 CE) formally merged them. The post of *Shuiheng Duwei* was abolished and *Shaofu* became the private office of the emperor.

As the executive officer of national finance, *Dasinong* managed local finance in three ways. First, local prefectures were required to hand over a quarterly account book, *Si Shi Bu*, containing a full record of their income and expenditure. Second, *Bucheng* (the subordinates of *Dasinong*), were established to oversee financial matters in every local government. Third, *Dasinong* took direct control of allocating finance to boundary counties (frontier commanderies) and to areas that were suffering from natural disasters.

Local government would collect taxes according to national regulations. In principle, all of this tax revenue belonged to the central government, but in practice local government was allowed to retain part of it to cover specifically local demands (such as those arising from natural disasters), always subject to regulations set centrally.

Fiscal management of local government covered *Shang Ji* and *Qi Hui*. *Shang Ji* required local government to give frequent reports on administrative matters, including economic and political developments, which would provide the basis for designing financial policies and examining officers' political achievements. *Qi Hui* referred to the implementation of policies within a prescribed time period.

It seems clear that the concept of a financial budget had taken shape under the Han. According to historical documents, Emperor Cheng (r. 33–7 BCE) once asked the Prime Minister Zhai Fangjin (53–7 BCE) to familiarise himself with every aspect of the existing budget.[26] Surpluses and deficits were recorded, efforts were made to keep expenditures within budgetary constraints, and attempts would be made (not always successfully) to manage shortages through the imposition of central and local economies.

Conclusion

The Qin and Han dynasties marked the beginning of the centralised Chinese state and had a lasting influence on the development of Chinese history. The brief Qin Dynasty provided little guidance on statecraft, leaving the Han rulers to fashion the state in response to the problems of the time. The system that evolved influenced China's development for the next two thousand years.

As to the monetary system, there were various types of currency in circulation during the Western and Eastern Han, not only metallic currencies but also real goods as the mediums of exchange. Copper coin was the major metallic currency. Gold was used mostly as a store of value, while silver currency was in circulation only for a very short period of time. In the early and middle Western Han, copper coinage experienced a series of reforms. At that time, government thinking and efforts were primarily directed towards monopolising the minting of coins. Also, adherence to the Nominal Theory of Money encouraged government to cause inflation by "lightening" coin in order to gather wealth. That policy resulted in social problems as frequent price fluctuations disordered market activity. In the late Western Han, with the economy declining, shortages of goods increasing and prices rising, people realised that the underlying problem was monetary, but no suitable solution had been found. The thought of replacing metal currency with real goods started to gain in popularity. In the Eastern Han, it was common for goods to perform the role of a medium of exchange, and this continued up to the Tang Dynasty, Compared to the monetary system in western countries at the time, where the Metallic Theory of Money was dominant and regulating standards emphasised, enquiry into the standards that might be applied to issuing currency did not attract much attention.[27]

Turing to the fiscal system, the types of tax in the Han Dynasty mainly followed those that had been levied in the Qin. Tax was collected both in currency and goods in accordance with the development of the commodity economy at the time. As the activities of the state increased, so too did government expenditure. Various ways to expand sources of revenue were explored, including property tax. However, the attempt to base the tax on self-reported property values merely encouraged people to take evasive measures, in turn leading to the direct confiscation of property by the government and a break on economic development. Although the property tax was imposed only for a short period, its negative influence was much longer lasting.

The state monopolies of salt and iron were another means by which the government attempted to increase revenue. Through adding tax to the prices of salt and iron, it was reckoned that the government could increase national revenue without increasing other taxes. After the successful implementation of the policy in the Han, this state-owned operation became the most important source of fiscal revenue for every succeeding dynasty. However, it also brought a series of problems, including low productivity, high prices and inferior quality of products. The debate over the merits of state-owned operations has continued to the present day.

A fact we should not neglect is that the emphasis in the Han was always on gaining more revenue rather than cutting down on expenses. Subsequently, the government of every dynasty followed suit, and the excessive interference of governments in their attempts to gather revenue led to a constrained development of the private economy in China.

In the Western and Eastern Han dynasties, the role of finance became more and more important and was related to every aspect of the empire. Over time, government and imperial finance converged, with government finance ultimately becoming the only financial department by the time of the Eastern Han. However, although the original intention was to expand the financial income of the government, the result was to open a door for emperors to embezzle the national treasury. Moreover, as governments were forced to place increasing burdens on the public to meet their burgeoning fiscal demands (and those of the emperors), social tensions were inflamed, sometimes to the point of explosion.

Throughout the changes of the monetary and fiscal systems in the Western and Eastern Han dynasties, the fundamental driving force was the need of the rulers to consolidate their regimes. The core idea was to increase financial income in order to maintain the operation of a thriving state. In this scenario, the government should have been the defender of the social order. As it was, its pursuit of expanding government authority and financial income turned it into a destroyer of the social order. How to restrain government from plundering the wealth of the society remained a key problem throughout Chinese history and was an important reason for the stagnant economic development in ancient times.

Notes

1 The legal currency in the Qin Dynasty was cast in copper and was called *Ban Liang*. It was round with a square hole at the centre. The diameter of the coin was about 3.2–3.4cm and it weighed approximately half a *liang* (about 7.8g).
2 Volume units in the Han Dynasty: 1 *shi* = 1 *hu* = 10 *dou* = 20 L. Weight units: 1 *liang* = 15.625 grams = 24 *shu* (1 *zhu* = 0.65 grams).
3 According to Sima Qian's account in *The Records of the Grand Historian* (*Shiji* 30).
4 Peng Xinwei (2015) Picture 25.
5 Jia Yi (200–168 BCE) was a political commentator and writer in the early Western Han.
6 Jia Shan was a political commentator in the early Western Han. The years of his birth and death are unknown.
7 *Fa Ma Qian* and *Cheng Qian Heng* are two parts of the means adopted from Han to Sui times to monitor the quality of the coinage. *Fa Ma Qian* was used to measure the weight of circulating coin relative to the standard, stipulated weight, and *Cheng Qian Heng* means that the coins in circulation should be weighed by *Fa Ma Qian*.
8 Peng Xinwei (2015) Picture 27.
9 Sima Qian, *Records of the Grand Historian* (*Shiji 30*).
10 Peng Xinwei (2015) Picture 28.
11 Sima Qian, *Records of the Grand Historian* (*Shiji 30*).
12 Gong Yu was an official of the late Western Han who once served as *Yushi Dafu* (the imperial censor).
13 Rong Geng (1931) *Qin Han Jin Wen Book (vol. 4)*.
14 They were famous generals in the Western Han. Wei Qing was Huo Qubing's uncle.

15 Sima Qian, *Records of the Grand Historian* ("The Treatise on the Balanced Standard", *Shiji* 30).
16 The inscription on the Juyan wooden slips read as follows: "a man named Wang Yan borrowed 100 *Qian* in May 20th, and he had to return goods valued 250 *Qian* on July 5th". Based on this record, the daily interest rate for borrowing was 3%. See Liu Hainian and Yang Yifan (1994), p. 407.
17 Lin Ganquan has argued that conscript labour in a feudal society creates value and is a source of invisible economic revenue. But for the conscript labourers themselves, it is a heavy economic burden. See Lin Ganquan (2007), p. 504.
18 Watanabe Shin'ichirou, Satake Yasuhiko (2008), p. 288.
19 Luo Qingkang (1985), p. 10.
20 *Pingshun*, *Junshu* and *Jiuque* were various policies adopted under Emperor Wu that were designed to increase government revenue. They will not be considered further in this chapter.
21 Kong Jin was a great iron merchant in his early years. Later, he served as *Dasinong* in charge of the salt and iron monopolies in the reign of Emperor Wu. The years of his birth and death are unknown.
22 Dongguo Xianyang had been a salt merchant and became *Danongcheng* in charge of the salt and iron monopolies under Emperor Wu. The years of his birth and death are unknown.
23 The inscription on the Dunhuang Xuanquan wooden slips read as follows: "When it came to the leap month and Lunar April, government expenditure reached 10,000. In Lunar April 9, the second year of Yang Shuo, *Xuanquan Zhi* took the money from *Shaonei Sefu*". *Shaonei* was the cash management organisation at the county level, from which we knew that government expenditure was based on postal zones. See Hu Pingsheng and Zhang Defang (2001), p. 74.
24 Yamada Katsuyoshi, in Satake Yasuhiko (2008), pp. 218–222.
25 Ma Daying (1983), p. 315.
26 Ban Gu. *The History of the Han Dynasty* ("Biography of Zhai Fangjin"). Beijing: Zhonghua Book Company (1962), p. 3423.
27 Ma Tao and Ma Xuedong (2016), pp. 107–120.

References

Original works

Ban Gu. *The History of the Han Dynasty*. Beijing: Zhonghua Book Company, 1962.
Liu Hainian, Yang Yifan. *The Integration of Valuable and Rare Laws and Classics in China*. Beijing: Science Press, 1994.
Rong Geng. *Qin Han Jin Wen Book*. Beijing: Institute of History and Philology, Academia Sinica, 1931.
Sima Qian. *Records of the Grand Historian*. Beijing: Zhonghua Book Company, 1959.

Secondary sources

Hu, P. and Zhang, D. (2001). *Dunhuang Xuanquan Han Wooden Slips*. Shanghai: Shanghai Classics Publishing House.
Lin, G. (2007). *Chinese Economic History: The Economy in the Qin and Han Dynasties*, 2nd ed. Beijing: The Economics Daily Press.
Luo, Q. (1985). "Discussions on the characteristics of the corvée labour system in the Western Han Dynasty". *The Journal of Chinese Social and Economic History* (4).

Ma, D. (1983). *The Financial History of the Han Dynasty.* Beijing: China Financial and Economic Publishing House.

Ma, T. and Ma, X. (2016). "The Features of Eastern and Western Ancient Monetary Axiology and Their Impact on the Monetary System". *World Economic Papers*, (6).

Peng, X. (2015). *The History of Chinese Currency.* Shanghai: Shanghai People's Publishing House.

Satake, Y. (2008). *The Basic Historical Questions of Yin, Zhou, Qin and Han Dynasties.* Beijing: Zhonghua Book Company.

5 Monetary thought in the Han Dynasty and Three Kingdoms period (220–280 BCE)

Gavin S.H. Chiu and S.C. Kwan

Introduction

The Han Dynasty instituted two systems for minting coin. One, which was set up during Emperor Wen's reign (180–157 BCE), allowed people to mint currency along with the central government. The other, beginning from the time of Emperor Wu (r. 141–87 BCE), imposed a central government monopoly on minting and, henceforth, minting without permission would result in a death sentence. Scholars during the two Han Dynasties debated incessantly over which system was better. The entire body of the literature that resulted left a legacy that continued to shape subsequent discussions. Scholars in the Qing Dynasty, some 1,500 years after the Han, still made frequent quotations from Han records to support their divergent views on the impact of the opium trade on the monetary system.[1] Of the legacy that the Han scholars had left, one was known as the "anti-monetary thought", which held that money had no use value and that its circulation was damaging to agriculture and, by extension, national security. This chapter seeks to analyse this anti-monetary thought and the background against which it developed.

Background

Bruno Hildebrand (1864) divided economic development into three stages, these being the natural (or barter) economy, the money economy and the credit economy. During the money economy, metal currency, especially precious metal currency, is the major medium of exchange as well as the medium for incomes and expenditures. In the first stage (the natural economy), commodities with high use values, such as grain and textiles, take the role of a medium of exchange, and wages, taxes, rents and so on, are mostly paid in terms of such material objects. However, as those objects are imperfectly divisible and inconvenient to carry around, transaction costs are high and economic development will be limited to a specific territory.[2]

Hildebrand believed that human economy developed from natural economy to a money economy, then ultimately to credit economy. But Chuan (2003) pointed out that as early as the beginning stage of the Western Han, China had already become a money economy. However, the Chinese economy had then reverted out of various causes (chiefly wars) to a natural economy by the time of the Eastern Han. Despite some short-lived revival of a money economy, towards the end of the Eastern Han a natural economy was again resurgent. With the interplay of different forms of economic systems, scholarly discussions sprang up in a fashion somewhat in correspondence with the economic fashions.[3]

As early as the end of the Warring States period (500–221 BCE) and the beginning of the Western Han, China had already become a monetary economy. According to Sung (2001), the Western Han departed from the age of barter by extensively using currency in exchanges such as transactions, loans, gifts, inheritance and collectibles, not to mention taxation and wages, until the reign of Emperor Zhang (57–88 CE), who decreed that currency be abolished for taxation purposes.[4] This saw the official revival of an ancient practice in which tax was paid in terms of real objects rather than currency.

During the period of Three Kingdoms (220–280 CE), one of the Kingdoms, Wei, decreed that tax must be paid in terms of grain and textiles. Although this policy did not eliminate cash transactions completely, it did succeed in reducing the supply of currency. The remains of an archaeological site discovered in Nanchang, Jiangxi, in June 1979, testify to the imbalance of the natural and money economies after the two Hans: of the currency found there, 96.8% belonged to the two Hans with the remaining 3.2% to the Three Kingdoms. Other archaeological discoveries seem to confirm the Nanchang finding.[5] The phenomenon was due to the fact that from the late Eastern Han to the Three Kingdoms (220–280 CE), the issue of currency was irregular, and the coin that was issued was of poor quality. That left few choices for the market, which ended up resorting to a non-currency system. Given this, it is clear that the money economic system had already given way to the natural variant.[6]

The low tide of the monetary economy

According to Chuan, the germination, as it were, of the natural economy in the late Eastern Han and Three Kingdoms periods could be attributed to wars and the lack of raw materials for making currency. He claimed that since the Yellow Turban Rebellion (184 CE) instigated by Daoists, China had run into a prolonged period of division. Wars led to economic recession, which further hampered the development of a money economy. To make matters worse, the post-Eastern Han period witnessed the widespread propagation in China of Buddhism, which generated a huge demand for copper to build statues and other religious artefacts.

Chuan's sketch of the state of the natural economy after the late Eastern Han and Three Kingdoms periods is no doubt an important contribution to scholarship. But a closer look reveals that its explanatory power is limited.

It is clear that war had an immense impact on the development of commerce. But, even in the later stage of the Western Han, the money economy was receding as anti-monetarist sentiment increased.[7] Long before the warlords went into constant battle with one another and large-scale rebellions broke out in the later Eastern Han, the money economy was already in retreat. War may certainly have had an impact, but it was not the only cause of the reversion to natural economy.

The falling back of monetary thought

Sung's work (2012) is complementary to Chuan's. He argued that the regression in the quality of monetary thought was yet another crucial factor accounting for the rise of natural economy after the late Eastern Han and Three Kingdoms periods.[8] But ideas will not gain popularity unless they reflect what people are thinking, which in turn depends on their experience. Hence the position taken in this chapter, that before anti-monetary ideas prevailed in the period under discussion, the market environment had already been suffering from extensive problems. It was the synergy between the experience of those problems and the articulation of anti-monetary thought that was to shape policies that finally led to the downfall of the currency economy. This chapter will examine the several stages involved in that process.

According to Sima Qian's account in *The Records of the Grand Historian* (*Shiji*) it was in 175 BCE, early in the reign of Emperor Wen (180–157 BCE), that the "people were allowed to mint [coin] at will"[9] on account of the apparent inadequacy of the currency supply. Once the supply of currency became stabilised, wealth was created and commodity price steadily rose.

With the development of commercial activities during the first 70 years of the new dynasty, at a time when policy was influenced by the teaching of the Yellow Emperor and Laozi,[10] a strong middle class and a growing number of entrepreneurs began to emerge.[11] During Emperor Jing's reign (157–141 BCE), the feudal lords had become so accustomed to their currency-issuing rights that they began to belittle the central government. That response finally culminated in the well-known "Rebellion of the Seven States" (154 BCE). After the rebellion was suppressed, Emperor Jing began to take over issuing rights, and in 144 BCE he established a statute making public coinage punishable by death. But these efforts were to no avail: opportunistic behaviour flourished and the currency was debased. As a result, people resorted to the currency issued during Emperor Wen's reign as the medium of transaction.

Jia Yi, who vehemently opposed Emperor Wen's monetary policy, was an important figure whose contribution marked the first stage in the articulation of anti-monetary thought. In 175 BCE, Jia robustly criticised the idea that the general public and feudal states be allowed to issue currency, not least on the grounds that peasants would disengage from farming, resulting in a drastic reduction in the supply of food. Social unrest would be the inevitable outcome, he argued. It is therefore not surprising that he proposed a state-planned economy in which non-government agencies were prohibited from engaging in copper mining, thus rendering private coinage impossible.[12]

Jia's proposal was highly unpopular. The government's policies of denationalising money had not only left agricultural industry intact, but also, with the impetus given by the quantity, quality and circulation rate of currency, had fuelled national economic development.[13] The central government's reserves still kept escalating in spite of drastic tax deductions. Jia's proposal therefore raised few eyebrows, if any.[14]

Established after almost 500 years of inter-state warfare, the early Han was a society that had barely begun a recovery. Its population, as Chuan (1941) claimed, was one of the lowest in Chinese history. Faced with this, the newly established government resorted to the teaching of the Yellow Emperor and Laozi in implementing policies with the aim of encouraging commercial development. As a result, a class of entrepreneurs rose to the fore whose activities stimulated the economy by promoting consumption.[15] Given this increase in economic activity, currency was in constant demand by the market. At the same time, the central government in the early Western Han was extremely prudent in its expenditure. During the reigns of Emperor Wen and Emperor Jin (180–141 BCE), the government regularly managed to cut agricultural tax, which was brought down initially to 6%, then to 3% and then, for a period of 12 years, to zero. Consequently, private capital accumulation continued to increase.

It was during this period that the "utility" of money (in Bentham's sense) was at its peak. This was evident as copper coins played a key role in the government's income and expenditure as well as in the majority of transactions. Wealth, as a result, was accumulated, which left a very favourable impression of money on the public mind.[16]

Apparently, Jia Yi's proposal, which represented the first stage of anti-monetary thought, not only took no account of the then pan-currency economy but also simply ran counter to it. It came to no surprise, therefore, that his proposal was neither accepted by Emperor Jing nor well received by society.

In 144 BCE, roughly 20 years after the death of Jia Yi, the central government abolished the policy of non-interventionism, which had run for 31 years, by disallowing private individuals from issuing currency (although provincial states were allowed to keep the privilege). Chao Cuo (200–154 BCE), a scholar during the reigns of Emperors Wen and Jing, held that currency achieved little other than offering government officials a temptation to walk out on the royal court, and the people to desert their homeland. Apparently, Chao gave much heavier weight to the concern for central authority and stability than anything else, and he simply ignored the benefits and advantages that currency could bring. For him, currency gave impetus to commerce. When people were engaged in it, they would leave their hometowns in pursuit of profits. But once it became difficult to ascertain people's whereabouts, it also became difficult to collect taxes (such as the poll tax), which was obviously a destabilising factor for the central government. As far as Chao was concerned, grains and textiles, not currency, were the commodities that had use value. At least they could feed and clothe people. That is why he proposed using them as the means of transaction in replacement of currency. Interestingly enough, this scholar-cum-minister had already anticipated the classical conception of commodity value. He was able to point out the function of currency, although he believed it was to the detriment of the ruling authority.[17] This perfectly reflects what Legalists like him had in mind: stability and central authority were the top priority, and everything else, including the people's livelihood, had to come second, at best.

Chao's voice was not initially heeded as the economy was still flourishing as a result of the implementation of policies influenced by the teaching of the Yellow

Emperor and Laozi, especially during the reign of Emperor Wen (180–157 BCE). Emperor Jing, who succeeded Emperor Wen, gave those policies further consideration. From his own experience, he noticed that although denationalising currency could bring about prosperity, it could also reduce the absolute power and authority of the central government over the provincial states, with potentially disastrous consequences, as exemplified by the Wu-Chu rebellion. On the one hand, government finances relied heavily on the circulation of currency, so any move to abolish the denationalisation of coinage could incur huge financial cost. But, on the other hand, the potential rise of provincial power – which was seen as a natural result of denationalising currency – might threaten the very survival of the central government. It was in pursuit of the lesser evil that Emperor Jing belatedly chose to follow the advice offered to him by Jia Yi. It was at this juncture that we see the confluence of forces – anti-monetary thought and political imperatives – that were to spell the demise of Yellow Emperor–Laozi policy.

Not long after Emperor Wu (r. 142–87 BCE) succeeded to the throne, he was determined to reduce further the strength of the provincial states. This was not surprising as his father, Emperor Jing, was plagued his entire life by threats from the provincial states and was so unfortunate as to have undergone the Wu-Chu rebellion mentioned above. If this were not bad enough, the empire during his reign was constantly intimidated by the Xiongnu in the north. However, Emperor Wu did not literally take Chao Chuo's proposal, for although he understood that to abolish the use of copper currency might perhaps weaken the provincial states, on the one hand, it would, on the other hand, adversely affect people's livelihood and commercial activities, which in turn meant a tremendous cut in revenue for the empire. As Sima Qian (1981) observed:

> By the time the present emperor had been on the throne a few years, a period of over seventy years had passed since the founding of the Han. During that time the nation had met with no major disturbances so that, except in times of flood or drought, every person was well supplied and every family had enough to get along on. The granaries in the cities and the countryside were full and the government treasuries were running over with wealth. In the capital, the strings of cash had been stacked up by the hundreds of millions until the cords that bound them had rotted away and they could no longer be counted. In the central granary of the government, new grain was heaped on top of the old until the building was full and the grain overflowed and piled up outside, where it spoiled and became unfit to eat. Horses were to be seen even in the streets and lanes of the common people or plodding in great number along the paths between the fields, and anyone so poor as to have to ride a mare was disdained by his neighbours and not allowed to join the gathering of the villagers. Even the keepers of the community gates ate fine grain and meat. The local officials remained at the same posts long enough to see their sons and grandsons grow to manhood, and the higher officials occupied the same positions so long that they adopted their official titles as surnames. As a result, men had a sense of self-respect and regarded it as a serious matter

to break the law. Their first concern was to act in accordance with what was right and to avoid shame and dishonour[18].

The officials therefore advised the emperor (Wu) that,

> in ancient times, currency made of hides was used by the feudal lord for gifts and presentations. At present there are three types of metal in use; gold, which is the most precious; silver, which ranks second; and copper which in third. The "half-tael" coins now in use are supposed by the law to weigh four Shu, but people have tampered with them to such an extent, illegally filing off bits of copper from the reserves side, that they have become increasingly light and thin and the price of good has accordingly risen. Such currency is extremely troublesome and expensive to use, especially in distant regions.[19]

With the 70-year reserve handed down from his predecessors in hand, Emperor Wu turned his back on his father's wish, resorted to Jia Yi's idea and began to take back the privilege of issuing currency from the provincial states and the general public. As a corollary, the central government monopolised the trade in salt and iron and closed all mines opened during Emperor Wen's rule. In short, unless sanctioned by the central government, no one was allowed to mine for copper and other metals for currency-issuing purposes. The teaching of Yellow Emperor and Laozi policy, which had dominated the economic scene for decades, finally came to a halt.

Poorly motivated and without the pressure of competition, the government officials' efforts in looking for mines and improving mining techniques could never be held in high regard. Mining techniques in China, even up to the Qing Dynasty, have never made any significant breakthrough.[20] Water drainage has been the predominant obstacle. As a result, deep mining has been impossible. Most important of all, private issuing of currency began to take place almost the first minute after it was banned. Although it had become illegal and ceased to attract a special property rights arrangement during Emperor Wen's time, opportunists, taking it as a single stage game, nonetheless were actively engaged in it. Such an institutional arrangement created an environment in which privately issued currency could never be worse in its quality.

From other archaeological findings, the quality of the currency issued, officially and unofficially alike, was perfectly up to the standard of Sizhu Coins (四銖 錢).[21] Chen (2008) has calculated the difference in the quality of currencies issued at various times in terms of standard weight, average weight, compliance rate of weight and average copper proportion. The quality index so compiled shows that the currency issued during the heyday of the teaching of Yellow Emperor and Laozi policy, which weighed the closest to the official 2.604 gram, reached a record high at 205, Qin's at 100, Emperor Wu's at 184 and Emperor Chao's and thereafter at 174. The currency of the non-intervention period literally outweighed all the others over a span of 200 years and was better than that of Emperor Wu's by 10%. It is not difficult to conclude that withholding private issuing of currency only led to a drastic decline in its quality. And with such a decline came deflation. Adam Smith (1976, p. 43) once lamented that all rulers in the world are vora-cious, taking pleasure in deceiving people by first standardising currency and then debasing it surreptitiously.²² Actually, this is inevitable when it comes to national monopolisation of currency. When a government, any government, has a politi-cal agenda in mind and begins to rock the economy by first tightening control, then monopolising the supply and finally shrinking the face value of money in an attempt to increase its reserves, a logical result is that the public will sooner or later lose their faith in money. The utility of money consequently abates. Under Emperor Wu's rule, merchants and entrepreneurs were oppressed. Their private properties were seized by the government under various groundless pretexts and so-called laws. Consequently, economic activities were subdued and the currency system became chaotic. Few would bother to raise objections to monetary econ-omy even at such times when it was in crisis.²³ It was only in Emperor Yuan's time (75–33 BCE), after a prolonged period of peace, that commerce began to revive. Yet, it could never be said to thrive as it had during the reigns of Emperors Wen and Jin. Historians had left only a few words on a few merchants' affairs during Emperor Yuan's rule, whereas much more had been said about the early Han. Nonetheless, commerce still fared better than it had in Emperor Wu's time, when the middle class mostly ended up facing bankruptcy. Those who had accumulated sufficient capital, entrepreneurs and government officials, turned to investments in land (agriculture or livestock farming), as profitable opportunities in trades such as salt, iron and forestry were blocked off to them.²⁴ The early Han did not see land acquisition on that scale. Occasionally there were some well-known cases like that of Xiao He, who assisted in the founding of the empire. However, it was government officials who did most of the land acquisition at that time. Yet, as late as the period under discussion, it was the merchants or entrepreneurs who flocked to the land market, thus assuming a dominant role in local districts. Apparently, the utility of currency was falling vis-à-vis that of land. And, natu-rally, this added more fuel to anti-monetary thought.

The third stage was around the time of Emperor Cheng's reign (33–7 BCE). Gong Yu (123–43 BCE), the deputy Prime Minister, pressed for an all-out aboli-tion of any form of currency, be it gold, jade or copper, and its replacement by a system of barter. By this time, the economy was much less vigorous than it had been before the reign of Emperor Wu. Anti-monetary thinkers put all the blame on the existence and circulation of money, failing to see that it was the inhibition of commerce, rather than money itself, that was to blame. But it was the popular association of widespread poverty and growing inequality with money that cap-tured the public's imagination.²⁵

Gong Yu's anti-monetary thought was initially well received by the govern-ment, and the emperor put it on the agenda for senior officials to discuss. Gong's opponents pointed out that unlike copper currency, grains and textiles were indi-visible and therefore inconvenient for exchange transactions. Moreover, they were also heavy (in weight), hence unsuited to facilitating long-distance transac-tions. Thus, if society returned to barter, commercial activities would doubtless suffer a heavy blow. As it transpired, it was the critics' argument that prevailed, but not for long.

We come to the fourth stage, which differs from the previous three in that anti-monetary thought was actually embodied in various policies.

Historians have long accused Wang Mang of being an impractical idealist, with good reason. In Wang's eyes, land acquisition was the prime cause of social ills and had to be dealt with by increasing transaction costs so that ownership was no longer profitable. During his reign as Emperor of the Xin Dynasty (9–23 CE), he first attempted to revive the monetary system of the Western Zhou, deliberately blind to an economic evolution that had taken 1,000 years to accomplish. But his reforms were resisted from the very beginning. To compel people to accept his policies, Wang tried all measures available to him: he declared it a criminal offence to use Western Han coins, and he decreed that his new currency was the sole means of payment for clearing customs and excise.[26] But his attempts to force the new coins on the people were to no avail, and several changes of coinage later the only beneficiaries were wily merchants who had taken advantage of the frequent currency changes and price fluctuations. For the mass of the people, the result was one of pervasive economic distress, ultimately resulting in large-scale rebellions.

Later, the market went back to using the Han 5-*shu* coin (the *Wu Zhu Qian*). It is here that the "good money" took the upper hand and edged out Wang's barter-type currencies – a classic case of anti-Gresham's Law. But, given the numerous upheavals, it comes as no surprise that people had completely lost faith in *any* currency. The lesson one can learn is, in short, that once anti-monetary thought has materialised into policy, the entire nation suffers loss.[27] According to historical records, Wang's reign had brought nothing but ubiquitous unemployment, high transaction costs, dwindling productivity and a standstill of food and commodity production.[28] His radical anti-monetary policy had not only failed to protect the peasantry, contrary to Wang's objective, but had actually made their situation considerably worse. Under such circumstances, it is at least understandable that people should have lost faith in a monetised economic system.

The new Eastern Han Dynasty, established in 25 CE after Wang Mang's demise, saw little change in people's perception of money, which in their eyes was synonymous with harm and chaos. As a reaction, they reverted to Western Han currency supplemented by barter trade using fabric, cloth, gold and corn.[29] Thanks to the currency reserves left over from Western Han, a limited number of transactions were still possible. The year 40 CE then saw a twist when Emperor Guangwu (r. 25–57 CE) was convinced by his ministers that currency – which he previously thought of as bordering on useless – should be re-issued.[30] The new Eastern Han Dynasty suffered much less turmoil than the previous dynasty, and this, for a country like China, meant a golden age of population growth. According to Ge (1991, p. 124), the population of Eastern Han grew from 20 million at its beginning to 60 million.[31] But, as the country expanded, the supply of copper – the principal raw material for currency – did not. Archaeological findings reveal that ever since Han 5-*shu Wu Zhu Qian* was issued, the government kept reducing its weight below its statutory value.[32] Over time, the currency issued by the Eastern Han government gave way to Western Han currency, thus continuing a trend that had begun under Wang Mang.

The fifth stage features two officials during the Eastern Han, Zhang Lin and Liu Tao. During Emperor Zhang's reign (75–88 CE), faced with an inflation brought about by natural calamities, one minister, Zhang Lin, mistakenly put the blame on the depreciation of currency.[33] The solution, he claimed, was to stop issuing new money, abandon the money currently in circulation and revert to real barter using fabric and cloth.[34]

The emperor initially favoured Zhang's proposal but a large number of his ministers and officials were opposed. The proposal was dropped.[35]

Liu Tao was another prominent anti-monetary figure. Towards the end of the Eastern Han, a minister submitted a file to Emperor Huan (r. 146–168 CE) in which he attributed inflation to the fact that copper money was getting lighter.[36] He then proposed that the government issue *Da Qian*, a new currency with its real value lower than its nominal value, to rectify the situation. Liu Tao rose immediately to reject the proposal and argued that the cause of inflation was bureaucratic corruption and local gang activities and had nothing to do with the quantity of money.[37] Therefore, inflation would prevail regardless of whether any new currency was issued. He even went so far as to contend that unlike the food supply, money was inessential to society.[38] But Liu knew nothing about the relationship between prices and money. What was more ridiculous is that he suggested that the government lift the ban on thinning the copper money. Copper was valuable at that time and people used it in a variety of ways. Because of this, many people clipped copper money and used the clippings to issue even thinner currency, resulting in a perpetual devaluation of copper money.[39]

Remarkably, Emperor Huan accepted Liu Tao's proposals, with predictably dire consequences: clipping continued apace, copper currency devalued further, commodity prices rocketed and widespread rebellions ensued. The people's faith in money had suffered a shattering blow, making them even more receptive to the suggestion of reverting to a natural economy.

The attraction of abolishing currency increased further as time went by. In 189 CE the capital of Eastern Han, Luoyang, was taken over by Dong Zhuo (134–192 CE), a warlord notorious for his brutality. One of the first things he did was to melt down prized artefacts (some more than 300 years old) in order to make copper money.[40] But the currency he issued was not the 5-*shu Wu Zhu Qian* but the *Xiao Chien*, literally "little money",[41] which was much lighter than the 5-*shu* coin but was stipulated as being of the same value even though its copper content was negligible. As a result, the money circulating around the capital was seriously devalued.

A while later, just prior to the Three Kingdoms period, Liu Bei (161–223 CE), at that time an Eastern Han official (but later the founder of Su-Han), issued *Da Qian*, a copper currency with a value much lower than its nominal value. To fund his army, he compelled people to exchange *Da Qian* with material produce, thereby managing in a short time to generate impressive revenue for his local government.[42] His success encouraged others to follow suit. The Suns, upon establishing Wu (also one of the Three Kingdoms), issued their own *Da Qian*.[43] These acts were seen by the people as nothing less than outright theft.

In 208 CE, Cao Cao (155–220 CE), the most prominent warlord at the time, resorted briefly to re-issuing *Wu Zhu Qian* in the name of the withering Eastern Han government. Yet, as it was not circulated widely enough, barter continued in the peripheral areas. His son, Cao Pei (187–226 CE), ordered a resurrection of currency only to abolish it soon after.[44]

By the late Eastern Han and early Three Kingdoms, public confidence in currency had been destroyed. What followed was an extended period of time in which natural economy ruled the Chinese economic world.

The monetarists' response

Under the auspices of the government, anti-monetary thought was enjoying its heyday. But that does not imply that all monetarists were silent. During the salt and iron conference (*Yantie lun*), intellectuals criticised Emperor Xuan's government (91–48 BCE) for monopolising the issuing of currency. They pointed out a number of benefits that denationalisation of currency brought about during Emperor Wen's reign. Naturally, they championed the teaching of Yellow Emperor and Laozi policies as regards salt, iron and money. This of course meant that state-controlled transactions had to be aborted and people should be allowed to mint money. Heated debates were nothing surprising. Sang Hongyang, the highest official in finance, flatly rejected the critics' arguments on grounds of national security and the authority of the central government. He insisted that interventionism was an effective guarantee of national revenue that could offset huge public expenditure.[45]

In passing, it must be noted that over the last 2,000 years, the teaching of the Yellow Emperor and Laozi have been side-lined by interventionism. Not until the nineteenth century, when the late Qing suffered an outflow of silver in the opium trade, did the debate between these two antagonistic positions once more return to the fore.[46]

When anti-monetarists like Zhang Lin urged that grains and textiles be adopted as media of transactions, Zhu Hui, a contemporary senior official, raised the objection that government officials should not contend with people in seeking profit. Policies like monopolisation or manipulating market prices were represented as typical acts of competing with the general public, which would inevitably give rise to poverty. A barter system would encourage counterfeiting and allow officials to engage in rent-seeking behaviour. Unlike money, objects used in barter lack a determined value and always end up in the hands of the opportunists, with the mass of the people as the losers.[47] Zhu Hui's analysis demonstrates that the adherents of Yellow Emperor and Laozi thought had never compromised with interventionism. What Zhu asked for from the royal throne was to revive Emperor Wen's non-interventionism. But Emperor Zhang was not persuaded. Although he briefly agreed to postpone the abolition of currency, that was only because Zhu Hui had threatened to kill himself.

Up to the beginning of the Three Kingdoms' era, which succeeded the two Hans, just six years after Emperor Wen of Wei had abolished the use of money, northern China had already experienced a financial crisis that lasted 40 years. In 227 CE, Xima Zhi, a minister of Wei, pointed out from a legal perspective that it was much easier to fake grains or textiles than to fake currency. At the time, it was not uncommon to find bandits increasing the weight of the media of transactions by pumping water into them. Consequently, the market became seriously chaotic and the costs to the judiciary system rocketed. The government faced a dilemma. Either it played blind to the unlawful acts, which definitely vitiated its authority, or it revived the use of currency for transactions. Xima Zhi begged the royal throne to opt for the latter. However, rather than minting a new currency, he suggested using the *Wu Zhu Qian* (五銖錢) as a way to increase national revenue and lessen the burden on the judiciary. From this we can see that *Wu Zhu Qian* had been banned during Emperor Wen (Wei)'s time.[48]

For the next 500 years until the Tang Dynasty, various governments alternated between using substantial objects like grains and textiles or *Wu Zhu Qian* as transactions' media.[49] A dependence path with its origins in the anti-monetary thoughts of Han could clearly be discerned.

Conclusion

It has been argued that the decline in the monetary economy in China can be attributed to two main factors: first, serious policy mistakes by successive governments; and second, a regression in economic (and particularly monetary) thought that was fuelled by people's negative daily experiences. Together, these influences paved the way for a reversion to natural economy.

Not realising the mutual relationship between the two factors, some historians have given a conventional inflation explanation of the rise in prices that occurred in the period under consideration.[50] From our discussions, both the quantity and circulation of currency had experienced a drastic plunge since the late Eastern Han. Commodity prices went up not because the supply of currency was on the increase, but because of incoherent policies of the monetary institutions, which pushed up transaction costs. It goes without saying, of course, that some price increases were the result of natural disasters and ceaseless wars. But the most important factor is that the weight of various kinds of currency was constantly and systematically reduced. When bad money took the stage, the rise in prices in this sense were apparently distinguishable from regular inflation caused by a mere increase in the supply of currency.[51]

The analysis of this chapter also clearly demonstrates that there were extended periods of deflation following the late Eastern Han.[52] The single most important function of currency is to reduce transaction costs. But the constant decrease in the money supply from these periods onward exerted a huge braking effect on this function of currency, which in turn made transactions tremendously difficult. Coupled with the increase in transaction costs caused by deflation, commercial activities plummeted and consumption plunged, leaving people with little choice but to eke out a bare subsistence. So, we see how a natural economy after the late Eastern Han Dynasty and Three Kingdoms period was consolidated and reinforced.[53]

We believe that the main contribution of this chapter has been to revise Chuan Han Sing's explanation of the rise and cause of the natural economy in the late Eastern Han and Three Kingdoms period. As we have argued, the decline in the money economy cannot be attributed simply to an insufficient supply of copper after the introduction to China of Buddhism. Rather, we suggest that account must be taken of the interaction between the negative consequences of misplaced government policy and the appeal of anti-monetary thought, which came to be seen as providing an answer to the people's woes when in fact it only made them worse. It was government policy, especially the attempts to impose a monopoly over currency, which unleashed a train of events – among them degradation and depreciation of coinage, loss of confidence and spiralling transactions costs – which both emboldened the anti-monetarists and facilitated a more favourable climate for the reception of their siren calls.

Notes

1 Lin (2006).
2 Hildebrand (1864), pp. 1–24; Quoted from Chuan (2003), pp. 73–74.
3 Chuan (2003), pp. 73–173.
4 Sung (1971, 2001), pp. 36–40.
5 Chen (2012), p. 53.
6 Fu (1982), p. 533.
7 According to Sung (2001), some officials held that the circulation of currency was detrimental to agricultural development and therefore to social morality.
8 Sung (2012), p. 37.
9 Sima Qian, *Shiji* 30 ("The Treatise on the Balanced Standard"). The original Chinese for "were allowed" (*fang zhu* 放鑄) conveys the sense that the government had adopted a non-interventionist attitude towards private minting.
10 In the context of the early Han, which could be characterised as verging on economic, if not just political, turmoil, the strategic use of the legacies of the Yellow Emperor and Laozi was highly relevant and pertinent. Their legacies, in short, could be likened to a minimalist state comparable to the one proposed by Robert Nozick in his *Anarchy, State and Utopia*. The governance of a state, in Nozick's view, should be severely limited to the protection of its citizens from military aggression, theft and breach of contracts, etc. The citizens, therefore, should be free, apart from violating others' rights, from any control over what they desire to do – including but not limited to the minting of money.
11 Sima Qian, *The Records of the Grand Historian*, "The Treatise on the Balanced Standard" *Shiji* 30.
12 One may wonder why we take Jia Yi as an anti-monetarist given that he did not advocate the abolition of currency. But Jia was recorded as saying that currency should be likened to jewellery, silver and gold which "could neither feed when one is starving nor keep warm when one shivers in coldness . . . and is clearly useless . . . therefore a wise ruler would discard them in favour of grains". See "Treatise on Food and Money", *Book of Han*, pp. 1131–1132. Thanks are due to Terry Peach who raised the query, which called for this explanation.
13 "As a result, the king of Wu, though only feudal lord, was able, by extracting ore from the mountains in his domain and minting coins, to rival the wealth of the son heaven. It was this wealth which he eventually used to start his revolt. Similarly, Deng Tong, who

was only a high official, succeeded in becoming richer than a vassal king by minting coins. The coins of the king of Wu and Deng Tong were soon circulating all over the empire, and as a result the rite minting of coinage was finally prohibited." Sima Qian, *Shiji* 30 ("The Treatise on the Balanced Standard").

14 Han and Bo (2015), pp. 1497–1519.
15 Merchants mentioned in *The Records of the Grand Historian* during the early period of Emperor Wu's reign were mostly in the trades of salt, mines or livestock, whereas those in the *Han Shu* after that period were landlords.
16 *Discourses on Salt and Iron*, pp. 57, 93.
17 Ban Gu, *Han shu* (1979), pp. 1131–1132.
18 Shiji 30, *The Treatise on the Balanced*, p. 1420.
19 ibid.
20 Rui, Huayan, Santosh and Shouting (2015), p. 722.
21

Time	Normal Weight (KG)	Real Weight	Result
Qin	7.81	4.78	61.20%
Kao & Lu	1.95	2.21	113.233%
Lu	5.21	3.85	73.90%
Wen	2.60	2.89	111.15%
Jin	2.60	2.33	89.62%
Wu	3.26	3.10	95.06%
Post-Wu	3.26	2.88	88.34%

From Chen (2008), p. 331.

22 Adam Smith, *The Wealth of Nations* (1976), p. 43.
23 Chiu (2017), pp. 19–24.
24 Sima Qian, *Records of the Grand Historian*, "The Biographies of the Money-makers", *Shiji* 129.
25 Ibid.
26 Zhao (1991), p. 720.
27 Though Wang attempted to replace the currency circulating at the time with his preferred coinage, he could nonetheless be taken as inclined to anti-monetarism. See Jiang (2005), p. 120.
28 Ban Gu, "Monograph on Food and Currency", *Han shu* p. 4112.
29 Nishijima (2007), p. 217.
30 Sung (2012), p. 45.
31 The population of Western Han peaked at 60 million; by the early Eastern Han it was less than 30 million, and thereafter gradually rose back to 60 million. See Ge (1991).
32 Chen (2007), p. 331.
33 Fang Qiao, *The Book of Jin* ("Food and Commodities"), p. 793.
34 Zhang (2001), p. 130.
35 Fan Ye, *Book of the Later Han* ("Biographies of Zhu, Yue, He"), p. 1460.
36 According to the report on the weight of *Wu-Zhu* money (五銖) in Han by an archaeological team in *Luoyang*:

Reign	Weight (nominal weight, 3.255kg)
Emperor Wu (Western Han)	3.5 g
Towards later stage of Western Han	3.5 g
First half of Eastern Han	3.0 g
Emperors Huan and Nin (later stages of Eastern Han)	2.4 g

See *The Han Tomb in Xiaogou, Luoyang* (1959), pp. 216–221. Also Chan Yan Liang (2009), whose extensive archaeological reports reached similar results.
37 Ibid.
38 Fan Ye, *Book of the Later Han* ("Biographies of Du, Luan, Liu, Li, Liu, Xie"), p. 1847.
39 Chen (2011), p. 26.
40 Nishijima (2007), p. 61.
41 Fan Ye, *Book of the Later Han* ("Annals of Emperor Xiaoxianp"), p. 370.
42 Chen Shou, *Records of the Three Kingdoms* ("Wei"), p. 981.
43 Fang Qiao, *The Book of Jin* ("Food and Commodities"), p. 795.
44 Nishijima (2007), p. 61.
45 *Discourses on Salt and Iron*, Chiu (2014), p. 2.
46 Ibid., pp. 4–6.
47 Yoshida (1966), p. 131.
48 Nishijima (2007), p. 251.
49 Shen Yue, *Songshu*, p. 156.
50 Hu (1998), p. 192.
51 Nishijima (2007), p. 238.
52 Pang (1987), p. 179: "the inflation rocketed by hundreds of times in a very short period".
53 Private mining was not a problem in the early Han, at least not during the reign of Wen and Jing. According to Sima Qian: "From the beginning of Emperor Wu's reign, because revenue in coin had been rather scarce, the government officials had from time to time extracted copper from the mountains in their areas and minted new coins, while among the common people there was a good deal of illegal minting of coins, until the number in circulation had grown beyond estimate. As the coins became more numerous and of poorer quality, goods became scarce and higher in price" (*Shiji* 30).

References

Ban Gu (1979). *Book of Han (Han shu)*. Taipei: Dingwen Publishers.
Chen, S. (1980). *Records of the Three Kingdoms (Sanguozhi)*. Taipei: Dingwen Publishers.
Chen, Y.L. (2007). "Sizhu Coins and the Monetary Reform of Emperor Wu in the Western Han Dynasty". *Tsing Hua Journal of Chinese Studies*, pp. 321–360.
Chen, Y.L. (2011). "Long-Term Inflation in the Eastern Han Dynasty: An Analysis based on Archaeological Evidence". *Tsing Hua Journal of Chinese Studies*, pp. 669–714
Chen, Y.L. (2012). "Characteristics of Monetary Liquidity in Medieval China". *The Journal of History of Taiwan National Chengchi University*, (38).
Chiu, G. (tr., ed.) (2014). *Discourses on Salt and Iron (Yantie lun)*, by Huan Kuan. Hong Kong: Chung Wah Press.
———. (2017). *Pioneer of the Free Economy in Chinese History: The Economic Thought of Sima Qian*. Taipei: Wan Juan Lou Books.
Chuan, H.S. (2003). "The Natural Economy in the Middle Ages". In *A study on Chinese Economic History*. Vol. 1. Taipei: Daw Shiang Publishing Co. Ltd. pp. 1–136. First printed in 1941, *Bulletin of the Institute of History and Philology, Academia Sinica*, (10).
Fan, Y. (1979). *Book of the Later Han (Houhan shu)*. Taipei: Dingwen Publishers.
Fang, Q. (1980). *The Book of Jin (Jin shu)*. Taipei: Dingwen Publishers.
Fu, Z.F. (1982). *An Economic History of the Feudal Chinese Society*. Vol. 2. Beijing: People's Publishing House.
Ge, J.H. (1991). *A History of Population Growth in China*. Fu Zhou: Fu Jian People's Publishing House.
Han, H.G. and Bo, K.C. (2015). "Denationalization of Money: Research Based on China's Experience in the Western Han Dynasty, 175 B.C.–144 B.C". *Economic Quarterly*, Vol. 4.
Hildebrand, B. (1864). *Jahrbuedher fuer Nationaloekonomie und Statistik*, vol. ii, pp. 1–24.

Hu, J. C. (1998). *A History of Chinese Economic Thoughts.* Vol. 2. Shanghai: Shanghai University of Economics & Finance Press.

Jiang, Z.Q. (2005). *A Synoptic History of China.* Taipei: Wu Nan Books.

Lin, Man-houng (2006). *China's Upside Down Currency, Society, and Ideologies, 1808–1856.* Boston: Harvard University Press.

Nishijima, S. (2007). *Shinoj shokkashi yakuchū.* Tōyō: Bunko.

Pang, W.X. (1987). *The History of Currency in China.* Shanghai: Shanghai People's Publishing House.

Rui, Z., Huayan, P., Santosh, M. and Shouting, Z. (2015). "The History and Economics of Gold Mining in China". *Geology Reviews,* (65).

Sima Qian (1981). *Shiji (Records of the Grand Historian).* Taipei: Dingwen Publishers.

Smith, A. (1976). *The Nature and Causes of the Wealth of Nations.* Oxford: Oxford University Press.

Sung, X.W. (2001). *A History of Currency in the Western Han.* Hong Kong: Chinese University Press. First printed in 1971.

Sung, X.W. (2012). "A Complimentary Note on Chuan's The Natural Economy in the Middle Ages". In Liu, B. Y (ed.), *The Structure and Change of Chinese Economy.* Taipei: Wan Juan Lou Books.

Yoshida, T. (1966). *Ryōkan sozei no kenkyū.* Tōkyō: Daian.

Zhang, K.S. (2001). *The History of Chinese Monetary Theory.* Wuhan: Hubei People's Press.

Zhao, J. (1991). *The History of Chinese Economic Ideas.* Beijing: Peking University Press.

6 The system of tribute equalisation in the Han

Li Chaomin[1]

Introduction

The policy of *junshu* (均输 tribute equalisation) is generally acknowledged to have been one of the most important fiscal measures to be introduced in the Western Han. According to Sima Qian in the *Shiji* (*Records of the Grand Historian*), a series of fiscal policies were applied during the reign of Emperor Wu of Han (147–87 BCE), including *junshu*, *pingshun* ("balancing standard"), the salt and iron monopolies, liquor tax, *Suanminqian* (capital gains tax) and *gaominqian* (surtax). As one of the greatest masters of public finance, Sang Hongyang has been praised regardless of time and ideology for his policy of *junshu*, commonly hailed as a measure "that helped enrich the state without increasing tax".[2] Thus, Jia Sixie in the Northern Wei (386–534 CE) believed that Sang Hongyang's law of *junshu* was "an immortal measure that benefited both the state and the people".[3] Li Zhi (1527–1602) in the Ming wrote a biography of Sang Hongyang in which he referred to him as "a famous minister who made his state rich" and "an indispensable talent for the state"; and he praised Sang's policy as "a great and indispensable undertaking of the state that can demonstrate authority under heaven, provide security to the borders, and bring satisfaction to the people".[4] In modern China, Dr Sun Yat-sen (1866–1925) remarked,

> Sang Hongyang's policy of tribute equalisation helped gather goods from across the state, buying at low prices and selling at high prices to equalise the overall supply of goods in the market and increase tribute, so that the state and the people can all benefit.

Dr Sun went so far as to claim that Chancellor Bismarck actually borrowed Sang Hongyang's policy in order to make Germany rich and powerful.[5] Chen Huanzhang (1911) perhaps went even further, suggesting that the policy of tribute equalisation was the first successful large-scale practice of National Socialism.[6] Nor has praise been forthcoming only from the Chinese: Esson M. Gale believed that Sang Hongyang was the Alexander Hamilton of China in the Han Dynasty.[7]

But what exactly *was* Sang Hongyang's policy of *junshu*? Could it relate to the system modelled in Chapter Six of the Han mathematical textbook, *Jiuzhang*

Suanshu (*The Nine Chapters on the Mathematical Art*)? How did Sang Hongyang manage to "enrich the state without increasing tax"? And, if the policy had such great power, why did people in later times not try to restore it? These and related questions are considered further below.

Sang Hongyang and *junshu*

The life of Sang Hongyang remains much of a mystery. Qing historian Zhang Xuecheng remarked that "*Zhiren Lunshi*" – understanding ancient people by knowing the time in which they lived and the lives they lived – serves as an important principle for historical research.[8] However, because of the absence of records of Sang Hongyang in both *Shiji* and *Han shu*, details of his life have been lost in the mists of antiquity. He is "a highly misunderstood historical figure".[9] But how would we know this? Despite a constant stream of defenders for Sang Hongyang, he still bears the accusation of being a schemer and usurper. All these conflicting voices have made Sang Hongyang something of a riddle, along with his policy of *junshu*. The only facts known to people in later times are that "he was the son of a merchant born in Luoyang who, because of his ability to work sums in his head, had been made a palace attendant at the age of thirteen".[10] Opinions concerning the date of Sang Hongyang's birth and death vary widely. Chen Huan-zhang maintained that Sang was born in 131 BCE and died in 80 BCE when he was 51.[11] Zhu Xizu held that he was born in 143 or 142 BCE, two years before the death of Emperor Jing of Han, and died at the age of 62 or 63,[12] while Ma Yuancai believed that Sang was born in 152 BCE, the fifth year of Emperor Jing's reign, and died at the age of 72. Yet another suggestion was made by Nancy Lee Swann and Wang Liqi, who put Sang's birth in the second year of Emperor Jing's reign, 155 BCE, and his death in 75 BCE at the age of 75.[13] But why should there be this mystery over Sang's dates? Ma Yuancai advanced his hypothesis that, "blinded by Confucian prejudices, both Sima Qian (author of *Shiji*) and Ban Gu (author of *Han shu*) regarded mention of profit-making as a taboo"; therefore, "he who considered financing as a priority was criticised as a courtier of profit-seekers" whose life did not merit the recording of personal detail.[14]

As to Sang Hongyang's policies, we find the following account from Sima Qian in the *Shiji* (*Records of the Grand Historian*):

> [In 110 BCE] Sang Hongyang was made secretary in charge of grain and put in control of the ministry of agriculture, as well as taking over . . . complete control of the salt and iron monopolies . . . Sang Hongyang believed that the reason prices had risen so sharply was that the various government officials were engaging in trade and competing against each other. Furthermore, when goods were transported to the capital as payment for taxes from various parts of the empire, their value often did not equal the cost of transportation. He therefore proposed that some twenty or thirty assistants be appointed to the ministry of agriculture, who would set out to supervise the various provinces

and kingdoms, where they would travel about and set up the necessary transport offices for the equalisation of prices [*junshu*], as well as salt and iron offices. In the case of distant regions . . . local products commanding a high price, such as would ordinarily be carted away and sold by the traders in other regions, should be transported to the capital in lieu of taxes. In the capital a balanced standard office [*pingshun*] was to be set up which would receive and store these goods brought in from various parts of the empire. The government artisans were to be ordered to make carts and other equipment needed to put the system into effect. All expenses would be borne by the ministry of agriculture, whose officials would then have complete control over all the goods in the empire, selling when prices were high and buying when they were low. In this way the wealthy merchants and large-scale traders, deprived of any prospect of making big profits, would go back to farming, and it would be impossible for any commodity to rise sharply in price. Because the price of goods would thereby be controlled throughout the empire, the system was to be called the "balanced standard" [*pingshun*].[15]

According to Sima Qian's account, the "balanced standard" (*pingshun*) system, established in the capital to receive tribute from the whole country and constrain prices at the same time, was distinct from the "tribute equalisation" (*junshu*) system, which required government officers to levy taxes on goods which were traded by merchants and to sell these items throughout the country. With the exception of *Pingshunshu* ("The Treatise on the Balanced Standard"), the *Shiji* barely talked about the idea of tribute equalisation and therefore cannot solve the mystery of what the policy really meant, and what the "equalisation" aspect of the policy amounted to. For that, we must first turn to Sang Hongyang himself, as represented in the *Yantie lun* (*Discourses on Salt and Iron*): a record by the Western Han essayist Huan Kuan of the debate on state policy held at the imperial court in 81 BCE, in which Sang Hongyang was one of the main protagonists.[16]

Junshu in the *Yantie lun*

According to the *Yantie lun*, Sang Hongyang expressed three roles of the system of tribute equalisation: first, "tribute equalisation increases national revenue which can be used to defray part of the military expenditure"; second, "it makes goods circulate and puts resources where they are most needed"; and third, "tribute equalisation makes people rich", and thus "officers of equalisation are set up in commanderies to facilitate the transfer of tribute from remote areas, which is what tribute equalisation means". All in all,

the implementation of the policy of tribute equalisation facilitates the equitable distribution of the work load. We implemented the two policies of tribute equalisation and stabilisation for the levelling of prices and for the convenience of our people, not merely for increased revenue.[17]

The *junshu* policy mainly comprised two parts: a tribute and tax-levying system, and a system that transferred tribute and tax. The two roles were like two sides of the same coin. Over time, however, owing to the paucity of historical records, people were left merely with a concept of "enriching the state without increasing tax". Although people mostly based their understanding on the brief accounts in the *Shiji* and *Yantie lun*, the relationship between the tribute equalisation problem in the Han mathematical text, *Jiuzhang Suanshu*, and the policy of tribute equalisation did catch some critical eyes.

Later misunderstandings

In *Shiji*, Sima Qian had written that

> in the case of distant regions . . . local products commanding a high price, such as would ordinarily be carted away and sold by the traders in other regions, should be transported to the capital [as tribute] in lieu of taxes.

But in the *Shihuozhi* chapter of *Han shu*, Ban Gu rewrote the explanation as, "people from remote areas were ordered to offer the items that would be resold by merchants when the prices were different as articles of tribute to the imperial court", so as to enrich the state without increasing tax.[18] Sima Qian was a contemporary of Emperor Wu of Han, and he most likely witnessed Sang Hongyang's policy reforms. Ban Gu's *Han shu*, written a hundred years later than *Shiji*, changed "commanding a *high* price" to "when the prices were *different*" and thus insinuated a policy of price-manipulation, quite different from Sima Qian's original intention. Xun Yue (148–209 CE) rewrote the historical record even more in his *Liang Hanji* by claiming that Sang Hongyang "established officers of equalisation and of the salt-iron business in major counties" and "ordered that people in remote areas pay taxes with items that were sold by merchants".[19] In his book, the establishment of the salt and iron offices and the policy of tribute equalisation were lumped together, and the premise of high prices was omitted.

Further misunderstandings occurred in later times. During the Wei era (220–265 CE), Meng Kang, in his collected commentaries on the *Pingshunshu* chapter in *Shiji*, claimed that the policy of tribute equalisation "ordered he who should pay tribute to hand in whatever he grew on his land, and officers then sold elsewhere what they received at an equalised price for the convenience of the people and the benefit of the government".[20] Sections in the *Cefu Yuangui* of the Song Dynasty have many descriptions of "tribute equalisation as a business". Sima Guang (1019–1086) omitted the policy of tribute equalisation completely in his *Zizhi Tongjian*, wrote only about stabilisation and asserted that "Sang Hongyang's system of stabilisation ordered that people from remote areas must offer the items that would be resold by merchants when the prices were high as articles of tribute, and local administrators then make these items circulate"; further, "every kind of good is transported within the country. That is, the government took everything as a levy".[21] We can therefore see that over the course of a thousand years, the policy of *junshu* was no longer considered a tax system, but had come to be regarded as a business that facilitated the government in gaining benefits at the expense of the people. A major misunderstanding had occurred.

Translation into Western languages did not help matters. Three misunderstandings stand out. The first was to regard *junshu* as a subsidiary part of stabilisation. The French scholar Chavannes believed that the *Pingshunshu* chapter in *Shiji* recorded the history of an office of Han named "Office of Stabilisation", whose basic function was to equalise prices, and he thus translated the phrase as "Balance du commerce".[22] When Esson M. Gale translated *Yantie lun*, he rendered officers of equalisation as officers to "equalise distribution" (*Chun-shu/junshu*, also described by him as "equable marketing"), and stabilisation became "bureau of equalisation and standardisation", meaning "making level, causing to be equal and stabilising". The implication was that the Office of Stabilisation was concerned with stabilising prices, with *junshu* a part of the price stabilisation policy.[23] Many people in later times,[24] including some contemporary Chinese scholars living in the West, have affirmed the same implication.[25] Nancy Lee Swann later translated *junshu* in the *Zhuanzan* chapter of *Shihuozhi* in *Han shu* in a totally different manner. She identified Sang Hongyang's control over market prices through offices that equalised prices by regulating transportation of supplies throughout the empire as *Chun-shu* (*junshu*).[26] Gale's translation of the concept of *junshu* was nothing but a temporary expedient. He said he used the words "equable marketing" to solve the problem of distribution but realised that he still had many other choices such as "equalised transportation" and "adjusted taxation", which all referred to the policy of *junshu*.[27] The meaning of *junshu* was therefore ambiguous to scholars in the West. Both Chinese and Western scholars understood its relation to tax, but the real puzzle was *how it worked*.

A second misunderstanding arising from translation is that scholars – including K.C. Hsiao[28] and Michael Loewe[29] – were confused about *pingshun* and *junshu*. Donald B. Wager, although he adopted the translation of "equable transportation", considered *junshu* as pertaining to the stabilisation of prices.[30] Kageyama pointed out the confusion and tried to explain it. However, he mistook the policy of *junshu* as a state-owned business.[31] The scarcity of historical records may partly account for these misunderstandings, but the translators' apparent ignorance of the background of the two policies was a more fundamental reason for the confusion.

Third, translations with a personal touch made the misunderstandings even worse. Nancy Lee Swann directly translated *junshu* as "offices for equalisation of price through transportation",[32] translated *junshu* as offices of "equal distribution" and *pingshun* as "stabilisation" or "standardisation of prices".[33] Kageyama's "equalisation through transportation" was nothing but a word-to-word translation from Chinese and did not reflect any of the true intention of the policy.[34] For those Western scholars who did not understand Sang Hongyang, it was all too natural to consider *junshu* and *pingshun* as government schemes for control over transportation or prices.[35]

The "righteousness" interpretation caused yet more misunderstanding of the policy of *junshu*. In *Wenxian Tongkao*, Ma Duanlin and his father, Ma Tingluan, noticed the difference between the two explanations of *junshu* given by Ban Gu and Sima Qian. But the authors adopted the account in Ban Gu's *Han shu* and Meng Kang's notes, leading to their conclusion that the policy of *junshu* was the practice of driving farmers to act like businessmen. Further, they decided that the description of "commanding a *high* price" by Sima Qian was not as clear as Ban Gu's "when the prices were *different*", leading them to the conclusion that the description in *Han shu* was more authentic and reliable. They also claimed that it was "righteous" for Sima Guang to follow the idea of "different price" in his book *Zizhi Tongjian*.[36] The word "righteous" here refers to the standard of "being righteous and beneficial" as applied to economic policy – a standard that dates back to the pre-Qin period. With regard to the "clearer description" favoured by the Mas, Li Zhi of the Ming Dynasty expressed his disapproval as follows:

> "As articles of tribute" is clear enough. Why would someone say it was not clear? The policy of tribute equalisation is mainly a tool for tribute, not for business. The former is like collecting grain or rent from different households, and the latter is like driving farmers to work like businessmen. If you ask farmers to do business, who else could you ask to work in farming? If all farmers have gone to do business and no one works in the fields, where would the grain or tribute come from? So why not let the businessmen do business and collect tax from them, and leave the farmers to their work? In this way we can collect tax from businessmen on one hand and grain from farmers on the other hand. Even a fool knows this is more beneficial, and Emperor Wu would certainly have known better. In fact Huo Guang from the Western Han Dynasty had already mistaken the policy of tribute equalisation or its merit, how could Ban Gu who came later in the Eastern Han Dynasty know the right way? Now I believe that one cannot discuss politics with the vulgar.[37]

Evidently, Ban Gu and Meng Kang had left a harmful legacy for those who would later write the history of the policy of tribute equalisation.

In the Song Dynasty, the statesman Wang Anshi implemented many policies in his quest for national security outwardly and economic benefits inwardly, including the hired service policy, the green sprouts money program and the market exchange system. He also implemented the law of tribute equalisation. According to his policy, transport commissioners were charged with organising the purchase and transportation of grain and supplies. The policy helped to reduce taxes and restrain the manipulative and exploitative actions of rich merchants and was described as "enriching the state without increasing tax".[38] However, understandings of the policy differed, with many courtiers comparing it to what they believed to have been the policy in the Han. Thus, Chen Xiang, Fan Chunren, Su Zhe, Su Shi and Sima Guang attacked Wang Anshi's policy one after another, denouncing it as a Han policy of buying goods at low prices and selling them when the price was high. Sima Guang was in total confusion over tribute equalisation and stabilisation, referring to them collectively as "the policy of stabilisation". Later, Ye Shi

(1150–1223) noted that the policy of stabilisation was the key financial policy of Emperor Wu, completely neglecting the policy of tribute equalisation.[39]

However, there were some people who understood, correctly, that the policy of tribute equalisation was the policy adumbrated in the *"Yugong"* chapter of the pre-Qin book, *Shangshu*. According to the historical records of Song:

> Li Chang . . . talked about the inconvenience of tribute equalisation. One day, the Emperor said to Ministers who managed state and political affairs: "I asked Li Chang what tribute equalisation was, and he answered that it was nothing more than buying goods when they were cheap and selling them when they were dear. I told him about the practice of contributing *su* [millet] and *jie* [stalk] in quantities according to distance, as in the Chapter *Yugong* [of *Shangshu*], which is what tribute equalisation really means. How can it be merely buying the cheap things and selling them at high prices!" Wang Anshi said: "What Li Chang said applies to stabilisation policy, not tribute equalisation. Perhaps Li Chang did not understand tribute equalisation." [40]

As we have seen, Li Chang was certainly not alone.

Among the reasons for the misunderstanding of *junshu*, three stand out as having been particularly important, the first being confusion over the origins of the policy.

The *"Yugong"* chapter in *Shangshu* is the first written source to demonstrate the origin of the equable tax-levying principle in ancient China. Sima Qian wrote in his *Xiabenji* [*History of Xia Dynasty*] in *Shiji* that "from Emperor Shun and the Xia dynasty, the empires never lacked tribute". Ma Duanlin pointed out that the *"Yugong"* chapter was one of the origins of the tribute equalisation policy.[41] According to the *Wufu* [Five Degree Graduation System] policy in pre-Qin times, tribute requirements depended on the distance from the emperor's capital. Those who occupied land within a radius of 100 *li* from the capital were required to bring as tribute the whole plant of whatever grain was cultivated; for the second 100 *li*, they brought the ears; from the third 100 *li*, the straw; from the fourth 100 *li*, grain in the husk; and from the fifth 100 *li*, unhusked grain.[42] What emerges here and in other, more complicated illustrations, is that the amount of tribute was related to the produce, and that the equalisation of tribute involved the equalisation of the sum of taxes and delivery costs. For example, the closer (or more distant) the payers of tribute were to the offices of tribute, the lower (or higher) the costs for transporting tribute; hence, an "equable" system required the equalisation of tribute *inclusive* of transport costs.[43] This logic was grasped by Chen Huanzhang,[44] and we can see from historical documents that it had also been understood by Emperor Shenzong of Song. But there was confusion between the tax system and other systems. For example, Ye Shi believed that tribute equalisation came from the time of Chunqiu and that the "goods circulated freely" description in *Suanshu* was a vulgarised understanding of tribute equalisation. Many people in later times claimed that the policy of tribute equalisation originated from the *Qingzhong* ("Light and

Heavy") theory in *Guanzi* and that it was merely a business practice.[45] These and other views notwithstanding, it is our contention that the idea of tribute equalisation clearly originated in the pre-Qin period, and that it was first recorded in the "*Yugong*" chapter of *Shangshu*.

The second common misunderstanding is that tribute equalisation was used by the government as a tool for the exploitation of market power. According to Professor Liu Shipei (1884–1919), "the policies of tribute equalisation and stabilisation made use of the power of the government to manipulate the market". Liu believed that these policies "ignore what the people have and ask for what they do not have", and that people were forced to sell their produce cheaply in order to meet government demands.[46] Similarly, Zou Zhenpu claimed that stabilisation policy was a state-run business, that the policy of tribute equalisation was a state-run transportation system and that the two policies could be collectively called "the policy of tribute equalisation and stabilisation".[47] More directly, the *Journal of the North-China Branch of the Royal Asiatic Society* simply asserted that "the policy of stabilisation and tribute equalisation was one of the state-run trading systems",[48] and variations on this same theme have been offered by several other scholars.[49] Such interpretations resulted not only from a misunderstanding of tax policies in pre-Qin and Han times, but also from the differences in the accounts given in the *Shiji* and *Han shu*.

The third important misunderstanding was over the function of tribute equalisation: was it a transportation policy, a tax policy or something else? According to the *Jiuzhang Suanshu*, the policy was designed to "balance the delivery costs". In the *Daju* chapter of *Zhoushu*, Zhu Xizu claimed that the policy was meant to prevent merchants from manipulating prices; by preventing price fluctuations, the people would be the beneficiaries.[50] Zhang Chunming translated *junshu* as "equable marketing", remarking that the policy was implemented to collect staples across the country as tribute and sell them where they were most needed, which benefited both the government and the people. According to Zhang, however, the policy did not pay off, so Sang Hongyang set up the balanced standard bureau (*pingshun*) in the capital to control the transportation system and constrain the see-saw in prices: a policy that combined *junshu* with *pingshun*, prevented the merchants from manipulating prices to reap excessive benefits and provided the government with new sources of revenue.[51]

According to Zhang Chunming's account, we can view the policy of tribute equalisation either as government control over prices or as a device for the government to reap benefits, which were indeed misunderstandings. In fact, after the implementation of the *pingshun* policy, the see-saw in prices was constrained and it became more convenient for the people to pay tribute, which had been the key objective all along. Western mathematicians could better understand the tax-related essence of the policy as a type of impartial taxation. Thus, Frank Swetz wrote that "consideration is given to the distribution of taxes and the various difficulties in transporting the taxes, as paid for with grain, to the capital (pursuit problems)".[52]

Utilising modern academic models when studying ancient thought, policies and systems is an effective way to cast new light on ancient knowledge and serve contemporary purposes. Chen Huanzhang's work is a case in point. His *The Economic Principles of Confucius and His School* established the "consumption–production–fiscal" research framework, which clearly explained the origin and formation of fiscal policies from pre-Qin times to the Western Han. Chen quotes from the *Yugong* chapter in *Suanshu* to dissect the historical, social and economic background of the idea and policy of tribute equalisation. Briefly, Chen shows that "equal transportation" (his translation of *junshu*) was established to equalise the sum of taxes and delivery costs across the country and raise funds for military spending. The policy of tribute equalisation, like a modern tax system, was a tax bureaucracy run by officers of equalisation. From central to local administrations, these officers took the place of businessmen to buy and sell goods. People in remote areas paid luxury items as tribute and other areas paid staples. At the top of the pyramid of the equal transportation system was the administration of level standards (*Pingshunshu* 平准署). The transportation of tribute was managed by this state-wide system with offices for stabilisation, but stabilising prices was only one of the system's roles. Therefore, although tribute equalisation and stabilisation did not share the same intention and function, they complemented each other and both were indispensable parts of the fiscal system at that time.

For all its undoubted merit, Chen's understanding of tribute equalisation as a *system of equal transportation* was far from comprehensive, for his translation did not reflect the *tribute* meaning of *shu* in *junshu*.[53] The translation of Sang Hongyang's *junshu* as "*tribute* equalisation" would have been far more appropriate.

Conclusion

Here we have six points. First, Sima Qian offered in his *Shiji* concise and correct records of the policy of *junshu* in the Western Han. In stark contrast, some interpretations of later commentators were based either on a deficient understanding of the subject matter or on the subjective evaluations of the authors. These works thus led to further misunderstanding, the greatest of which can be found in the erroneous comments by Meng Kang of Wei and *Wenxian Tongkao* by Ma Duanlin of Song, the deficiencies of which have been exposed by scholars including Li Zhi of Ming.

Second, the intention of the policy of tribute equalisation was to make sure of the equalisation of the sum of tribute and delivery costs in the tax system of the Western Han – regardless of whether they inhabited border regions or the inner cities, people paid the same rate of money for their tribute and relative delivery cost. Presumably, the policy of tribute equalisation comprised mainly of two parts – collecting tribute and transferring it.

Third, the policy of tribute equalisation had two origins: in the fiscal and economic practice of ancient China, and in the conclusion of the *Yugong* chapter in *Suanshu*.

Fourth, the development of the policy of tribute equalisation was possibly related to the establishment of offices for the salt–iron business and the national transportation system, which collectively achieved the result of "enriching the state without increasing tax".

Fifth, later generations furthered misunderstanding by using "righteousness" as their guiding ideology, to the detriment of historical accuracy.

And finally, it is submitted that the tribute equalisation problems in *Jiuzhang Suanshu* hold the key to unlocking the mysteries of the *junshu* policy in the Western Han.

Notes

1 Presented at the 48th Annual UK History of Economic Thought Conference, Shanghai University of Finance and Economics, 2–4 September 2016. I would like to thank Professor Wu Ge of Fudan University Library, Professor Zhou Deming of Shanghai Library and Gong Deyu of Shanghai University of Finance and Economics Library for their help with historical documents.
2 Sima Qian, *Shiji* ("Records of the Grand Historian"), p. 1729. Wang Anshi (1021–1086) claimed that Sang Hongyang had "enriched the state without increasing tribute on people".
3 Jia Sixie (2007), p. 6.
4 Li Zhi (2000), pp. 337, 338, 339–340.
5 Sun Yat-sen (2011), p. 123. Cf. S.C. (1936), pp. 168, 170.
6 Chen (1911), p. 559.
7 Gale (1953), p. 102.
8 Zhang (1998), p. 55.
9 Hu (1963), p. 72.
10 Sima Qian, "The Treatise on the Balanced Standard", *Shiji* 32. In B. Watson (tr.) (1993), p. 70.
11 Chen (1911), p. 555.
12 Zhu (1926), p. 150.
13 Swann (1950), p. 40.
14 Ma (1934), pp. 1, 3.
15 Sima Qian, "The Treatise on the Balanced Standard", *Shiji* 32. In B. Watson (tr.) (1993), p. 82.
16 Wang (1992).
17 Ibid., pp. 3–4.
18 *Han shu* pp. 1174–1175.
19 Xun Yue, *Lianghan Ji.*, p. 219. It is notable that when Xun Yue rewrote the 800,000-word *Hanshu* as the 180,000-word *Lianghan Ji*, he did not cut out anything relating to the stabilisation policy or the policy of tribute equalisation, thus reflecting the importance attached to these historical phenomena.
20 Sima Qian, *Shiji*. Beijing: Zhonghua Press, 1982, p. 1720.
21 Sima Guang, *Zizhi Tongjian* p. 228.
22 Chavannes (1895–1905), in Blue (1948), p. 82, explanation no. 22.
23 Gale (1967), p. xxv.
24 Spengler (1964), pp. 223–243; Blue (1948), pp. 1–118.
25 Ming (2012), p. 150.
26 Swann (1950), p. 359.
27 Gale (1967), pp. xxv, 2.
28 Kung-chuan (1979), p. 458.

29 Loewe (2008), p. 515.
30 Wager (2001), pp. 13, 30.
31 Tsuyoshi (1982), p. 1.
32 Swann (1950), pp. 314–315.
33 Kung-chuan (1979), p. 458.
34 Kageyama (1982).
35 De G. (1965), pp. 4–5.
36 Ma (1986), p. 194.
37 Zhang (2000), p. 208.
38 Li (2010), p. 886.
39 Li (2001), p. 83.
40 Ma (1986), p. 196.
41 Ibid.
42 Yingda et al. (1998), p. 88.
43 See the Appendix to this chapter for a more detailed account of the analysis in the *Suan shu*.
44 Chen (1911), p. 556.
45 Zhao (1985), pp. 75–76.
46 Liu (1909), pp. 5, 6.
47 Zou (1943), pp. 91–93.
48 Chen (1936), p. 170.
49 See Swann (1950), p. 62; Kageyama (1982), p. 1; Wang (2013), p. 396; Yi (1994), pp. 68–69.
50 Zhu (1926), pp. 133–163.
51 Zhang (1933), pp. 17–18.
52 Swetz (1972), p. 427.
53 Chen (1911), pp. 555–556.

References

De G., A. (1965). "The Great Salt and Iron Debate in Ancient China". *American Behavioral Scientist*, June.

Ban Gu (1962). *Hanshu*. Beijing: Zhonghua Press.

Blue, R.C. (1948). "The Argumentation of the *Shih-Huo Chih*: Chapters of the Han, Wei, and Sui Dynastic Histories". *Harvard Journal of Asiatic Studies*, 11:1–2.

Chen, H. (1911). *The Economic Principles of Confucius and His School*. New York: Columbia University.

Chen, S.C. (1936). "Sang Hongyang (143–80 B.C.): Economist of the Early Han". *Journal of the North China Branch of the Royal Asiatic Society*, 67.

Gale, E.M. (1953). *Salt for the Dragon: A Personal History of China, 1908–1945*. Ann Arbor: Michigan State University.

Gale, E.M. (1967). *Discourses on Salt and Iron (Yantie lun)*, by Huan Kuan. Taipei: Cheng-wen Publishing Company.

Hsiao, K. (1979). History of Chinese Political Thought, Volume 1: From the Beginnings to the Sixth Century A.D. Princeton, NJ: Princeton University Press.

Hu, J. (1963). *History of Chinese Economic Thought*, Volume 2. Shanghai: Shanghai People's Press.

Jia Sixie (2007). *Qimin Yaoshu*. Shanghai: The Shanghai Classic Books Press.

Kageyama, T. (1982). "Sō Kōyō no kin'yūhō shiron 桑弘羊の均輸法試論". *Tōyōshi kenkyū* (東洋史研究), 40:4.

Kong, Y. et al. (eds.) (1998). *Shangshu*. Beijing: Zhonghua Press.

Li, W. (ed.) (2010). *Collections of Sima Guang*. Chengdu: Sichuan University Press.

Li, X. (2001). "On the *junshu* System". *Journal of Shandong University (Philosophy and Social Sciences)*, 1.

Li Zhi, (2000) *Collections of Li Zhi*. Volume I. In Zhang Jianye (ed.), with the collaboration of Liu Yusheng. Beijing: Social Sciences Academic Press (China).

Liu, S. (1909). "On the State-Control Malady of Finance in Ancient China". *Guocui Journal*, 5:55.

Loewe, M. (2008). "The Organs of Han Imperial Government: Zhongduguan, xianguan and xiandaoguan". *Bulletin of the School of Oriental and African Studies*, 71:3.

Ma, D. (1986). *Wenxian Tongkao*. Beijing: Zhonghua Press.

Ma, Y. (1934). *Chronicle of Sang Hongyang*. Shanghai: The Commercial Press.

Ming, W. (2012). "Discourses on Salt and Iron: A First Century B.C. Chinese Debate over the Political Economy of Empire". *Journal of Chinese Political Science*, 17:2.

Sima Guang (1990). *Zizhi Tongjian*. Changsha: Yuelu Book Press.

Sima Qian (1982). *Records of the Grand Historian (Shiji)*. Beijing: Zhong Hua Press.

Spengler, J.J. (1964). "Ssu-Ma Ch'ien, Unsuccessful Exponent of Laissez Faire". *Southern Economic Journal*, 30:3.

Sun Yat-sen (2011). *Collections of Sun Yat-sen (Sunyixian canshu)*. Beijing: The People's Press.

Swann, N.L. (1950). *Food and Money in Ancient China*. Princeton, NJ: Princeton University Press.

Swetz, F. (1972). "The Amazing *Chiu Chang Suan Shu*". *The Mathematics Teacher*, 65:5.

Tsuyoshi, K. (1982). "Sō Kōyō no kin'yūhō shiron" (桑弘羊の均輸法試論). *Tōyōshi kenkyū*, 40:4.

Wager, D.B. (2001). *State and the Iron Industry in Han China*. Cobenhagen: Leifsgade.

Wang, L. (ed.) (1992). *Discourses on Salt and Iron (Yantie lun)*, by Huan Kuan. Beijing: Zhonghua Press.

Wang, Z. (2013). *An Outline of Qin and Han Transportation History*. Beijing: The People's University of China Press.

Watson, B. (tr.) (1993). *Records of the Grand Historian: Han Dynasty*, by Sima Qian. New York: Columbia University Press.

Xun, Y. (2002). *Lianghan Ji*. Beijing: Zhonghua Press.

Yi, J. (1994). "The Business Role of *junshu* Officials". *Journal of Beijing Normal University (Social Sciences)*, (3).

Zhang, C. (1933). "Background of *Yantie lun* and an Analysis of Its Content". *Quarterly Journal of Economics and Statistics*, 2:1.

Zhang, J. (ed.) (2000). *Collections of Li Zhi: Volume I (Fenshu, Xu Fenshu)*. Beijing: Social Sciences Academic Press.

Zhang, X. (1998). *Wenshi Tongyi*. Shenyang: Liaoning Education Press.

Zhao, M. (1985). "On the Economic Thought of Sang Hongyang". *Qilu Journal*, Issue 5.

Zhu, X. (1926). "The Economic Policies of Sang Hongyang". *The National Beijing University Social Sciences Quarterly*, 65:1–2.

Zou, Z. (1943). "A Review of Sang Hongyang's State Fiscal Policies". *Financial Review*, 65:4.

Appendix

The chapter *Junshu* in *Jiuzhang Suanshu.*

The first four problems in *Junshu*, the sixth chapter of *Jiuzhang Suanshu*, fall into three categories. The first problem, *junshusu* (均输粟), is about equalising the delivery costs of millet among four counties as they pay their tribute. The second problem, *junshuzu* (均输卒), solves the problem of evenly dividing up the quota of conscripts among five different counties considering their respective distances from the frontier. The third and fourth problems, *junfusu* (均赋粟) concern equalising the sum of tribute and delivery costs among six counties. These four problems, the first being the simplest and the last being the most complicated, demonstrate the tribute and conscription system of Western Han.

The fourth problem best represents how tribute or land tax was paid in Han:

> **Problem 4.** Now we have the problem of *junfusu* (均赋粟), which is equalising the sum of tribute and delivery costs among six counties. County A should pay land tax of 42,000 *suan* (1 *suan* equals 120 *Qian*) with millet at the price of 20 *Qian* per *hu*, which should be brought to the office in the county by the owner. County B should pay land tax of 34,272 *suan* with millet at the price of 18 *Qian* per *hu*, and they should hire labourers to bring their tribute to the office of transportation (in county A), which is 70 *li* away and the delivery cost is ten *Qian* per day; County C should pay land tax of 19,328 *suan* with millet at the price of 16 *Qian* per *hu*, and they should hire labourers to bring their tribute to the office of transportation, which is 140 *li* away and the delivery cost is five *Qian* per day; County D should pay land tax of 17,700 *suan* with millet at the price of 14 *Qian* per *hu*, and they should hire labourers to bring their tribute to the office of transportation, which is 175 *li* away and the delivery cost is five *Qian* per day; County E should pay land tax of 23,400 *suan* with millet at the price of 12 *Qian* per *hu*, and they should hire labourers to bring their tribute to the office of transportation, which is 210 *li* away and the delivery cost is five *Qian* per day; County F should pay land tax of 19,136 *suan* with millet at the price of ten *Qian* per *hu*, and they should hire labourers to bring their tribute to the office of transportation, which is 280 *li* away and the delivery cost is five Qian per day. The total amount of tax from the six counties should be 60,000 *hu*, all delivered to County A. Six people drive a carriage and every carriage is loaded with 25 *hu*. A fully

loaded carriage travels 50 *li* per day while an empty carriage travels 70 *li* per day. Both loading and discharging take one day. Prices of millet vary and so do the delivery costs. You are required to figure out the amount of millet (land tax) that should be paid for each county to equalise the sum of tribute and delivery costs.

As we can see from Problem 4, out of the six counties in question, County A was the place to receive tribute and all six counties should deliver their tribute or millet to the office of equalisation in this county for storage. However, not only did the distances vary between individual counties and the stipulated destination, so too did the delivery costs and prices of millet in the different counties. What was required, therefore, was a set of land taxes that would equalise the sum of tribute and delivery costs across counties.

7 War economy during the Western Han Dynasty

Elisa Levi Sabattini[1]

Introduction

The early decades of the Western Han empire (西漢 202 BCE – 9 CE) are crucial for the construction of the imperial system and its later stability. The conquest of the independent states by the Qin 秦 in 221 BCE and the foundation of the empire were not enough to consolidate the project of keeping the world (*tianxia* 天下) together. After the collapse of the Qin empire and years of civil war, when anarchy reigned, in 202 BCE the Han 漢 empire was founded and Liu Bang 劉邦 (Gaozu 高祖, r. 202–195 BCE) ascended the throne as the first emperor of Han. The new-born empire, far from being tranquil (*an* 安), faced, among others, the challenge of foreign relations.

The early decades of the Han experienced a tension between the desire for a stronger centralisation of political and economic power – which according to the supporters of this policy was crucial in order to have a stable empire – and actual reforms that were essentially decentralising political and economic control in favour of powerful families. In foreign relations, the Han policy was ultimately one of border[2] development and territorial expansion through immigration, which caused a war-demography. This approach followed the plans instituted in the pre-Qin and Qin periods, although the unification of the empire radically changed both the conception of frontier and the identification of the frontier's location, and opened a new phase in foreign relations. The border control and the control of the passage of travellers was adapted to the new political situation and, during the first decades of the Han, changed often.

Since the beginning of the Han empire, the northern borders were constantly pressured by incursions from the Xiongnu 匈奴, a semi-nomadic confederation which, by that time, had expanded over a territory that extended from Manchuria to the west of the Yellow River, and had absorbed over time many other nomadic tribes.[3] The result was a strong army with a centralised structure. Since history begins *in medias res*, it is difficult to tell exactly when troubles with the Xiongnu started.[4] The beginning of the relationship is dated to the time of the military expansion of the Central States at the end of the fourth century BCE.[5] The shift in political circumstances that accompanied the foundation of the Han empire certainly posed new political struggles for the populations who originally lived at the northern borders. Moreover, the situation in the northern regions was exacerbated by the connivance between domestic rebels and the Xiongnu. At the beginning of the Han, these northern territories required special attention in terms of enforcement of authority, involving additional costs of military activities and also of emigration. Coupled with other demands on state revenue, the result was a more general financial crisis that forced the Han government to adopt revenue-increasing measures such as reform of the currency, new monopolies, market controls and the sale of offices and aristocratic ranks, just to mention a few.[6]

This chapter studies the perspectives of Jia Yi 賈誼 (200–168 BCE) on foreign relations, specifically the diplomatic and economic strategies that he suggested for the purpose of degrading the Xiongnu confederation. Since the Han empire could not yet afford to attack such a great military power and lacked suitably trained troops (in steppe warfare) even if it had the requisite financial resources, the problem was one of identifying the political and economic strategies that might be used as an effective alternative. In line with the Warring States tradition of demographic warfare, of which the "*Lai min*" 徠民 (Attracting the People) chapter of the *Shangjun shu* 商君書 (*Book of Lord Shang*) is the *locus classicus*,[7] Jia Yi's proposal was to encourage the immigration of Xiongnu subjects, thereby weakening their capability as an external adversary.

Jia Yi

Based on his biographies in the *Shiji* 史記 and *Han shu* 漢書,[8] we know that Jia Yi was a native of Luoyang 洛陽. Because of his literary skills, his talent was recognised early in his youth while in his home commandery of Henan 河南. Jia Yi was an expert in the *Shi* 詩 (*Odes*), *Shu* 書 (*Documents*) and the *Zuozhuan* 左傳 (*Zuo Commentary*). Venerable Wu 吳公, governor of Henan and a former student of the Qin minister Li Si 李斯 (d. 208 BCE), promoted Jia Yi to a position in his entourage. When Wu became Commandant of Justice (*tingwei* 廷尉) around 179 BCE, he recommended Jia Yi to Emperor Wen of Han 漢文帝 (Liu Heng 劉恆, r. 179–157 BCE) as a scholar learned in the writings of the Masters (*zi* 子). Jia Yi presented memorials to the emperor on several issues. The emperor appointed Jia Yi as an Erudite (*boshi* 博士). The other officials, who were much older men, viewed the young Jia Yi with envy, particularly after he rose within one year to the post of Grand Master of the Palace (*taizhong dafu* 太中大夫). Because of the growing resentment against Jia Yi among the court officials, Emperor Wen sent him to be Grand Tutor (*taifu* 太傅) to the King of Changsha 長沙, in the south, in 177 BCE. A few years later, Jia Yi returned to the capital and was appointed Grand Tutor to the favourite son of emperor Wen, Liu Yi 劉揖 (King Huai of Liang 梁懷王, d. 169 BCE). During this period, Jia Yi did not stop writing memorials. Liu Yi died as a result of a riding accident. Jia Yi died one year later, convinced he had failed to carry out his duties as a tutor.

Jia Yi's memorials have been partly incorporated in his biographies and other chapters in the *Shiji* 史記 (*Records of the Historian*) and *Han shu* 漢書

(*History of the Former Han Dynasty*). His writings were assembled in the book named *Xinshu* 新書 (*New Writings*).[9] In this chapter, I shall utilise all of these three sources.

Up north

Walls and watchtowers were built during the period of the Warring States (453–221 BCE) to defend the recently conquered territory and to extend it.[10] The construction of military installations known as "long walls" (*chang cheng* 長城), together with the adoption of chivalry, were two major events in the late Warring States period and were part of the expansionist project of the states fighting for supremacy. With the foundation of the Qin empire, wall building in the north became a single system of walls to mark its expansion into the steppe.[11] It is important to note that, according to the account in the *Shiji*, the expansion of the states of Qin 秦, Zhao 趙 and Yan 燕 had reached the border with the territory inhabited by the Xiongnu during the late Warring States period[12] (*Shiji* 110, pp. 2885–2886). Military walls were part of the expansionist, offensive project of the warring states.[13] However, the stronger militarisation of the north was not enough to defend the empire from the incursions of the people who originally populated that area, the Xiongnu.

From the very beginning of the empire, the Han were forced to recognise the Xiongnu as a "rival state" (*di guo* 敵國). According to the *Han shu*, at the beginning of the Han Dynasty the Xiongnu considered themselves as equals of the Han (*Han shu* 94A, pp. 3754–3755). Soon after ascending the throne as first emperor of Han, Liu Bang had to deal with the danger of invasion. In 200 BCE, the Han army was defeated by the Xiongnu, who had taken advantage of Han's internal problems and reconquered much of the territory they had previously lost. Liu Bang was forced to accept a humiliating treaty with the Xiongnu, which involved Han acceptance of equal diplomatic status with the Xiongnu and the imposition of tributary conditions (*Shiji* 110, p. 2895). In 199 BCE, what is described in the *Shiji* as the *heqin* 和親 (harmony through family relations) policy – *heqin* here being used for the first time to denote a diplomatic policy[14] – was accepted.[15] The *heqin* policy of securing alliances with northern people through the creation of bonds via intermarriage and political infiltration had been already used by the independent states before the unification of the Qin empire, but was not to referred to as *heqin*. In order to avoid invasions and the devastation of frontier settlements in the northern part of the empire, Liu Jing 劉敬, advisor to Liu Bang, suggested a diplomatic resolution: to send an imperial princess to become the wife of Chanyu 單于[16] Modun 冒頓 (d. 174 BCE),[17] leader and architect of the Xiongnu's great military power. In this way, Modun would have become the son-in-law of Liu Bang and his children would be Liu Bang's grandchildren. The result would have been to place the Xiongnu in a position of subordination to the Han empire. Moreover, Liu Jing stressed the desirability of two additional ploys: corrupting the Xiongnu by sending them valuable things of which the Han had a surplus; and sending them scholars who would impart the rules of proper conduct. These measures would, according to Liu Jing, reduce the Xiongnu to the level of subjects of the Han (*Shiji* 99, p. 2179). One year later, in 198 BCE, the *heqin* treaty was signed by the two parties and a marriage alliance was then guaranteed. In addition, the Han agreed to send an annual tribute of silk, cloth, grain and foodstuff (*Shiji* 110, pp. 2894–2895; *Han shu* 94A, p. 3754). In other words, the Han empire was buying a truce. The *heqin* treaty was not enough to guarantee peaceful control at the borders and the Han were not ready for a military response because the Xiongnu army was too strong. Therefore, the payment of a tribute was needed, which also put the Han in a position of political inferiority. This agreement nominally put the two political entities on par, but in fact it subordinated the Han empire in a relationship similar to agreements that the Xiongnu had garnered with other surrounding states and tribes. On a practical level, in the context of this foreign policy, the payment of tribute put the Han into a hierarchical relationship that favoured the Xiongnu.

The political inferiority of the Han was clearly in evidence when Chanyu Modun sent an official letter proposing marriage to the Empress Dowager Lü. Considering the fact that they were both alone, unhappy and anxious, he wrote:

孤僨之君，生於沮澤之中，長於平野牛馬之域，數至邊境，願遊中國。陛下獨立，孤僨獨居。兩主不樂，無以自虞，願以所有，易其所無。

I am a bereft and lonely ruler, born in marshes and raised in lands populated by cows and horses. I have reached your borders numerous times and desired to travel to the Central States. Your Majesty stands on her own, bereft and alone. We two rulers are unhappy. We have nothing with which to please ourselves. I wish we could exchange what we have for what we lack.[18]

The empress was furious (*nu* 怒) and wanted to send her troops in a punitive expedition against the Xiongnu. However, her assistant Ji Bu 季布 warned her of the great and powerful Xiongnu army. She eventually declined Chanyu Modun's proposal and sent gifts instead, replying as follows:

單于不忘弊邑，賜之以書，弊邑恐懼。退日自圖，年老氣衰，髮齒墮落，行步失度，單于過聽，不足以自汙。弊邑無罪，宜在見赦。竊有御車二乘，馬二駟，以奉常駕。

The Chanyu has not forgotten me and sent a letter to me. I am frightened and anxious. I withdraw in daytime and make plans for myself. I am old and my vital energy is weak. My hair and teeth are falling out. When I walk I lose my balance. The Chanyu [must have] misheard; I am not worthy of his self-abasement. I am without blame and deserve to be pardoned. I humbly own two carriages and two teams of four horses, which I offer you respectfully for regular excursions.[19]

Chanyu Modun was satisfied and offered horses to fulfil the agreement. He replied:

未嘗聞中國禮義，陛下幸而赦之。

I have not yet heard of the rituals and etiquette of the Central States; may Your Majesty be so generous as to pardon me.[20]

A contemporary reader might understand this episode as a cross between comical and grotesque. However, the exchange of letters shows that, from the point of view of the Xiongnu, the newly founded Han Empire was just another state, or even a "younger brother" state, not an invincible empire. Tamara Chin stresses that Chanyu Modun was actually proposing "to enact the Xiongnu custom of 'brothers marrying their [deceased] brothers' wives'.[21] In this light, his marriage to the empress Dowager would impose Xiongnu kinship practices onto Han ones". This, of course, would have been a mirror image of Liu Jing's *heqin* proposal. The fact that Chanyu Modun dared to propose a marriage to empress Lü reveals that he conceived of himself as being in position to do so. The Han was too weak to face a conflict with the Xiongnu and preferred to respond with grace and gifts.

In 169 BCE, Chao Cuo 晁錯 (d. 154), in a memorial presented to Emperor Wen of Han, offered an analysis of the military talents of nomadic cavalry in the steppe that were related to various factors, including the configuration of terrain, the ability to both ride and shoot arrows in narrow passages and dangerous roads and the habituation of nomadic people to atmospheric adversities, hunger and thirst. In contrast, according to Chao Cuo, the Han army was stronger in the open and flat terrain; Han crossbows had a longer range than the bows of the Xiongnu; the Han infantry was equipped with long and short bows; and the Han were more accurate with bows and arrows, and more disciplined in dismounted formations. Therefore, Chao Cuo argued that the key to vanquishing the Xiongnu army was to fight on foot, because the Han forces were stronger and more prepared. Chao Cuo then asked for the formation of a corps of light cavalry to fight the Xiongnu in order to repel a future intervention.[22]

From Emperor Gaozu to the time of Jia Yi, there were four gift agreements with the Xiongnu. Under Emperor Wen, the total amount of gifts was increased, and cash, such as coins and copper, also formed part of the gift (*Shiji* 110, p. 9. *Han shu* 94A, p. 7).[23] According to *Han shu*, during the time of Emperor Wen, the amount of gold was increased to 1,000 pieces a year (*Han shu* 94B, 12b). From the point of view of state economy, these regular payments could soon pose a problem. In fact, this policy was originally conceived as a temporary expedient, not as a lasting solution. In 162 BCE, Emperor Wen wrote that he and the Chanyu were the "father and the mother" (*fumu* 父母) of the people (*Shiji* 110, p. 2896; *Han shu* 94A, p. 3756), effectively conceding that they had equal status. In the treaty drawn up in the same year, it was determined that the Xiongnu should rule over the nation to the north of the Great Wall, and the Han should rule over the settled people living to the south (*Shiji* 119, p. 2902, *Han shu* 94A, pp. 3762–3763). With this treaty, the Xiongnu and Han defined the borders between the two countries and their respective "spheres of influence", implying a mutual recognition of the rights of political supremacy over the stipulated peoples and areas.[24]

The process of political centralisation of the tribal confederation of the Xiongnu took place between 215 BCE and 209 BCE.[25] It amounted to a political and military response to the Qin and early Han invasions that had caused the Xiongnu to move into the northern steppes; and it also served to create a more cohesive military organisation to face other Inner Asian people. The coming to power of Modun and reorganisation as a process of centralisation of political and military power coincides with the foundation of Qin and Han empires. Modun was able to win over other nomadic people responsible for paying tribute, crucial for the support of the Xiongnu court and army and for the provision of other economic benefits. Jia Yi knew that it was dangerous to face the Xiongnu on the battlefield, but also knew that gifts were succulent bait to lure the heart of the Xiongnu leaders. Jia Yi realised that in order to weaken and control the Xiongnu, it was necessary to exploit their weaknesses by accentuating the internal divisions within the newly formed and centralised Xiongnu confederacy, the goal being to make them subjects of the Han.

Jia Yi's plans for the economic containment of the Xiongnu

During the Former Han, diplomacy utilised various techniques that had been developed during the Warring States period. The *Xinshu* never discusses the *heqin* contract (strategic marriages), although there are references to the strategy of gifting more generally. The expression used in Jia Yi's memorials is *gongzhi* 貢職, usually rendered as "tribute", which refers to taxes or goods paid regularly to a ruler by a distant subject. In particular, Jia Yi refers to the *gongzhi* that the Han had to pay to the Xiongnu, thus recognising that there was a tributary relationship that favoured the Xiongnu. For this reason, what follows will deal mainly with Han tributes to the Xiongnu rather than the *heqin* agreement.

The *Xinshu* devotes a whole chapter to the Xiongnu and mentions problematic relations with them in other chapters. Jia Yi repeatedly alerts Emperor Wen to the urgent need to change his policy toward the Xiongnu, who are defined as *huo* 口 (calamity) for the Han (*Xinshu* 3.10, p. 128). As portrayed, the Xiongnu extensively invade and humiliate, causing the world endless suffering, and to enter into a "tributary agreement" (*gongzhi*) with them was a big mistake that offered no respite from their hostile activities (*Xinshu* 3.10, p. 128).

The problem with paying gifts to the Xiongnu was mainly twofold: the burden could have a long-term negative impact on the Han economy, and paying tribute to the Xiongnu implied a recognition of their superiority.

The "Xiongnu" chapter of the *Xinshu* develops the strategy of "three models" (*san biao* 三表) and "five baits" (*wu er* 五餌) as a way to contend for the Chanyu's people by undermining his authority. With this multifaceted tool, Emperor Wen of Han would win over the tribesmen.[26] The idea was to present gifts such as chariots, feasting meat and court ladies to the multitude of Xiongnu nobility, not to the Chanyu.

The "three models" to follow are "trustworthiness" (*xin* 信), "cherishing" (*ai* 愛) and "approval" (*hao* 好). In the "Xiongnu" chapter (*Xinshu* 4.1, pp. 134–153), Jia Yi stresses the importance of applying these models to the Xiongnu peoples. Charles Sanft, who studied this chapter in his PhD thesis, argues that the "three models", which he translates as "three manifestations", serve two purposes: "First and foremost, they function as part of the creation of virtues. Second, they are necessary conditions for Jia Yi's plan to bring the Xiongnu under Han sway".[27] The aim of Jia Yi's idea of the "three models" is to develop and practice the "warring virtues" (*zhande* 戰德), which are related to the emperor (帝者戰德) (*Xinshu*, 4.1, p. 135). Jia Yi was probably influenced by Liu Jing when dealing with the importance of attracting the Xiongnu with a sense of virtue: by teaching the rules of proper conduct to the Xiongnu, they would learn about the hierarchy in family relations and would come to respect the Han emperor accordingly. For Jia Yi, though, the key to defeating the Xiongnu confederacy was to establish the "three models" and to provide the "five baits" in order to contend with the Chanyu for his people (*Xinshu* 4.1, p. 135) and make them subject of the Han empire. Jia Yi stresses the crucial point of keeping one's word with the Xiongnu people: the good influence of "trustworthiness" would guarantee their allegiance to the Han:

夢中許人，覺且不背其信，陛下已諾，若日出灼灼。

Even if the emperor would have agreed in a dream, once awake he would not turn his back to his trustworthiness. The promise just made by your Majesty is like the brightness of the sunrise.[28]

The second model, "cherishing", is another technique to motivate the people and thereby to govern them.[29] By extending to the Xiongnu[30] the use of "cherishing" as the instrument to govern them, the Han empire would expand its supremacy and be stable at the same time. The last model is "approval": by instilling in them a desire for approval, they will come naturally to act in support of the Han empire, thereby securing the greatest approval (*Xinshu* 4.1, p. 125).

The "three models" are usually read from a moral point of view: the Xiongnu can be the beneficiaries of a moral transformation that is an end in itself.[31] However, it may be doubted if the "three models" deal *only* with morality. "Trustworthiness", "cherishing" and "approval" are instruments to persuade the Xiongnu people that they can feel secure and appreciated under the Han political umbrella. Conquering the people from other states was the method promoted by scholars of the pre-imperial period in order to unify the world or, as expressed in the *Xunzi*, *sihai zhi nei ruo yijia* 四海之內若一家 (to be like one family within the four seas).[32] The aim was expressed in the ode *Wen wang you sheng* 文王有聲 (King Wen is famous) as follows: "From the west to the east, from the south to the north, there is none who does not obey".[33] The idea in the *Xunzi* is that according to what the ruler does, the people will respond like an echo. If the ruler's behaviour towards the people follows the methods mentioned above, then people from distant places will come happily to join his reign.[34] Similarly, Jia Yi's idea of the "three models" shares the same goal of *Xunzi*, but with a crucial difference: Jia Yi focuses on the elite, not the commoners.[35] Attracting and conquering the leaders was the basic move to win over the Xiongnu because the people would naturally follow them. This would have been possible due to the configuration of the Xiongnu state. The "three models" are the means by which the Han could extend their influence over the Xiongnu.

The idea of "attracting the people" (*Lai min* 徠民) is originally developed in the *Shangjun shu*.[36] This chapter, probably written between 262 and 230 BCE,[37] deals with the importance of improving the demographic balance with Qin's rivals. Qin, which suffered from under-population mainly in the recently conquered territories such as Sichuan,[38] had abundant land but insufficient labour. To the contrary, rival states such as Wei and Han (韓) suffered from overpopulation relative to land. The Qin was thus able to attract settlers from the east.[39] To facilitate immigration, the *Shangjun shu* recommends the exemption of immigrants from military service (with no great loss, because their loyalty to Qin would be questionable), and from taxes for three generations. Moreover, in order to attract immigrants and thus seize the people, the Qin ruler must be lenient with the men of service (*shi* 士) who surrendered. Giving the people what they do not have, namely, benefits from farming and exemption from taxes, would be the means by which to win them over.[40]

To seize the people by seducing them with the lure of material prosperity was precisely what Jia Yi would suggest a few decades later. According to his plan, the "three models" would be supplemented with "five baits", which were: elaborate clothes and carriages to seduce their eyes; fine food to seduce their mouths; music to seduce their ears; high halls and deep chambers,[41] granaries and slaves to seduce their stomachs; and gifts and favours for [those] who surrendered (*Xinshu* 4.1, pp. 136–137). According to this plan, you first win the enemy by making them feel secure and then nurture them with blandishments to make them dependent. The idea behind the plan of using the "five baits" is to control the five senses in order to neutralise the Xiongnu peoples and control them.

In the *Xunzi*, the five senses are related to *xing* 性, the genuine and unrefined elements of human nature. *Xing* is what is not refined by ritual and music.[42] Hence Jia Yi, by referring to the five senses as the means to reach the hearts of the Xiongnu leaders and corrupt them, stresses the fact that in order to domesticate them, you need to appeal to their materialism. For Jia Yi, there is no intent of moral refinement: the aim is to play with basic and intrinsic instincts in order to control them.

The idea of attracting the Xiongnu peoples so as to domesticate them can be seen as the germ of the later idea of *yi yi fa yi* 以夷伐夷 (using non-Han people to attack non-Han people) developed by Chao Cuo and usually explained as a strategy of diplomacy. Here the term *yi* 夷 is a generic term for non-Han populations. Although this expression is not attested in the *Xinshu*, we might consider Jia Yi's idea as its precursor. Jia Yi knew that the Xiongnu commanded the northern regions and took advantage of disruptions that the raids of their tribesmen caused to extort goods and subsidies from the Han court. They maintained a monopoly on this flow of Han goods to the steppe, which gave them great economic power and stability.[43] This was the reason why it was crucial, according to Jia Yi, to divide the confederacy by winning over the people and overturn the situation in favour of the Han. The *Xinshu* states that:

故三表已諭，五餌既明，則匈奴之中乖而相疑矣。

Therefore, as soon as the three models are made understood and the five baits are clear, then among the Xiongnu there will be dissent and [they will be] suspicious of each other.[44]

Jia Yi's plan was to turn the Xiongnu into subjects of the Han empire. The aim was to disrupt the stability of the people from within: by offering the various baits to their leaders at the borders, the Han would be able to corrupt and win them over to its side. The Xiongnu wanted border markets (*guan shi* 關市) so badly that they tried to obtain them with violence. For this reason, Jia Yi suggests sending envoys to tell the Xiongnu about the decision to establish large-sized border markets. These markets should be open in locations of strategic importance for the Han, and military forces should be stationed for Han self-protection. Every border market must include shops selling cheap meat, cooked rice and delicious raw and dry meat. These shops must be able to serve one or two hundred people. Thus, at the borders there will be hordes of Xiongnu. In this way, according to Jia Yi, if their king and generals would have tried to force them to go back to the north, the Xiongnu people would turn against their king. The Xiongnu will be starving for Han food and wine, and this will be their fatal weakness (*Xinshu* 4.1, p. 41).

According to this plan, which was probably first developed and suggested to Emperor Wen by Chao Cuo,[45] it was less costly and more effective to defend the northern frontiers of the empire by employing non-Han peoples to contain other non-Han peoples instead of committing Han troops and waging campaigns. The idea *in nuce* was to introduce non-Han elements into the Han military system, notably the *shuguo* 屬國 (Dependent State)[46] soldiers of the captured Xiongnu as public officials (*Xinshu* 4.2, p. 153).[47] Using non-Han people as allies against their own tribesmen would have allowed the Han empire to control – *divide et impera* – the territories beyond its frontiers. In contrast, the goal within the borders was to create stability through unity. In order to control the northern regions, the establishment of border markets, a precondition for cross-border trade, would have allowed the Han to provide the Xiongnu elite at the borders with Han merchandise. Ideally, for Jia Yi, this plan would have increased Han profit twofold: the Han would have divided the control of the Xiongnu over the elite and made them economically dependent on the Han. Thus, the borders would come under Han political control.

Jia Yi deals with the problem of the Xiongnu with a policy of economic containment. The gift agreement was important to maintain the military truce between the Han and the Xiongnu, but it had to be used to corrupt the leaders at the border with the Han empire. The potential results of Jia Yi's plan have to be seen as a long-term alternative to the existing policy in the context of a stable political economy: to win over the Xiongnu people at the borders by providing them with Han goods would allow the Han empire to weaken the enemy by winning over the tribesmen and have them by their side.

In the "Tong bu" 銅布 (On Copper Distribution) chapter,[48] Jia Yi deals with the problem of centralising economic power during the reign of Emperor Wen. In particular, this chapter seeks to persuade the emperor to take control of copper and monopolise the issue of currency. The policy, which dealt with the more urgent matter of inflation, aimed at controlling the dissemination of copper among the subjects in order to centralise and consolidate economic power. Jia Yi identifies three disasters (*san huo* 三禍) resulting from unconstrained copper distribution: the creation of a disaffected class of people convicted for illegal coinage whose social status had been reduced as a consequence of mutilating punishment; the circulation of counterfeit currency that was increasing suspicion among the people; and, the greatest disaster of all, the famine that would result from the widespread abandonment of fields and agricultural activities by those who chased after profits from coinage (*Xinshu* 3.5, p. 110). To avoid these disasters, the solution was to attain the "Seven Blessings" (*qi fu* 七福): practical measures to be applied in order to prevent economic crisis. The climax of the blessings is to compete with the Xiongnu for their people:

> 挾銅之積，制吾棄財，以與匈奴逐爭其民，則敵必懷矣，此謂之七福。故善為天下者，因禍而為福，轉敗而為功。今顧退七福而行博禍，可為長太息者，此其一也。

> If [Your Majesty] seizes the copper supplies and deploys our disposable property in order to compete with the Xiongnu for their people, then the enemy is certain to be assimilated. This is what is called the Seventh Blessing. Therefore, one who is good at governing the empire will transform calamities into blessings and turn defeat into achievement. Now, on the contrary, to reject the "Seven Blessings" and to wreak large-scale calamities, this is one of the reasons for which one can sigh long.[49]

Jia Yi, aware of the fact that a thriving economy can play a key role in promoting political stability, wanted to moderate expenditures in order to keep centralised control of the economy in the hands of the emperor, who should ensure the economic well-being of the people. Therefore, he suggested allocating domestic goods to the Xiongnu. In this way, the Han would be able to secure its northern borders and "then the enemy is certain to be assimilated" (則敵必懷矣). In his plan, it was important to send them only the Han's surplus goods in order to minimise the cost to the empire. In fact, by recommending the shipment of "disposable property" (*qicai* 棄財),[50] Jia Yi showed dissatisfaction with the current policy, which threatened to damage the Han economy and transform the empire into a tributary state, because the Xiongnu increased their requests every year. His idea was to use excess production for the purpose of corrupting and dividing the Xiongnu by tying them economically to the empire.

This policy would have probably constituted a double benefit for the Han: surplus product would be used beneficially without the need for the people of the Han empire to sacrifice anything; and the Han empire's affluence and abundance of property would have attracted the Xiongnu, resulting in a competition with the [Chanyu] Xiongnu for their people and the destruction of the stability of the confederation: by making them dependent on Han goods and corrupting them, the Han could undermine their loyalty to the Chanyu (*Xinshu* 3.5, p. 111).

As part of Han diplomatic strategy, Jia Yi, like Liu Jing before him, suggests saving on expenditures by trading surplus property.[51] On the one hand, Jia Yi recognised that carefully considering the Xiongnu problem was important to keep the Han state stable and secure because the enemy posed a real threat; on the other, he was not inclined to concede too much. He considered gift agreements to the Chanyu Xiongnu as being disadvantageous and even dangerous for the Han, because they tended to turn the Xiongnu into "lords above" and the Han into "vassals below" (*Han shu* 48, p. 2240). Jia Yi stresses that an economic plan that also dealt with the problems on the northern borders was needed in order to prevent the collapse of the empire.[52]

Trade was thus used as a political weapon not only by the Han government but also by the semi-nomadic populations on the northern frontier.[53] The plan was to turn the Xiongnu into subjects ready and trained to defend the Han empire.

將必以匈奴之眾為漢臣民，制之令千家而為一國, 列處之塞外，自隴西延至遼東，各有分地以衛邊，使備月氏、灌窳之變。

We must make the multitudes of the Xiongnu subject of the Han [and] command one thousand households to become one polity, arrayed beyond the passes, stretching from Longxi to Liaodong, with each [polity] possessing a part of the territory at the border to safeguard it, and charged with preparing for possible calamities by Yuezhi and Guanyu [populations].[54]

Since the empire could not subdue them because of their military power (and the state's own weakness), Jia Yi aims to transform the Xiongnu into a network of foreign *clientes*, which would act as a defensive belt against other nomadic tribes.[55] The political economy related to the Xiongnu might be seen as part of Jia Yi's idea of diplomacy in order to avoid the battlefield: economically, going to war would have been much more demanding in terms of both material resources and human lives. Moreover, the result of a major campaign against the Xiongnu would not only be difficult to predict but also violate the principles of "cherishing the people", the root of political stability. In line with the Warring States tradition of demographic warfare, Jia Yi's concern is to encourage the immigration of Xiongnu subjects and subjugate them to the Han empire.

Conclusion

Due to military operations and tributary agreements, Xiongnu–Han relations became part of the economic expenses of the empire. From the perspective of

Jia Yi, the empire could conquer the Xiongnu federation with material goods as baits and, at the same time, incorporate foreign policy within the empire's economic plan.

At that time there was no "Chinese" superiority in terms of military power: the fact that the Han had to pay tribute to the Xiongnu shows that they were inferior. Therefore, the idea of northern borders had to be reconsidered from an economic point of view, taking account of the fact that the Han and the Xiongnu shared cross-border economic links. Jia Yi was persuading Emperor Wen to integrate the border economy into the larger imperial economy. Gift agreements could be transformed into an economic weapon in order to take the control over that sensitive border area. Jia Yi understood that cross-border economic activity is often based on pre-existing networks of kinship, friendship and, more generally, common interest.[56] Borderlands connect two – or more – economic systems. The plan was to control these interactions. This was the only way to conquer the Xiongnu peoples and bring them to the side of the Han. The desire to control the northern frontier areas was a by-product of imperial ideology, which did not belong only to Han: the concept of "the Son of Heaven" extended to the Xiongnu as well.[57] The "five baits" and other material goods were meant to conquer the Xiongnu population in order to build an economic belt favouring the Han empire, the very last purpose of which would have been to drive the Xiongnu from a nomadic life to a more sedentary one. Since the Xiongnu was dominant both militarily and economically at the borders, Jia Yi's plan aimed to overturn this situation by wresting economic control: using the "five baits" and other tasty goods, the Han would be enabled to exert its economic influence and win over the Xiongnu people. This economic belt, which eventually led to the agricultural colonisation of frontier regions, was a trans-border economic grouping, which allowed shifting loyalties and allegiances in accordance with political organisation and reorganisation. If we consider borders as markers of the actual power that states wielded over their own society, it is clear that during the time of Jia Yi this region was totally unstable.

Jia Yi's plan to corrupt the people's senses using tasty baits was later applied, and also criticised.[58] In the comments attached to Jia Yi's biography in the *Han shu*, Ban Gu 班固 (32–92) wrote of the strategy:

及欲試屬國，施五餌三表以系單于，其術固疏矣。

As for his attempt to try to establish subordinate states and tie down the Chanyu by means of the "five baits" and "three models", these methods are indeed shallow and distant.[59]

Rather than adopting Jia Yi's proposal (which was to corrupt leaders at the borders, not the Chanyu) the state pursued Chao Cuo's policy of acquiring new territories from the non-Han people. In 167 BCE, Chao Cuo suggested that the government bestow higher orders of rank upon people willing to move to the frontier to guard it.[60] But not until Emperor Wu 武 (r. 141–87) would Xiongnu generals surrender to the Han.

Notes

1 I am grateful to Paul R. Goldin, Terry Peach and Yuri Pines for their precious comments on previous drafts of my chapter.
2 In this chapter I refer to "border" when emphasising regions rather than lines drawn on the map. "Frontier" commonly refers to the territorial expansion of civilisations into "empty" areas. See Baud and Van Schendel (1997).
3 On the formation and organisation of the Xiongnu confederacy, see, among others: Barfield (1981), Yamada (1982), and Di Cosmo (2002), pp. 167–190.
4 Material culture attests that already during the last part of the Warring States period, contacts between northern populations and what will soon become the Chinese empire became more significant. See Jacobson (1988), So and Bunker (1995), and Di Cosmo (2002), pp. 83–87.
5 Di Cosmo (2002), p. 157.
6 Chang (2007), p. 176
7 I am indebted to Yuri Pines for this observation.
8 For Jia Yi's biography: *Shiji* 84: 2491–2503, and *Han shu* 48: 2221–2265. The editions used here are: *Shiji*, Beijing: Zhonghua shuju, 1959; *Han shu*, Beijing: Zhonghua shuju, 1997.
9 The title simply denotes a new edition of the collation of texts ascribed to Jia Yi and edited after his death. See Cai Tingji (1984), pp. 23–27. On the authenticity of the *Xinshu*, see Nylan (1994), pp. 161–170; Wang Xingguo (1992), pp. 39–72; and Chen Weiliag (1958), pp. 1–30. The methods of philological analysis in Svarverud (1998) have been sharply criticised by Shaodan Luo (2003, pp. 270–299). In this chapter I translate the title as *New Writings* with the meaning of "New Edition of Jia Yi's Writings". In early Han, the practice of naming written works with "new edition" (*xinshu* 新書) was common. In this chapter I use the *Xinshu jiaozhu* 新书校柱, Beijing: Zhonghua shuju 2000. Hereafter, I will refer to the text as *Xinshu*.
10 Wall building was originally a military concept and a technology imported from the Central Plain. It was later adapted to a new context and changed accordingly. See Di Cosmo (2002), pp. 138–158.
11 Di Cosmo (2002), p. 128; Lewis (2007), p. 130.
12 The standard interpretation of wall building is that it was essentially a defensive measure.
13 Di Cosmo (2002), p. 143.
14 In pre-imperial texts, the expression *heqin* was used to explain the ritual and social etiquette within the family and by extension within the state. For instance, the *Yueji* 樂論 (Treatise of Music) of the *Xunzi* 荀子 says: "在閨門之內，父子兄弟同聽之則莫不和親。 Within the internal walls [of the female part of the household], if fathers and sons, elder and younger brothers, listen to [music] together, everybody will be in harmony and intimate [with each other]". The same passage occurs in the "Yueji" 樂記 (Record of Music) chapter of the *Liji* 禮記 (Record of Rites) and in the "Liyue" 禮樂 (Ritual and Music) chapter of the *Baihutong* 白虎通 (Discourse on General Virtues at the White Tiger Hall). The *heqin* policy has been the focus of extensive scholarship. Among others, see: Di Cosmo (2002), Sophia-Karin Psarras (2003), pp. 55–236, Lin Gan (2007), pp. 44–116, and Yan Mingshu (2003). For *heqin* and the tributary system, see also Goldin (2011) and Selbitschka (2015).
15 From 201 to 174 BCE the Xiongnu and Han concluded six treaties, which put the Han in a dangerous position.
16 Chanyu is the Xiongnu title equivalent to the word *huang* 皇 "immense" in the Chinese title *huangdi* 皇帝 "emperor". Shiratori (1923), pp. 76–78 argues that Chanyu is not a Xiongnu word because the characters used to transcribe it have the same meaning in Chinese as in the Xiongnu term they transcribe. To the contrary, Pulleyblank considers the term to be of Mongol origin (1963, p. 256). See also Psarras (2003), p. 128. Chanyu is sometimes read as "Shanyu".

17 Goldin (2011) discusses the term in 238 n.33.
18 *Han shu* 94B.3755.
19 *Han shu* 94B.3755.
20 *Han shu* 94B.3755.
21 Chin (2010), p. 348
22 *Chao Cui ji zhushi* 晁錯集注釋. Shanghai: *Shanghai renmin chubanshe*, 1975, p. 8.
23 Yü (1967), p. 42.
24 Di Cosmo (2002), p. 197.
25 Di Cosmo (2002), p. 186.
26 There are different modern interpretations with regard to the functions of gifts to the Xiongnu: they were said to have been intended to control the Xiongnu through Han culture (see Yü 1967, p. 388) or to "soften and corrupt" them (see Loewe 2000, p. 189) or to "dazzle and corrupt" (see Di Cosmo 2002, p. 202); or gifts as example of exoticism (see Miller 2009, p. 98).
27 (Sanft (2005), p. 292.
28 *Xinshu* 4.1, p. 135. The meaning is that what the emperor says, even what he says hypothetically in a dream, must be fulfilled as a promise. In this way, his influence would reach any place, like the brightness of the sunrise. This is clearly a rhetorical exaggeration, but it says a lot about the importance of trustworthiness in government as a means of conquering through virtue.
29 The idea of "cherishing the people" in Jia Yi is strongly influenced by *Xunzi*, where we read that: "if one who rules over people desires stability, there is no alternative to governing wisely and cherishing the people" (*Xunzi* 9: 152–153). Just like the *Xunzi*, Jia Yi's "cherishing the people" is an instrument for governing, not its purpose. I discuss this idea in Levi Sabattini (2012, p. 180).
30 Here Jia Yi refers to the Hu 胡 population. However, in Han times the term became synonymous with the Xiongnu. Di Cosmo (2002), p. 129.
31 Zhou (2012), p. 259.
32 *Xunzi* 8, 9 and 15.
33 *Zi xi zi dong, zi nan zi bei, wu si bu fu* 自西自東，自南自北，無思不服. See *Xunzi* 8, and 15.
34 *Xunzi* 8.
35 Jia Yi develops this idea in the "Jun dao" 君道 (The Way of the Ruler) chapter.
36 The *Shangjun shu* is traditionally ascribed to Shang Yang 商鞅 (d. 338 BCE), political reformer of the state of Qin. Jia Yi's general attitude toward Shang Yang is somewhat controversial (Pines 2017, p. 264). Jia Yi is identified as a connoisseur of Shang Yang and Shen Buhai (*Shiji* 130: 3319). To the contrary, the *Han shu* recalls Jia Yi as Shang Yang's critic (*Han shu* 48: 2244). Jia Yi praises Shang Yang political reforms in the "Guo Qin lun" chapters, discussed in Levi Sabattini (2017).
37 Pines (2017), p. 198.
38 Sage (1992), pp. 132–134.
39 Pines (2017), p. 199.
40 Trad. Pines (2017), p. 203.
41 David Hawkes gives "high halls and deep chambers" (高堂邃宇) in his translation of the *Chuci* 楚辭. See Hawkes (1985), p. 226. I follow his interpretation.
42 As for Jia Yi's general indebtedness to *Xunzi*, see Goldin (2007).
43 See Barfield (1981), pp. 45–61. In this connection, Armin Selbitschka notices that "the Xiongnu were not at all corrupted by the opulence of Chinese products, as Jia Yi assumed they would be. Instead, the magnitude of goods extorted from the Western Han was essential to the internal stability of the nomad confederacy" (Selbitschka 2015, p. 97 n.129). Actually, I think that Jia Yi was aware of this situation; this is the reason why he argued that it was important to corrupt and divide the Xiongnu nobility.
44 *Xinshu* 4.1:29.
45 *Han shu* 49:5 a–b. See also Yü (1967), p. 14.

46 This expression refers to subordinate non-Chinese states or peoples that accepted China's overlordship and submitted tribute to the Chinese ruler.
47 See also Yü (1967), p. 14.
48 I study this issue in depth in "To Ban or Not to Ban: Jia Yi on Copper Distribution and Minting Coins" (Brill, forthcoming).
49 *Xinshu*: 353.
50 The importance of creating a surplus in order to avoid famine and guarantee the stability of the empire is also discussed in *Xinshu* 1.4, p. 30.
51 This idea was also related to the formation of the tributary system among the populations at the southern frontiers, whereas the use of Han goods as economic weapons was aimed to bring about control over the population. Selbitschka (2015) highlights that tribute as "gift" has secular functions in early China.
52 One of the premises of *Yantie lun* 鹽鐵論 is that military expenses to contain the Xiongnu have forced the imperial government to devise new methods of acquiring revenue.
53 See also Barfield (1981), pp. 45–61.
54 *Xinshu* 4.1, p. 134. The Yuezhi and Guanyu were populations from Inner Asia and enemies of the Xiongnu. Charles Sanft has analysed the chapter on the Xiongnu in "Economic Communication in the Western Han", a presentation for the panel on "Early Chinese Economic Thought in Its Socio-Political Context: Arguments, Approaches, Objectives" at the European Association for Chinese Studies Conference (EACS), University of Minho, Braga (Portugal), 24 July 2014.
55 For the institution of foreign *clientelae* in the Roman Republic, see Badian (1958) and compare with Pina Polo (2015).
56 See, for instance, Baud and Van Schendel (1997), pp. 229–230.
57 Goldin (2011).
58 In *Shiji* 99, 110 we read that the policy that involved gifts and border trade was precisely an attempt at "corruption".
59 *Han shu*: 2265.
60 *Han shu*: 2286. Chun-Shu Chang (2007), p. 187. See also Chang (2007).

Bibliography

Badian, E. (1958). *Foreign Clientelae (264–70 B.C.)*. Oxford: Clarendon Press.
Barfield, T. (1981). "Hsiung-nu Imperial Confederacy: Organization and Foreign Policy". *Journal of Asian Studies* 41.1.
Baud, M. and Van Schendel, W. (1997). "Toward a Comparative History of Borderlands". *Journal of World History* 8.2.
Brosseder, U. and Miller, B.K. (eds.) (2011). *Xiongnu Archaeology: Multidisciplinary Perspective of the First Steppe Empire in Inner Asia*. Bonn: Bonn Contributions to Asian Archaeology 5: Vor und Frühgeschichtliche Archäologie, Rheinische Friedrich-Wilhelms-Universität Bonn.
Cai, Tingji 蔡廷吉 (1984). *Jia Yi yanjiu* 賈誼研究. Taipei: Wen shi zhe xue jicheng 113.
Chang, Chun-shu (2007). *The Rise of the Chinese Empire: Frontier, Immigration, and Empire in Han China*. Ann Arbor: University of Michigan Press.
ChaoCui ji zhushi 晁錯集注釋 (1975). Shanghai: Shanghai renmin chubanshe.
Chen Weiliag 陳偉良 (1958). "Jia Yi Xinshu tanyuan" 賈誼新書探源. In Jiang Runxun 江潤勳 et al. (eds.), *Jia Yi yanjiu* 賈誼研究. Hong Kong: Qiujing, 1–30.
Chin, T.T. (2010). "Defamiliarizing the Foreigner: Sima Qian's Ethnography and Han-Xiongnu Marriage Diplomacy". *Harvard Journal of Asiatic Studies* 70.2.
De Crespigny, R. (1984). *Northern Frontier: The Policies and Strategy of the Later Han Empire*. Canberra: Australian National University.

Di Cosmo, N. (1994). "Ancient Inner Asian Nomads: Their Economic Basis and Its Significance in Chinese History". *The Journal of Asian Studies* 53.4.

Di Cosmo, N. (2002). *Ancient China and Its Enemies: The Rise of Nomadic Power in East Asian History*. Cambridge: Cambridge University Press.

Goldin, P.R. (2007). "Xunzi and Early Han Philosophy". *Harvard Journal of Asiatic Studies* 67.1.

Goldin, P.R. (2011). "Steppe Nomads as a Philosophical Problem in Classical China". In Paula L.W. Sabloff (ed.), *Mapping Mongolia: Situating Mongolia in the World from Geologic Time to the Present*. Philadelphia: University of Pennsylvania Museum of Archaeology and Anthropology.

Ban Gu (ed) (1997) *Hanshu* 漢書 . Beijing: Zhonghua shuju.

Hawkes, D. (1985). *The Songs of the South: An Anthology of Ancient Chinese Poems by Qu Yuan and Other Poets*. London: Penguin Classics.

Jacobson, E. (1988). "Beyond the Frontier: A Reconsideration of Cultural Interchange between China and the Early Nomads". *Early China* 13.

Levi Sabattini, E. (2012). "'People as Root' (*min ben*): Rhetoric in the *New Writings* by Jia Yi (200–168)". *Political Rhetoric in Early China: Extrême-Orient, Extrême-Occident* 34.

Levi Sabattini, E. (2017). "How to Surpass the Qin: On Jia Yi's Intentions in the *Guo Qin lun*". *Monumenta Serica* 65.2.

Levi Sabattini, E. (forthcoming). "To Ban or Not to Ban: Jia Yi on Copper Distribution and Minting Coins". In E. Levi Sabattini and C. Schwermann (eds.), *Between Command and Market: Economic Thought and Practice in Early China*. Leiden: Brill.

Lewis, M. (2007). *The Early Chinese Empires: Qin and Han*. Cambridge, MA: Harvard University Press.

Lin Gan 林幹 (ed.) (1983). *Xiongnu shi lunwen xuanji* 匈奴史論文選集. Beijing: Zhonghua shuju.

Lin Gan (1984). *Xiongnu tongshi* 匈奴通史. Beijing: Zhonghua shuju.

Lin Gan (2007). *Xiongnu shi* 匈奴史 (rev. ed.). Hohhot: Neimenggu Renmin chubanshe.

Loewe (2000). *A Biographical Dictionary of the Qin, Former Han and Xin Periods, 221 B.C.-A.D 24,* Leiden: Brill.

Luo Shaodan (2003). "Inadequacy of Karlgren's Linguistic Method as Seen in Rune Svarverud's Study of the *Xinshu*". *Journal of Chinese Linguistics* 31.2.

Ma Xiaoli 馬曉丽 (2006). "Jia Yi's Thoughts on the Han: Xiongnu Relationship 贾谊的民族关系思想". *Yantai daxue xuebao* Issue 119.

Miller, B.K. (2009). "Power Politics in the Xiongnu Empire". PhD dissertation. University of Pennsylvania.

Nylan, M. (1994). "Hsin shu". In Michael Loewe (ed.), *Early Chinese Texts: A Bibliographical Guide*. Institute of East Asian Studies. Berkeley: University of California.

Pina Polo, F. (2015). "Foreign *Clientelae* Revisited: A Methodological Critique". In Martin Jehne and Francisco Pina Polo (eds.), *Foreign Clietelae in the Roman Empire: A Reconsideration*. Franz Steiner Verlag: Mul Edition.

Pines, Y. (2012). *The Everlasting Empire: The Political Culture of Ancient China and Its Imperial Legacy*. Princeton, NJ: Princeton University Press.

Pines, Y. (2017). *The Book of Lord Shang: Apologetics of State Power in Early China*. New York: Columbia University Press.

Psarras, S.K. (2003). "Han and Xiongnu: A Reexamination of Cultural and Political Relations". *Monumenta Serica* 51.

Pulleyblank, E.G. (1962). "The Consonantal System of Old Chinese (II)". *Asia Major* (new series) 9.2.

Pulleyblank, E.G. (1963). "The Hsiung-nu language". *Asia Major* (new series) IX.2.

Purdue, C.P. (2009). "Nature and Nurture on Imperial China's Frontiers". *Modern Asian Studies* 43.1.

Qi Yuzhang 祁玉章 (ed.) (1974). *Jiazi Xinshu jiao shi* 賈子新書校釋. Taipei: Zhongguo wenhua zazhishe.

Sage, S.F. (1992). *Ancient Sichuan and the Unification of China*. Albany: State University of New York Press.

Sanft, C. (2005). "Rule: A Study of Jia Yi's Xin shu". PhD dissertation. Münster (Germany).

Sanft, C. (2014). "Economic Communication in the Western Han". Presented for the panel on "Early Chinese Economic Thought in Its Socio-Political Context: Arguments, Approaches, Objectives". European Association for Chinese Studies Conference (EACS), University of Minho, Braga (Portugal).

Selbitschka, A. (2015). "Early Chinese Diplomacy: Realpolitik versus the So-Called Tributary System". *Asia Major* 28.1.

Sima Qian (1986). *Shangjunshu zhuizhi* 商君書錐指. Beijing: Zhonghua shuju.

Shiji 史記 (1959). Beijing: Zhonghua shuju.

Shiratori, K. (1923). "Sur l'origine des Hiong-nu". *Journal Asiatique* 202.

So, J. and Bunker, E.C. (1995). *Traders and Raiders on China's Northern Frontier*. Seattle and London: Arthur Sackler Gallery and University of Washington Press.

Svarverud, R. (1998). *Methods of the Way: Early Chinese Ethical Thought*. Leiden: Brill.

Van Ess, H. (2012). "The Ethos of the Envoy and His Treatment by the Enemy in Han History". *Crossroads* 5.

Wang Xingguo 王興國 (1992). *Jia Yi pingzhuan fu Lu Jia Chao Cuo pingzhuan* 賈誼評傳附陸賈晁錯評傳. Zhongguo sixiangjia pingzhuan congshu 15. Nanjing: Nanjing Daxue.

Wang Zijin 王子今 (2010). "On the Preparations for the Changes of Yuezhi and Guanyu 論賈誼新書備月氏、灌窳之變". *Social Sciences* 社會科學 Issue 3.

Xie Jian 謝劍 (1968). "Xiongnu zhengzhi zhidu de yanjiu" 匈奴政治制度的研究. *Bulletin of the Institute of History and Philology (Academia Sinica)* 40.2.

Yamada Nobuo (1982). "The Formation of the Hsiong-nu Nomadic State". *Acta Orientalia Academiae Scientiarum Hungaricae* 36.1–3.

Yan Mingshu 閻明恕 (ed.) (2003). *Zhongguo gudai heqin shi* 中國古代和親史. Guiyang: Guizhou Minzu chubanshe.

Yan Shengguo 閻盛國 (2004). "Discussion on the Han Strategies to Attract the Xiongnu Surrenderers 漢朝招降匈奴策略述論". *Junshi lishi yanjiu* 軍事歷史研究 Issue 2.

Yü Ying-shih (1967). *Trade and Expansion in Han China*. Berkeley: Berkeley University Press.

Zhou Ying (2012). "Jia Yi's Proposal of the 'Three Exemplifications and Five Means of Allurement' and the Han-Xiongnu Relationship in Early Western Han Period". Victor H. Mair, *The "Silk Roads" in Time and Space: Migrations, Motifs, and Materials: Sino-Platonic Paper* 228. http://mongolschinaandthesilkroad.blogspot.com/2012/08/blog-post.html.

8 The "land quota" system in the Han Dynasty and its historical influence

Wang Fang

Introduction

The thought of "land quota" (限田) in Chinese history is about limiting the amount of land owned by private individuals. In traditional Chinese society, "land quota" was often proposed as an ideal scheme to ease social crises and consolidate governance at times when rapid expansion of privately owned land led to land annexation and social conflict. Such thought, or similar ideas, became "an important thought or policy on land of the subsequent feudal dynasties in China",[1] so that in each dynasty after the Han there were people who proposed similar ideas or attempted to implement similar policies. Even up to the time of the Republic of China, there were discussions about the applicability of "land quota" and attempts to solve contemporary land and social issues by imposing limits upon privately owned land. Based on a systematic review of the evolution of "land quota" thought from the Han Dynasty to the time of the Republic of China, this chapter explores the question of how "land quota", as an idea that thrived in theory but failed in practice, could exist for such a long time and have such a profound influence on later generations.

Literature review

According to information from the National Library, Shanghai Library, the Library of Shanghai Academy of Social Sciences, Fudan University Library, SSreader and Dacheng Journal Database, there was a great deal of work undertaken on land issues before the foundation of the People's Republic of China. The number of works on modern land issues from the 1920s to the 1940s exceeds 210, while in the Dacheng Journal Database, the number of papers in modern times (1840–1949) with the keyword "land" is over 7,600. The topics covered involved various aspects of land issues, including land policy, the history of land systems, land tax and land rent. Various academic journals, such as the *Economics Quarterly* of the Chinese Economic Society, *Chinese Economy* of the China Economic Research Association and *Land Administration News Report* and *Rural Construction* of the Department of Land Administration of the Kuomintang, were founded during this period, and it is noteworthy that they carried a considerable number of papers on rural economy and land issues.

After 1949, research on the land system of the Han Dynasty fell into two categories. One is general research on land issues in ancient China and the Han Dynasty. The second category is research on (ideas about) one or several specific land systems, including the *Ming-Tian* land system (a land allocation system based on title or rank), rent and tax issues, the army farming system and the King's land system (王田), among others. Research on Han Dynasty land systems by scholars in modern times can be divided into two time periods, the first marked by the 1975 excavation of Qin bamboo slips at Shuihudi (睡虎地秦简), the second by the 1983 excavation of Han bamboo slips at Zhangjiashan (张家山汉简). Before the excavation of the Han bamboo slips, research mostly focused on the discussion of land ownership; after the excavation, research broadened to include the contents of land systems, land planning, the land and village system (庄田) and the essence of the land system.

The thought of "land quota" and its core content

Background and basic conditions

The private ownership of land established in Qin was carried over to the Han Dynasty. When the regime of Western Han was founded, the primary task was to recover and develop agricultural production. Because large quantities of labour had been enlisted in the army and the supply was insufficient, Liu Bang (256–195 BCE), Emperor Gaozu of Han, embarked on large-scale demobilisation. The former officers and soldiers were not only exempted from forced (corvée) labour for the government but were also allocated different quantities of land and housing according to their military exploits. Also, the *Ming-Tian* land system was put into practice, whereby people in exile could return home and register in the household system to recover their ownership of land.

In the early years of the Han Dynasty, although the private ownership of land was permitted, various limitations were placed on the transfer, trade and inheritance of land in order to protect the existing social hierarchy and to control land annexation. The *Ming-Tian* land system was a system of long-term land occupation under which land allocated would not be taken back. As long-term occupation gradually became private ownership, land annexation would come back again, so the *Ming-Tian* land system suffered total destruction.[2]

By the time of Emperor Wu of Han (r. 141–87 BCE), following a period of economic recovery and growth in population, land annexation had come to be seen as a serious problem: "in some cases, despotic landlords who build their fortune and power by land annexation run amuck among the people".[3] Officials, nobles, local despots and merchants all joined the party of land annexation, leading to a situation where "the rich have boundless land while the poor have not even a tiny plot".[4]

It should be pointed out that land annexation in the Han was predominantly of two types: one was annexation by landlords through violence; the other, annexation by merchants through unfair trade. As observed by Chao Cuo (晁错 200–154 BCE), a famous politician and writer in the Western Han, farmers

> already endure so much toil and hardship, but they still have to suffer from floods and droughts, urgent conscription and harsh taxation, frequent apportionment of tax, and constant changes of government orders. At these times, those who have grain will sell at half price, while those who do not have grain must pay the tax with funds borrowed at usurious rates. The result is that some people will need to sell land and houses and even their children to pay off their debt. . . . That is why merchants can annex the land of farmers, and farmers become homeless.[5]

Hu Jichuang observed that "land annexation in ancient Rome was half by trade and half by seizure. Land annexation in China as from the middle of the second century BCE was also through the same way"[6] However, land annexation after the middle of the second century BCE was different. Before the middle of the second century BCE, annexation was through the appropriation of land by rich merchants, but after the middle of the second century BCE, one important feature was annexation of small holders' land by large landlords. The offspring of the King of Huainan and the King of Hengshan (contemporaries of Dong Zhongshu) "deprived farmers of their land and houses", "seized farmers' land several times, destroyed their tombs and took it as their own land".[7] Land annexation not only harmed agricultural production but also impacted on social stability. As Dong Zhongshu remarked, "poor people were often dressed in rags and ate as meagrely as dogs and pigs";[8] they therefore "fled to the mountains and forests and turned into robbers and thieves".

Core elements of "land quota" thought

To counter land annexation, Jia Yi (贾谊 200–168 BCE) put forward the policy of "establishing more vassal kings and weakening their power", which involved establishing more vassal kings on land that originally was allocated to only one king, thus weakening their power. The primary aim of the policy was to deal with land annexation. The manor of vassal kings would be divided into smaller pieces generation by generation until the land was too small to be divided further. This kind of "land division system" attempted to solve the problem of land annexation brought about by rich families by limiting the land of vassal kings. But it was not realistic.

At the time of Dong Zhongshu (董仲舒 179–104 BCE), the conflict between powerful landlords and peasants became fiercer. Dong believed that annexation was due to the abolition of the *jing* land system (井田制),[9] the result of which was to "allow people to trade in land". This trade had resulted in an increasingly large gap between rich and poor, which would finally lead to serious social problems. Therefore, he suggested that

> although the ancient *jing* land system cannot be revived, the present land system should more or less approximate to it. That is, the amount of land

privately owned by people ought to be limited to satisfy the needs of those who have not enough land, thereby blocking the road to annexation.[10]

Dong Zhongshu thought that by limiting the amount of land owned by private individuals, the polarisation between rich and poor could be prevented and social order stabilised. Influenced by Dong's argument, Emperor Wu implemented the policy of "land quota", carrying out a series of measures to restrain powerful landlords and thus alleviate, to an extent, the social conflict at that time. The measures included the imposition of a land quota decree upon registered merchants and their families, and "Suan-Min" (算缗) and "Gao-Min" (告缗) decrees[11] that indirectly supported the practice of the land quota system. The series of policies implemented by Emperor Wu led to the bankruptcy of a large number of merchants.

In the fifth Yuanfeng year (106 BCE) of Emperor Wu's reign, the whole country was divided into 13 sections (states), and each section was assigned a governor (刺史) whose duties were specified explicitly. The first duty was supervision, requiring the governors to report to the emperor the cases of powerful families "who own more land and houses than is allowed, oppress the weak, and harm the minority".[12] Hence we see that the target of Emperor Wu's land quota policy was not only the merchants but also "powerful families". After Dong Zhongshu's death (104 BCE), the land quota decree fell into disuse. Then, from the mid-Western Han to the time of Emperor Ai (25–1 BCE), more land annexation occurred on a grand scale. What is more, frequent natural disasters such as earthquakes and floods wreaked havoc, so that by 7 BCE the country was beset with social crises:

> Vassal kings, Lie-Hou [nobility of the highest rank], princesses, high officials, and rich people keep many slaves, own limitless land and houses, and scramble with the people for profits, so the people lose their livelihood and live in great poverty and deficiency.[13]

In the later stage of Western Han, Confucianism developed in an unprecedented way. Emperor Yuan (74–33 BCE) strongly supported Confucianism, while great Confucian scholars, including Kuang Heng (匡衡) and Shi Dan (师丹), emerged at the time of Emperors Cheng and Ai. During the reign of Emperor Ai (r. 7–1 BCE), three of his ministers, Shi Dan (师丹 d. 3CE), Kong Guang (孔光 65BCE-5 CE) and He Wu (何武 d. 3 CE), revived Dong Zhongshu's thought of "land quota" and designed specific measures to tackle the problem of annexation. Their decree stipulated the maximum quota of land owned by individuals ranging from vassal kings to officials and ordinary people:

> vassal kings and Lie-Hou [marquises] can own land within their manor; Lie-Hou living in the capital city of Chang'an, and princesses who own land in different counties, as well as Guannei-Hou [nobility of the second highest rank], officials, and ordinary people, can own no more than 30

qing of land [1 *qing* equals 6.666667 hectares]. . . . Those who violate the law will be punished according to the law. Those who own more land and slaves than is allowed according to their rank will be expropriated by the government.[14]

The decree also imposed restrictions on merchants. Although there have been different opinions about whether it was implemented, it was the first decree in Chinese history that had provisions for land possession and the land quota system.

The views underling the decree were as follows: annexation by despotic landlords caused peasants to lose land, which threatened agricultural production and state security; and the destruction of the *jing* land system and free trade in land were seen as the root of land annexation. The land quota scheme put forward by Shi Dan's party specified the targets of the system. Whereas Dong Zhongshu spoke of the applicability of the system to "the people", Shi Dan, together with Kong Guang and He Wu, disaggregated the target group into vassal kings, marquises, princesses, second-rank officials, other officials, ordinary people and merchants. Also, it stipulated specific amounts of land quota. Although it did not specify a precise quantity of land for vassal kings, it allowed them to own land only "within their manor" and forbade them to annex land elsewhere; for others, specific limitations on land ownership were proposed, and merchants were not allowed to own any land. Further, it stipulated a time limit on compliance with the system and imposed strict punishment on violation. Shi Dan gave those powerful families who broke the provisions of the system three years to make adjustments, after which the government would expropriate land beyond the limit of 30 *qing*. Merchants who owned land would "be punished according to the law". Measures of land quota system were also accompanied by restrictions on owning slaves – "vassal kings can own two hundred slaves, Lie-Hou and princesses can own one hundred, and Guannei-Hou, officials, and ordinary people can own thirty".[15] However, the land quota scheme put forward by Shi Dan harmed the interests of the nobility, officials and big landlords and met with strong opposition from the powerful, so its implementation was thwarted.[16] In addition, Shi Dan's scheme was more rigorous and wide-ranging than the policy under Emperor Wu, which had been applied only to new annexation by registered merchants and did nothing about the land they possessed already. The land quota scheme put forward by Shi Dan's party stipulated the maximum quota of land owned by private individuals, with land exceeding the limit expropriated by the government.

Wang Mang (王莽 46–23 CE), who was later to develop Dong Zhongshu's and Shi Dan's thought, attempted to recover the *jing* land system; he also implemented the King's land system (王田制), which decreed that all land belonged to the state and forbade trade of land. Wang Mang believed that trade in land was the cause of annexation, so the King's system was, in effect, another type of land quota system. However, difficulties with its implementation were such that the system was abandoned after only three years.

The development of "land quota" thought in the Eastern Han

Problems of land annexation and possible solutions received further consideration in the Eastern Han. Xun Yue (荀悦 148–209 CE), a historian and ideologue, argued that attempts to implement the *jing* system, as proposed by Dong Zhongshu and Shi Dan, were impractical because the system could operate only in vast and sparsely populated areas.[17] Hence, Xun Yue proposed his own idea of limiting private ownership of land by allowing people only "to farm but not to own the land":

> Families occupy land according to the size of their households, for which a restrictive decree is established to allow people to farm the land but not to trade in it, so as to aid the weak and prevent land annexation.[18]

Zhong Changtong (仲长统 179–220 CE), a philosopher, also supported a land quota to curb annexation: "a limitation should be imposed …"

> limitation should be imposed upon large families . . . If their land is covered with grass, it will be taken by the government; if they are competent at farming, then just allow and accept the situation. If they are allowed to have absolute discretion to take land as their own, in future they will do evil things for sure.[19]

The long-term influence of "land quota" thought

Ideas about land quotas were discussed repeatedly in later dynasties. From Tang to Qing, there were thinkers who supported the idea of land quotas and believed they could solve contemporary land problems. Even during the Republic of China, discussion about land systems was still influenced by ideas dating back to the Han Dynasty.

"Land quota" thought from Tang to Qing

Lu Zhi (陆贽 745–805 CE), a politician in the Tang Dynasty, believed that the system that allots one hundred *mu* of land to each man was a "land quota system". Land annexation had come about because of the destruction of the *jing* system, but it was impossible to return to that system in view of the spread of private ownership in the Tang. He therefore proposed to limit private land ownership and to reduce rent and taxes paid by those who worked the land:

> All land occupied will be bound by regulations to reduce rent and benefit the poor. . . . [Set] up rigorous decrees to punish violation, so affluence is slightly lessened and poverty lightly eased to the extent that the rich will not lose their wealth but the poor will be relieved.[20]

The Song Dynasty marked an important transition in the land system in ancient China with the abandonment of a nationwide policy. Land issues were discussed from two perspectives. Some thinkers believed that the fundamental cause of land annexation was the destruction of the *jing* system but, as it was impossible to recover that system, most people inclined to the implementation of a "land quota" policy.

Su Xun (苏洵 1009–1066 CE), a writer in the Northern Song Dynasty, and Lin Xun (林勋), a political thinker in the Southern Song Dynasty, advocated a "mild" land quota policy. Su Xun suggested the policy should only be applied to future cases, not retroactively. He believed that the destruction of the *jing* system and privatisation of land had caused the separation of the ownership and the right to use land ("land is not owned by those who farm the land, while those who own the land do not farm")[21] which had further led to the polarisation between the rich and the poor. However, Su Xun did not propose a return to the *jing* land system on the grounds that the cost of its (re-)introduction would be prohibitively high, involving a massive irrigation project. He supported Dong Zhongshu's idea of "land quota" providing it did not involve the expropriation of land in excess of the quota and was not applied retroactively: the limitation will not be imposed upon "those who already own land more than allowed, but will in the future keep people from occupying more land than is allowed".[22] Su Xun proposed a relatively low limit of land quota. Although he did not give a specific number, he believed that the 30 *qing* proposed by Kong Guang and He Wu was too high: "Though it cannot be the same as the land system of the Zhou dynasty, it is still too much for one man to occupy the amount that should be farmed by 30 labourers".[23] People owning land below the limit could obtain new land as long as the sum did not exceed the limit.

At the same time, however, He Wu suggested that "modest limitations should be imposed, instead of expropriation of land", in the hope of reducing the land owned by the rich in a gradual way so as to resolve the contradictions of the private ownership of land and secure "the benefit of the *jing* land system without irritating or disturbing the people by implementing that system".[24]

The land quota scheme proposed by Lin Xun required that farmers were classified according to the amount of land owned and was based on the assumption of insufficient land for the large population in Zhejiang and Fujian provinces at the time. It abandoned the distribution principle of traditional *jing* thought of "one hundred *mu* for one man" and was in fact an equalised land distribution system under which one man was allowed to occupy 50 *mu* of land. The scheme designed by Lin Xun was neither "nine men constituting one *jing*" as proposed in the Rites of Zhou, nor "eight households as one *jing*" as put forward by Mencius; rather, his *jing* land was only a unit of taxation. Lin Xun also abandoned land rent in the form of labour but suggested the combination of rent in kind and rent in money. As rent in kind had been the only form of rent payment since the dynasties of Qin and Han, Lin Xun's attempt to include the money form of land rent in the *jing* land scheme was unprecedented. Moreover, before Lin Xun, those who supported the recovery of *jing* land systems also supported a tax of one-tenth, but Lin Xun suggested a tax rate lower than 2 *sheng* rice per *mu* of land (the *sheng* being an ancient unit of mass equal to 4 kg) and less than five coins in money, amounting to a rate significantly below 10%. As Lin Xun's scheme was rather elaborate and included adjustments according to circumstances, it received much attention in Song and subsequent dynasties. The scheme may have purported to recover the "ancient *jing* land system", but it was actually a combination of ideas discussed in the Rites of Zhou, the Sima's Military Science and Mencius, together with elements of the land occupation system.

Emperor Ren and Emperor Hui of the Northern Song Dynasty both issued decrees on land quotas. At the time of Emperor Ren (r. 1022–1063 CE), the decree on land quota stipulated that

> those with ranks below Gong and Qing [the noble and high-ranking officials] should own no more than 30 *qing*, logistics officials [responsible for the supply and escort of government-related goods, usually undertaken in turn by rich families] who are obliged to return to the army should own no more than 15 *qing* in one *Zhou*.[25] Those who exceed the limit will be judged in violation of the decree, and those who report such violation will be awarded with land. . . . Officials intimate with the emperor are forbidden to buy big houses in the capital city, and those in charge of temples are forbidden to trade land.[26]

This decree was severe, but it was not easy to carry out in practice. When Emperor Shen (r. 1067–1085) succeeded to the throne at a time of serious crisis,[27] he entrusted Wang Anshi (王安石 1021–1086 CE), a politician and reformer in the Northern Song, with important responsibilities for political reform. He also enacted the square land tax system (方田均税法) for the purpose of thoroughly investigating land occupation and determining the amount of land tax. During the 14 years when the system was effective, over 2.4 million *qing* of land was surveyed, accounting for more than a half of all the arable land nationwide. However, due to repeated attacks from the opposition, it was abandoned in 1085 CE.[28]

At the time of Emperor Hui of Song (r. 1100–1126 CE), a decree on land quotas for officials of different ranks and temple estates was issued:

> Officials of different ranks should own land within the quota limit, which is 100 *qing* for first-rank officials and 10 *qing* for ninth-rank officials, decreasing successively with their ranks; the amount exceeding the quota limit will be taxed the same as land owned by regular households. Temples in and out of the capital city can buy land of no more than 50 *qing* in the capital and no more than 30 *qing* outside the capital, and tax, labour, and tax transit will not be exempted.[29]

This amounted to a mild policy of "land quota", the aim of which was not to limit the land occupied by officials of different ranks but to provide the legal quotas within which they could enjoy the privilege of tax and labour exemption; only the amount exceeding the limit would be taxed according to the regulation. The legal quotas for officials of different ranks to enjoy the privilege greatly exceeded the limit set up in the decree on "land quota" in Emperor Ren's time.

Zhao Tianlin (赵天麟) an expert on law, and Zheng Jiefu (郑介夫), a Confucian scholar, both of the Yuan Dynasty (1271–1368 CE), also suggested solving social problems with "land quota" systems. Zhao Tianlin thought the ideal objective was to recover the ancient *jing* system, but only as the end-point of a gradual transition. Thus, in his *Peace Golden-Mirror Strategies* (太平金镜策, publication date unknown) he proposed a detailed land quota scheme as follows. First, the quota limit for royal families was set at hundreds of *qing*, while for common families of officials and the people the limit was in the dozens. Second, if people voluntarily turned over their surplus land to the government, official ranks were to be conferred on the head of the family according to the amount of land they returned. Third, concerning the distribution of the returned land, land returned from landlords would be granted to the tenant farmers who had originally rented those areas of land. If the land returned was uncultivated, it would be allotted to dispossessed farmers who would receive a full exemption from the land tax in their first year of tenure and a 50% rebate in their second year. As for those landless farmers who did not want to occupy a plot of land, the injunction was to just let them be.[30] Fourth, trade in land within the quota limit should be allowed. Fifth, violations of the decree would be punished with heavy penalties. The above measures applied to privately held land. For public land, Zhao Tianlin had a different scheme. He proposed to allot public land according to the nine official ranks: first-rank officials could occupy 20 *qing*, second-rank officials 18 *qing*, third-rank officials 15 *qing*, fourth-rank officials 12 *qing*, decreasing to 2 *qing* for the ninth-rank officials. His aim was to reintroduce the *jing* system in a mild and progressive way over a period of 50 years.[31] But his main purpose was to solve financial problems. As remarked by Hu Jichuang:

> Before that, thoughts on land often started from solving the problem of land for farmers and involved various plans that met farmers' requirements of land but might not come into effect. Zhao Tianlin's plan put the focus on the solution of problems concerning feudal government revenue instead of giving enough attention to farmers' requirement of land.[32]

According to Zhao:

> The tax shall be totally remitted in the first year, reduced by half in the second year, and levied as usual in the third year. . . . thus it will not be too hard for people to gain permanent properties and officials to cultivate honesty.[33]

In fact, the upper limit of land quota suggested by Zhao Tianlin was too high and exceeded the actual amount of land owned by most landlords, thus nullifying the redistributive intent of the policy.

Zheng Jiefu suggested restraining major landowners through a land quota system. In *Peace Strategies: On the Situation of Jing Land*, his scheme was expounded as follows. The land quota limit was to be set at 10 *qing* for all, regardless of titles and the size of families, and five years would be given for landlords to dispose of surplus land (over the quota) by distributing it among relatives or selling it to others. Surplus land remaining after five years would be expropriated by the government and sold to poor farmers, with 50% of sales revenue taken by the government and the rest be paid to the landlord. Zheng also suggested limiting the land quota of temples according to their size: 10 *qing* for big temples, 5 *qing* for the medium-sized, and 2 *qing* for small temples, with all land above these quotas expropriated by the government.

Moving to the Ming Dynasty (1368–1644), Yuan Yongzhi (袁永之), a poet, and Liu Tongsheng (刘同升 1587–1645), a military leader and poet, were both advocates of land quotas. Yuan Yongzhi thought that the uneven distribution of land[34] had arisen because no limit was imposed on land annexation by major landowners, while Liu Tongsheng claimed that quotas were necessary for the government to fulfil its responsibility of "supporting the people".

In the Qing Dynasty, the scholars Huang Yizhou (黄以周 1828–1899) and Yun Gaowen (恽皋闻) both advocated land quotas, believing that the polarisation between rich and poor was caused by uneven land occupation.[35] In Yun's view,

> the best way to implement a land distribution system is to adopt a land quota system first. One household should own no more than 50 *mu* of land; those who violate the regulation and own more than 50 *mu* must have no other choice than to give the surplus part to others or sell it to the government.[36]

Of all the opinions of different ages, some were a direct inheritance and development of Dong Zhongshu's "land quota" thought, while some developed by way of criticism of his ideas, often on grounds of their alleged lack of realism. Thus, Li Gou (李觏 1009–1059), a philosopher, educator and reformer in Northern Song Dynasty, held that Dong's proposals may have been feasible in the reign of Han Emperor Wu, because at that time, "annexation by despotic landlords was not that prevalent and the problem of land occupation was not critical".[37] By the time of Emperor Ai, however, the strong would not tolerate dispossession, while the weak were reconciled to their position, and hence the implementation of land quota system "could do nothing but disturb the people".

Wang Fuzhi (王夫之 1619–1692 CE), a philosopher in the Ming Dynasty, was also opposed to land quotas. He saw wealth annexation and polarisation as an inevitable trend and opposed the use of force to check it. He believed that private ownership of land was the most reasonable and the most natural system and should not be constrained. Instead, he argued that reducing tax and labour duties and punishing corruption were better strategies, because in that way, "people would not be afraid to own land" while major landowners would "have no land to annex"; as a result, "annexation will naturally stop even without adopting a land quota policy".

Though there were different ideas about the specific criteria of land quota systems and treatment of land possession exceeding the limit, the purposes of the systems were quite similar in different dynasties: they were regarded as transitional measures to recover the *jing* land system, and they were means to restrict land annexation.

Scholarly perspective in the Republic of China (ROC)

China went through drastic changes in modern history, one of the most fundamental being the transition from natural economy to commodity economy, from an economy that counts on conventions or commands to distribute resources to a market economy that relies on market signals to allocate resources. Social changes in China's rural areas emerged with the historical progress of industrialisation, urbanisation and modernisation. But ideas about the construction of a rural land system still focused on the solution of problems arising from a big population with proportionately little land. The land system of modern China also confronted development issues of an agricultural country in pursuit of industrialisation, with expanding population and scarce resources. Land distribution in the rural areas was uneven: land ownership was centralised while the right to use it was decentralised. Also, the right to use of land tended to be commercialised, which caused increasingly severe conflict between the decentralised demand for the use of land and the centralisation of land ownership.

Land issues facing the rural area of China in the first half of the twentieth century

The severe economic crisis in rural areas during the 1920s prompted renewed interest in ideas about land systems of previous dynasties. Though people had different opinions on land issues facing China in the modern period, a prevalent point of view was the "theory of centralisation", based on the perception that the landlords controlled most of the arable land and collected high rents from the tenant peasants who farmed it for them. With farmers deprived of funds for reinvestment, rural areas for a long time remained trapped in an underdeveloped, semi-feudal situation. Such an analysis of the plight of agriculture constituted the theoretical foundation not only for the land revolution of the Communist Party of China, but also for the land reforms in the early period of the People's Republic (PRC). From the 1920s to the 1950s, although many scholars and government departments had estimated the distribution of land ownership differently, the shared judgment was that rural land was mostly owned by landlords and rich peasants and rarely owned by yeoman.[38] The most extreme estimation was that landlords and rich peasants, who took up 14.31% of the population, held 81% of the land in total, while middle-ranking and poor peasants and farm labourers, who took up 85.6% of the population, held only 19% of the land in total.[39] At the same time, merchants and moneylenders also purchased land. Therefore, in the face of a land distribution situation similar to that in the Han Dynasty, scholars attempted to seek solutions to contemporary problems from the study of ancient systems and thought.

Discussion of "land quota" systems in the R.O.C.

In 1937, the economist Li Honglve (李宏略) published "The History of Land Quota Theory" in issue 3–4 of *Rural Economy*, in which he discussed Dong Zhongshu's ideas about land quotas. Li argued that it was the development of commercial capital in the Western Zhou that had facilitated the collapse of the enfeoffment system and had made land a tradable commodity. Land quota policy was used as the bridge to recover the *jing* system and eliminate land annexation. In the early Han, some thinkers already associated land quotas with *the jing* system; later, people proposed similar ideas one after another and believed that although the *jing* system was an ideal solution, it was impossible to implement under existing conditions, leaving land quotas (including equality of land distribution) as the only feasible option. Li Honglve thought of land quota policy as the core of all ancient thought on land, which explained that land annexation was the cause of a series of land and social problems, and that the root of the problems was the private ownership of land.

By examining the significance and limitations of the land quota system in the Han Dynasty, Wan Guoding (万国鼎 1897–1963), an agricultural historian, proposed measures to counter the problem of uneven land occupation in modern China. He believed that although the land quota system could not eliminate land annexation immediately, it could change the situation gradually over time.

In "Land Quota System Is Not a Thorough Solution", published in *People and Land* (1941), Wan Dingguo quoted and discussed two clauses of the land law of the ROC government. Clause 14 provided that

> local government should take the following aspects into consideration to set limits on the maximum quota of land owned by individuals and groups, which, however, should be verified by the central governmental agency: one, local demand; two, types of land; three, land characteristics.

Clause 15 stated:

> If the limitation set up by the previous clause applies to someone's privately owned land, the land administration department should prescribe solutions by asking that the surplus land be separated and sold within a certain time. Those who do not separate and sell the land as provided by the previous clause will have their land confiscated by local government according to the law.

Wan pointed out that the

> land quota system is not a good solution to the problem of land annexation. At the time of Emperor Ai of Han [r. 7–1 BCE], the land quota [30 *qing*] was not a small amount. The land quota system only seeks to limit the excess; it does not provide for absolute equalisation.[40]

Wan's conclusion was that although the land quota system could not eliminate land annexation, it could at least impose a restriction on its progress.

In *A History of China's Land System*, Wan Guoding stated,

> the malady of annexation is because the rich occupy immense areas of land. Land is concentrated in the hands of the few, while the general public is cornered and the farmers cannot have their own land. If limitation is imposed to forbid despotic landlords occupying more land than is allowed by the regulation, then the emergence of large landlords can be prevented, and the poor and the weak can have more opportunities to own land. Although the objective is equalisation of land distribution . . . at least a move can be made in that direction, which is much better than the limitless expansion of land occupation by the few.[41]

According to his analysis, the underlying problems were "the relative deficiency of land because of the increase of population" and "the uneven distribution of land because of class differentiation".[42]

Wang Heng (王恒), a scholar in the ROC period, presented similar opinions in his *Land System of the Han Dynasty* (1945), holding that the land quota policy of the Han Dynasty had barely any influence upon land distribution:

> In the system of private ownership of land, the possession of land could be obtained by buying, so the phenomenon of excessive land possession would happen inevitably. To counter such a phenomenon, government would use the method of land quota. The land possession of merchants was also checked, but the effect was not that good. Land distribution was not significantly influenced.[43]

As the inevitable result of land privatisation and trade in land, land annexation can be restricted by land quota measures, but it cannot be eliminated in that way. When the maximum quota is too high, the land quota policy may do more harm than good, which was proved by outcomes in previous dynasties. Moreover, because of the difficulties in framing rigorous decrees, and the imperfect implementation of land quota policies, the result may be to increase the suffering of peasants, thus subverting the whole purpose of the exercise.

Another work published in the ROC period, *Collection of Notes on Land Tax* by Chen Dengyuan (陈登原), analysed the land quota policy in the Han Dynasty. According to Chen:

> [Dong] Zhongshu's idea of land quota is only a general suggestion. At the time of Emperor Ai, Shi Dan initiated the formulation of the specific policy and named it "land equalisation", which reveals that land distribution at that time was uneven; the policy included the prohibition of private land ownership by merchants, so we know the system was also intended to strike at the merchant group; the limitation on both land and slaves shows there were slaves attached to land at that time; the maximum quota of 30 *qing* and the

compliance limit of three years indicate that Shi Dan dared not to infringe on the rights and interests of landlords; from Dong Xian's reception of the grant of two thousand odd *qing* of land, we can tell that the largest landlord at that time was still the imperial family. To sum it up, there surely were contradictions among the imperial family, the despotic landlord and the merchant, but there were also shared interests. For such reason, Shi Dan's proposal was finally put to an end.[44]

Chen Dengyuan thought that neither the land quota system nor equal distribution of land ever impinged on the rights and interests of the landlord class, and because the biggest landlord of that time was the imperial family, the policies either could not be implemented or turned out to be toothless.

Scholars in the ROC analysed land quota ideas from the Han Dynasty in the hope of solving the problem of uneven land distribution in contemporary China.[45] Some scholars believed that land annexation was the crux of rural economic depression, and that although land quota policies had done something to ameliorate social conflict, they could not provide a comprehensive solution to land problems. Moreover, it was pointed out that land quota policies in ancient times were all premised on the need to protect the feudal land ownership system. Therefore, whatever the precise policy, they all served as a means for the ruling class to protect their own interests. Only through radical reform of the land system could the problem of land annexation be solved once and for all.

Why did the "land quota" system have such lasting influence?

Ever since "land quota" ideas were put forward in Han Dynasty, they were seen as the basic means to solve land problems, even in modern times. But that raises a conundrum, because "land quota" policies were by no means a success in practice. Why, then, should "land quota" thought have exerted such a lasting and profound historical influence?

The philosophical basis and appeal of "land quota" systems

Dong Zhongshu's view of human nature was the theoretical foundation for his thought on "land quotas". He extended the idealism of the Confucian school in the pre-Qin period and presented the theory of "interaction between heaven and mankind", according to which everyone is born with "nature and sensibility".[46] People's "sensibility" was Dong Zhongshu's term for human desire. He held that people should control their desires, or else have them controlled for them by government decree.[47] Land quota policy was a case in point, by placing a limit on the extent to which the rich could indulge their desire to increase their land holdings. Moreover, the policy could also help satisfy the basic daily needs of peasants. Then, with rich and poor both contented, the emperor could promote morality and turn the peoples' nature to goodness.

Dong Zhongshu had developed traditional thought on morality and applied it to a contemporary problem. Not only was his policy designed to improve the well-being of the poor (a core Confucian virtue), it could also be commended as being in the true interests of the rich: by curbing their desires, they could be enlightened to "show dignity but not extravagance" and embrace morality, to their benefit and the benefit of others.

The land quota system was the inheritance from and development of people-oriented thought. In traditional Chinese society, people-oriented thought meant to value agriculture and peasants, which resonated with the objectives of the land quota system to improve the standard of living of peasants and reduce the gap between rich and poor. People-oriented thought included the idea of "equal treatment", that is, the equal distribution of social wealth. Although the "equitable treatment" promoted by the "land quota" system did not amount to distributional *equality*, it at least represented a step towards the realisation of an ancient ideal.

The periodic cycle of traditional Chinese society

The feudal society of China presented a periodic cycle of the alternation between peace and upheaval, which led to the periodic cycle of land annexation. Judging from the evolution of various land systems, it can be seen that the government had always attached great importance to the distribution of land and had exerted state power to control land resources. When a dynasty began, much attention was paid to problems of unequal land distribution but, as major landlords and officials took advantage of their economic superiority or political influence to occupy more land, land once again was gathered in the hands of the few and annexation became intensified, leaving more and more farmers with no land at all. Disorder and wars ensued, followed by new attempts at land redistribution. As expressed by Qin Hui, "with 'no restriction on annexation', there would be vicious expansion of powerful and rich families, but with 'restriction on annexation', there would be vicious expansion of the 'extractive capacity' of the imperial court",[48] hence the repeated cycle of annexation–restriction on annexation–annexation–restriction on annexation, described by Arnold Toynbee as the "Chinese pattern".

In such periodic cycles, most rulers would face very similar situations to those that confronted the Han Dynasty, i.e. the expansion of privately owned land, severe land annexation and outbursts of social crises. So, when they looked back in history, the thought of "land quota" in the Han provided an important lesson to learn. Though this thought could not thoroughly solve the problem of land annexation, it could provide certain restrictions and a buffer to lessen social conflicts. Hence, echoes of Han thought on "land quota" were often heard in later generations.

The fundamental reason behind annexation was that land was seen as the most desirable form of wealth in an agricultural society, so that even rich merchants would rather consolidate their wealth by holding large quantities of land. Therefore, the combination of capital in trade with land constituted one of the important characteristics of Chinese feudal society. The traditional Chinese values of emphasising agriculture and restraining commerce also made people more willing to invest in land with the fortunes accumulated in commerce. Moreover, the returns of investment in land were more stable than commercial investments, further increasing the concentration of land ownership.

"Strong government" and the "land quota"

From the allowance of private ownership of land in the Warring States period to the rejection of curbs on annexation in the Song Dynasty, nationwide land systems had included land quota systems (限田), the King's land system (王田), land occupation systems (占田) and land equalisation systems (均田). Although these systems were implemented at different times against different historical backgrounds and their specific provisions were not the same, they were all designed and implemented by the national government. Reasons for the acceptance of the systems were not only that they were popular with peasants but also that they were authorised by the type of "strong government" that commanded respect and compliance in traditional Chinese society.

A condition for the implementation of a land quota system was therefore a strong and powerful government. Since the Qin and Han dynasties, private ownership of land had developed gradually and trade in land led to a diversified, multi-layered social structure. In the landowning class, there were not only landlords with titles but also a large number of new landlords coming from the merchant class, as well as Confucian scholar–landlords, among others. As for farmers, there emerged a large number of yeomen[49] as well as poor peasants and farm labourers. The annexation was inflicted not only by large landlords on small-scale landowning peasants: "The domination of powerful or noble families in annexation gradually changed to the domination of common families, and some medium and small landlords also gradually became the target of annexation just as the small-scale landowning peasants".[50] Furthermore, not only big landlords and the nobility but also temples were motivated to expand their land holdings.

Lyu Zuqian (吕祖谦 1137–1181), a philosopher, revealed the fundamental reason for the lack of a "land system" in the Song Dynasty: the development of private ownership and increasing scarcity of land directly under the control of the government had fatally weakened the land-distributing power of the feudal state. He observed:

> Today's scholars indulge in empty talk about land systems, but the government does not have land and the control of trade is in the hands of the people; today, people all know the benefits of the even distribution of land but cannot put it into practice.[51]

This perhaps was the fundamental reason for the frequent failures of the practice of land quota systems. The implementation of land quotas required a strong government in control of a large amount of land available for distribution. Strong government alone was not enough.

Conclusion

Dong Zhongshu's ideas about the "land quota", although concise in words, became the guideline for land ownership in China's feudal landlord economy, as well as the basic principle for the design of land systems in traditional Chinese society. The thought of "land quota" also influenced land systems in different periods, including the land occupation system of the Western Jin Dynasty, and ideas about the even distribution of land in the Sui and Tang *Dynasties*. It is one of the most important legacies in economic thought of the Han Dynasty, and the one with the most far-reaching influence.

Some scholars hold that the *jing* system, land quotas and the "equal distribution of land" policy were the three most important proposals to emerge on land systems. The *jing* was the most ideal and impractical system, whereas land quota systems and approximation to even distribution of land could serve the purpose of "stabilising the people".

As we have seen, however, there were differences in the criteria for "land quota", and in the measures taken in different historical periods, and different thinkers put forward different propositions about "land quota". In terms of its target, "land quota" before the Tang Dynasty was mainly for the purpose of preventing land annexation by big landowners, whereas the "land quota" which was "not limiting annexation" in the Song Dynasty and afterwards was not to address "unequal land ownership" or "unequal taxation" but to tackle the problem of the government's unequal assignment of unpaid labour. Land systems thus differed in their details and in their objectives.

Table 8.1 Research on the Han Dynasty's land system by modern scholars

Subject investigated	Author	Title of work
Research on the thought of land quota of Han Dynasty	Li Sanyuan	*Discussion on Land Quota System Since Ancient China*
	Wan Guoding	*Land Quota System Is Not a Thorough Solution*
	Wan Guoding	*The Road to the Rejuvenation of Villages – The Cause of Economic Depression in Rural Areas*
	Lyu Zhenyu	*Complete Works of Lyu Zhenyu*
	Wan Guoding	*A History of China's Land System*
	Chen Dengyuan	*Collection of Notes on Land Tax*
	Li Honglue	*The History of Land Quota Theory*
	Zhang Yinlin	*The Development of Han Empire*
	Hou Wailu	*Ancient China and Asiatic Mode of Production*
Research about land tax of Han Dynasty	Tao Xi	*On the Essence of Tax*
	Liu Shipei	*An Article about Sympathy on Peasants*
	Tang Caichang	*An Investigation on the Gain and Loss of Tang's Law on Zu (submission of grains to the government), Yong (labour service substitution with silk), and Diao (submission of silk to the government)*

	Li Da	*Reasons for the Sluggish Social Development in China*
	Nagano Rou	*Research on China's Land System*
	Xie Wuliang	*An Investigation of China's Ancient Land Systems*
	Wang Heng	*Land System of Han Dynasty*
Wang Mang's land reform	Hu Shi	*Wang Mang*
	Hu Shi	*Re-exploration of Wang Mang*
	Li Dazhao	*Land and Peasants*
	Xie Wuliang	*An Investigation of China's Ancient Land Systems*
	Chen Dengyuan	*Collection of Notes on Land Tax*
	Ma Yinchu	*China's Economic Reform*
	Chiang Kai-shek	*Chinese Economic Theory*
	Zhang Yinlin	*The Development of Han Empire*
	Wang Feilie	*Xin Mang Reform and Reasons of Its Failure*
	Jian Bozan	*On Wang Mang's Reform and Its Failure*
Jing land system	Feng Guifen	*Xiaobinlu Protest*
	Hu Shi	*Debate about Jing Land – A Letter to Mr. Liao Zhongkai*
	Liao Zhongkai	*Response to Hu Shi's Letter About jing Land*
	Hu Hanmin	*Debate About jing Land – Attached With Mr. Liao Zhongkai's Response*
	Cai Hesen	*A History of Social Evolution*
	Wan Guoding	*A History of China's Land System*
Army farming system	Tang Chenglie	*An Article About Army Farming*
	Wan Guoding	*A History of China's Land System*
	Lyu Simian	*An Essay on the Phenomenon of Migration in the Time of Qin and Han*

Notes

1 Hu Jichuang (1998), vol. 2, p. 43. Hu Jichuang (1903–1993) was an economist and one of the pioneering scholars in the area of the history of Chinese economic thought.
2 Scholars in China hold different opinions on the relation between the *Ming-Tian* land system and land annexation.
3 *Book of Han*, Records of Food and Commodities I.
4 *Book of Han*, Biography of Wang Mang.
5 *Han shu* (*Book of Han*), Records of Food and Commodities I.
6 Hu J. (1998), vol. 2, p. 40.
7 *Han shu* (*Book of Han*) Biography of the King of Huainan and Biography of the King of Hengshan.
8 *Han shu* (*Book of Han*), Records of Food and Commodities.
9 The *jing* land system (井田制) was allegedly an ancient system of farming and land distribution that involved dividing a piece of farmland into nine hundred-*mu*-square areas in the pattern of the Chinese character 井 (*jing*). The central square was cultivated collectively and the produce went to the state, whereas the other squares were cultivated by individual families who owned the entire produce of their labour. Whether or not such a land system ever existed remains an unsettled question.
10 *Han shu* (*Book of Han*), Records of Food and Commodities.
11 The Suan-Min Decree required that people report their properties to the government and pay taxes accordingly. Those who failed to report or reported falsely would be exiled to the border region for one year and expropriated of all their property. The Gao-Min Decree encouraged people to inform on the rich who failed to report or reported

falsely, the inducement being that the informant would get half of the expropriated wealth as reward. The implementation of Suan-Min and Gao-Min decrees greatly suppressed the merchants of that time.

12 *Han shu (Book of Han)*, volume 19, "Memorial of Officials of All Ranks", p. 742.
13 *Han shu (Book of Han)*, Record of Emperor Ai.
14 Ibid.
15 *Han shu (Book of Han)*, Records of Food and Commodities.
16 Zhao Jing (2002), p. 710.
17 Xun Yue and Yuan Hong, commented and proofread by Zhang Lie (2005), pp. 114–115.
18 Ibid., p. 115.
19 Ma Duanlin (Song Dynasty), commented and proofread by SHNU (Shanghai Normal University Ancient Books Research Institute and ECNU (East China Normal University Ancient Books Research Institute) (2011), p. 22.
20 Lu Zhi (Tang Dynasty), commented and proofread by Wang Su (2006), p. 768.
21 Ma Duanlin (Song Dynasty), commented and proofread by SHNU and ECNU (2011), p. 22.
22 Ibid., p. 24.
23 Ibid.
24 Ma Duanlin (Song Dynasty), commented and proofread by SHNU and ECNU (2011), p. 24.
25 An administrative area similar to city.
26 *History of Song*, Records of Food and Commodities I.
27 When Emperor Shen of Song came to the throne, the Northern Song encountered a series of crises. Huge military expenditure, a bloated bureaucracy and various administrative fees, along with large amounts of money given away annually to Liao and Western Xia dynasties, led to repeated annual budget deficits.
28 Beginning with Emperor Ren of the Northern Song Dynasty, there were constant outbreaks of peasant uprisings due to budget deficits and hardships in people's livelihood as a result of the country's defeat in the wars with the northern minorities. After Emperor Shen of Song came to throne, he entrusted Wang Anshi to carry out a comprehensive reform covering political, economic, military, social and cultural aspects. Various sections of the population suffered as a result of the reform measures. In particular, new measures harmed the fundamental interests of the large landlords and thus evoked strong opposition and, ultimately, failure to apply the measures.
29 *History of Song*, Records of Food and Commodities I.
30 "Advice of Famous Officials to the Emperors in Past Dynasties". Zhao Tianlin: *Peace Golden-Mirror Strategies*, volume 112.
31 Ibid.
32 Hu J. (1998), vol. 3, p. 43.
33 "Advice of Famous Officials to the Emperors in Past Dynasties", volume 112. Zhao Tianlin: *Peace Golden-Mirror Strategies*.
34 Chen Zhenhan (1955) argued that there was severe land concentration in the late Ming Dynasty: "manors of the royal families, their relatives and ministers reached more than 200,000 *qing* in area during the years of Jiajing (1522–1566). . . . taking up 1/200,000 of all the taxable fields at the time. The number of landlords who owned land from several thousand to tens of thousands of *mu* was large judging from the extremely incomplete records we can access now". The concentration of land continued until the early eighteenth century. The idea of "continuous concentration" of land proposed by Chen Zhenhan was dominant for a long period of time. After the 1980s, some scholars challenged this opinion. Recent research, using calculations based on the data in land register books from the Ming and Qing Dynasties, suggests that the Gini coefficient for the distribution of land ownership should be 0.613 for the Ming and Qing dynasties and 0.523 afterwards, reflecting a huge difference in the distribution of land ownership .

35 Regarding the degree of land concentration in Qing Dynasty, Chinese academics have different opinions. See Li Wenzhi and Jiang Taixin (2005).
36 Wang Yunwu. (1937). *A Preliminary Compilation of Book Series – The Book of Pacifying Volume 7 – Land System 5*. Beijing: The Commercial Press, 1937, pp. 61–62.
37 Wang Fuzhi: Commentary on *Reading History as a Mirror* – Volume 5, Emperor of Ai.
38 Li and Zou (2003).
39 The data comes from the investigation by the land committee under the Central Executive Committee of the Kuomintang in 1927.
40 Wan G. (1933).
41 Wan G. [1934] (2011), p. 98. Originally published by Zhengzhong Press, 1934.
42 Wan G. (1933).
43 Wang H. (1945), p. 15.
44 Chen Dengyuan, *Collection of Notes on Land Tax*. Beijing: China Financial & Economic Publishing House, 1987, p. 53.
45 In the 1920s, China's traditional countryside was faced with the challenge of social transformation. During the 1920s and 1930s, China set off a wave of empirical research on its rural society, with the distribution of land ownership being the main focus. Most surveys were undertaken by scholars, academic institutions and institutions of higher education, as well as government agencies and social organisations. Chen Hansheng et al. used a method of class analysis and reached the conclusion that the uppermost problem in rural China was unequal land distribution and that the solution was to redistribute land and properties. This idea developed into what Carl Riskin called the "School of Distribution". Opinions of the "Technical School", with Bu Kai as the best representative, set the basis for the Kuomintang government's formulation of agricultural policies, while the ideas of "School of Distribution" became the theoretical cornerstone for the social revolution of the Communist Party of China. Based on his surveys into Hunan and Jiangxi provinces, Mao Zedong held that the fundamental problem for rural China and the farmers was the issue of land, the core of the problem being irrational land ownership. Only by adopting the policy of "land to the tiller" and equalising land ownership could the farmers' land problems be addressed satisfactorily.
46 Su Y. (2010), p. 298.
47 Ban Gu, *Book of Han*, Volume 56, "Biography of Dong Zhongshu", pp. 2515–2516.
48 Qin Hui (1997).
49 That is, farmers who owned land and other means of production and were engaged in individual agricultural labour combining both farming and weaving in the economic unit of the household.
50 Hu J. (1998), vol. 2, p. 41.
51 Lv Zuqian (1990). *Detailed Comments on Systems of Each Dynasty* Volume 9 – *Land System*.

References

Ban Gu. (2010). *Han shu (Book of Han)*. Beijing: Zhonghua Book Company.
Hu, J. (1998). *A History of Chinese Economic Thought*. Shanghai: Shanghai University of Finance and Economics Press.
Li, J. and Zou, X. (2003). "New Exploration of Rural Economic History of Modern China in Last 20 Years". *Historical Research*, Issue 4.
Li, W. and Jiang, T. (2005). *On China's Landlord Economy: Development and Changes of the Feudal Land Relations*. Beijing: China Social Sciences Press.
Qin, H. (1997). "The Strange Circle in the Economic History of China: 'Restriction on Annexation' and 'No Restriction on Annexation'". *Strategy and Management*, Issue 4.

Su, Y. (2010). *The Luxuriant Dew of the Spring and Autumn Annals: An In-Depth Investigation of Names*. Beijing: Zhonghua Book Company.

Tian, C. and Jia, S. (2003). "An Empirical Study of the Influence of the Agricultural Land Market on the Allocation of Land-Use Rights". *Chinese Rural Economy*, Issue 10.

Tian, C., Zhang, L. and Zhang, X. (2013). "Distribution of Land Ownership in Chinese History: Estimations Based on the Land Register Books". *China Rural Studies*, Issue 2.

Wan, G. (1933). "Land Quota System Is Not a thorough Solution". *People and Land*, Volume 1, Issue 60.

Wang Heng. (1945). *The Land System of Han Dynasty*. Zhengzhong Publishing House.

Zhao, J. (2002). *A History of Chinese Economic Thought*, Volume 1. Beijing: Peking University Press.

Zhao, L. (2005). *A History of China's Land System*. Jinan: Shandong Qilu Press.

Other works cited

Lu Zhi. (2006). *A Collection of Lu Zhi's Works II Volume 22: Zhong-Shu's Memorial to the Throne VI*. (2006). Edited and proofread by Wang Su. Beijing: Zhonghua Book Company.

Lv Zuqian. (1990). *Detailed Comments on Systems of Each Dynasty, Volume 9: Land Systems*. Yangzhou: Jiangsu Guang Ling Ancient Books Printing House.

Ma Duanlin (Song Dynasty). (2011). Edited and Proofread by SHNU (Shanghai Normal University Ancient Books Research Institute) and ECNU (East China Normal University Ancient Books Research Institute).

Wang Yunwu. (1937). *A Preliminary Compilation of Book Series: The Book of Pacifying, Volume 7: Land System 5 I*. Beijing: The Commercial Press.

9 A Western perspective on the *Yantie lun*

Bertram Schefold

Introduction

The *Yantie lun* is a great testimony of Chinese intellectual life in the Han period (early first century BCE) because, recording a debate which actually took place in 81 BCE, it mirrors the antagonism between high-ranking Legalist officials of the empire and, in the main Confucian, Literati and scholars about primarily economic matters, in particular the state monopolies of salt and iron production.[1] In a broader historical and philosophical context, it reveals political dissent about whether the borders of the realm should be pushed outward to keep off "barbarian" tribes, or whether all governmental efforts should be concentrated on autarchic development in the homeland.[2] Both sides argue relentlessly by buttressing their positions with historical precedents, affirming or criticising the deeds and beliefs of earlier statesmen and philosophers – to this extent one is carried backwards in historical time through the first millennium BCE, when the Chinese identity took shape in the Warring States period, and further back to mythological origins (Mende 2002). The book also carries the reader forward in that the text has been an object of discussion for 2,000 years and has been reprinted and used to buttress contemporary positions for and against Confucianism, against and for Legalism, down to the late imperial, republican and communist periods. Vogel (2002) summarises interpretations of the *Yantie lun* in the People's Republic of China. Exponents of the Cultural Revolution saw the Legalists in the *Yantie lun* as progressive representatives of the centralised State and the Confucians as adherents of a reactionary clique of slaveholders, while a more differentiated picture emerged in the reformist period; discussions continue. A book on, at first sight, such special matters (imperfect competition and indirect taxation in the salt and iron markets two millennia ago) must in a deep sense be connected with persistent Chinese characteristics if it has remained a controversial classic in China throughout its history without having had much impact abroad. Hence, the challenge is to compare the Chinese development with that of the West by means of a comparison of the ideas and institutions that come up in the *Yantie lun* with their counterparts in Europe. To this end, this chapter will lead from an introduction to the historical context and a summary description of the economic content of the *Yantie lun* to a novel confrontation with the pseudo-Aristotelian *Oeconomica*, a work dating from the Hellenistic period in Ancient Greece and also concerned with problems of public finance, monopolies, money and the like. The *Oeconomica* reflected a European approach, taken up again, as will be shown, in cameralism, the period when public finance dominated the then existing economic discourse in the German states and beyond.

Our focus here will be on the understanding of economic matters. We do not know how accurately the author Huan Kuan reported the real debate, but the impression made on this reader is one of authenticity. One is deeply impressed by the seriousness and intensity with which both sides defend their policies and views; their speeches evoke the political drama which plays on the vast stage of much of East and Central Asia. There are the gardens and palaces of the Court, nobles, the rich (including some merchants); there are wild forests where fortunes are made in mining in a wilderness which invites to arrogate local power and to defy the central authority; there are vast plains and deserts of the nomadic tribes, the mountains of Tibet and, most importantly, innumerable fields of small farmers, sometimes congregated in villages of moderate affluence, but mostly poor and often hungry, subject to taxation, corvée labour and conscription.

How to keep this world together and to make it prosper? Both sides are convinced that there is a cosmological order into which human institutions ought to fit, and that power is at the centre and must rule to maintain security and the forms of decent conduct. How this is to be achieved is at the root of the debate, which therefore starts from common concerns. It also seems to be a matter of course that what we call economic institutions are a central factor for the safeguarding of the political order, in which there is a correspondence between the rule of the realm as a whole and the individual family. Individual well-being is not so much regarded as a primary and independent goal as it is the likely result of the realisation of this order. A recurrent theme is that a state cannot survive unless the people are "contented". According to such formulations, the survival of the state is the end and well-being the means. This switching of ends and means may seem paradoxical, but it is easily explained. The rulers want to maintain their position, and they therefore allow the people to reach a certain level of well-being, not out of generosity or because of humanitarian feelings, but in the interest of power. But shall government be oriented towards development and acquisition of riches, permitting luxury, by means of forceful intervention of the state through redistribution and strong legal constraints on individual action? Or is the ordered intercourse between well-educated people, who know their station and are happy to pursue the tasks associated with it, the main aim? Both positions have in common that they ascribe not only the will but also the ability to the ruling elite to shape the destiny of the people through the appropriate formation of the imperial state. We are therefore far from the modern recognition of the economy as an autonomous force. The positive role of markets is recognised by both sides, but this force is seen as an instrument of politics which can be and must be controlled, and its results must be corrected by legal means or by stabilising the rules of behaviour: while the Confucians insist on philanthropy and obedience within both the upper and the lower ranks of society, the Legalists want to use laws and controls.

The author of the *Yantie lun*, Huan Kuan, is known to us as an official from the province of Henan, who lived under the Emperors Zhaodi (87–74) and Xuandi (73–49) and who was last an assistant of the prefect Lujiang in what is today Anhui (Mende 2002, p. 52). The book is subdivided into 60 sections; it seems only later to have been subdivided into ten chapters. Not knowing Chinese, I have worked with three translations. There is the translation of Esson M. Gale of the first 28 sections into English, of 1931 and 1934 (Gale 1931, 1934). This translation emphasises philological rigour with an extensive apparatus. There is a French translation, edited by Georges Walter and translated from the Chinese by Delphine Baudry-Weulersse, Jean Lévi and Pierre Baudry, of 1978 (Walter 1991 [1978]). This is a very free translation, dramatic and readable, but not complete and with a rearrangement of some sections, such that it is on occasions difficult to find out to which section the translated text belongs. Finally, I have used a translation of selected sections made by my former student of economics Sabine Ludwig, who was, as a sinologist, also a student of Erling von Mende; this was edited (Ludwig 2002), with comments added by Erling von Mende, in a book *Huan Kuan: Yantie Lun*, together with essays by Erling von Mende (Mende 2002) and Hans Ulrich Vogel (Vogel 2002), and with an introduction by myself (Schefold 2002a), as a companion volume to a facsimile reprint of the *Yantie lun*, based on a print of 1501 in the series *Klassiker der Nationalökonomie* (Schefold 2002b). The translations differ considerably. For instance, the Confucians (who presumably were not all Confucians; Mende 2002) are designated in the text as "Worthies" and "Literati" (Gale 1931, 1), as "sages et lettrés" (Walter 1978, 44) and as "fähige und aufrechte Männer", and, as a group, as "Gelehrte" in the translation by Ludwig (2002, p. 109). Needless to say, I try to concentrate on conclusions that are invariant to the translation chosen.

We know little of the 60 scholars (or Literati). Mende (2002, p. 61) mentions two who could be identified as historical personalities. The scholars were invited by the government to discuss with officials, as had been done on other occasions in the Han period, in momentous debates which did not necessarily concern primarily political matters; preserved is one other dialogue of the year 79 CE on classical texts (Mende 2002, p. 60).

Only a small number of people speak on the government side. The emperor (who is only 13) remains silent. There is a chancellor, a secretary and other personalities, but the most important by far is Sang Hongyang, one of the most eminent economic politicians of the time and a personality who has remained controversial down to the present day (Vogel 2002, p. 101). His speeches betray that he commands respect. He may be seen as pompous but Huan Kuan's readers knew that this minister was executed a year later because of an alleged participation in a coup. He originated from a merchant family, which was untypical for the time (later, merchants were banned from becoming officials). His knowledge of practical affairs does not prevent him from also extensively making reference to classical writings and historical precedents in order to argue his position.

The debate centres around the following institutions: the monopoly of salt and iron, introduced in 117; the system of equitable distribution, instituted in 115; the system of price controls, instituted in 110; the monopoly of alcohol, instituted in 98; and the monopoly of minting, which had existed since 113 (Vogel 2002, p. 82). Sang Hongyang had been involved in particular in the establishment of the system of price equalisation. It is worth quoting extensively from the economic chapter of the history of the Han Dynasty (*Han shu*) in order to illustrate by way of an example how the state created institutions and how its main inventor reflected upon the mechanism of price equalisation. The declared aim was to stabilise prices. The government thus was able to appropriate profits which would otherwise have gone to traders. And the reform helped to move from deliveries in kind to payments in cash:

> Sang Hongyang, [at that time] . . . (a subordinate of the ministry of agriculture) became acting chief of the ministry [in 110 BCE] . . . in control of salt and iron throughout the empire. [Sang] Hongyang considered that government offices . . . wrangled in competition, and that merchandise for this reason [rose] by leaps and bounds, and that [furthermore], when imperial poll taxes . . . were transported, at times they did not compensate for the cost of cartage. Then he proposed [the following:] that there be established in the ministry of agriculture as assistants several tens of men. [Let] them be divided into sections to have charge in provinces and fiefs, where from time to time in each [according to the need] there would be set up . . . (offices for equalization of prices through transportation); and offices for salt and/or iron. [Let] orders be given that in places far distant [from the capital], each in lieu of poll taxes deliver [for sale by local authorities] in other places load after load of its native products which in the past have been carted out of the locality for sale by travelling traders and resident merchants. In the imperial capital [as central office] establish the . . . (office for standardization of prices) to receive [paid up taxes from sale of goods, or merchandise in lieu thereof], transported cartload after cartload from all over the empire. Call upon the office of labour [subordinate to the ministry of agriculture] to manufacture carts and the several [kinds of] equipment. [Let] all [the above agencies] look for sustenance to the ministry of agriculture. [Allow] the several offices of the ministry to corner completely the money and merchandise of the empire. When prices are high, then they will sell; when prices are low, then they will buy. In this manner will rich traders and great merchants lose that by which they gained excessive profits. Then will [the people] return to the fundamental (that is, agricultural pursuits); and [prices of] merchandise of all sorts will have no chance [to rise] by leaps and bounds. By these means [prices of] all the merchandise of every kind throughout the empire will be restrained. [Let] the name [of the system] be the . . . (standardization of prices) The Son of Heaven looked upon [the plan] as right, and gave his approval.[3]

Sang Hongyang explains in the debate that he had had the honour of serving the imperial family for more than 60 years (he had entered service at 13) and that he had risen through various positions and had now become minister. He declares to have received favours from the monarch, but that he also had to spend much for chariots and horses, for the support of the family, for servants, and that he, nevertheless, had been able to build up a fortune. The scholars, challenged by this self-representation, refer to the old times in which one did not accumulate offices and did not make private business with the income from the state. Sang Hongyang combines Confucian and Legalist arguments and is the prime representative of the idea of the strong extended empire based on the military defence of a fixed border.

I am used to distinguishing between a positivistic, a relativistic and a political approach to the history of economic thought (Schefold 2016a). The *Yantie lun* does not contain much that might count as analytical economics in the sense of the positivistic approach, and a mere contextualisation in the sense of a relativistic interpretation would miss the most important element, the political, for the entire discourse of this Chinese classic revolves around the contribution of the state to the organisation of social life. Western histories of economic thought mostly seek to reconstruct the history of the discovery of economic insights and, for the more recent period, of contributions to economic theory. Hu Jichuang, in his history of Chinese economic thought (Hu 1988), tries to construct a Chinese parallel to a Western history of economics, giving special emphasis to analytical insights, but not without explaining the specific philosophical background. He establishes parallels with Aristotelian economics with regard to the distinction between value in use and value in exchange and, in monetary theory, the parallel between the ideas of "light" and "heavy" coins and the explanation of price level changes via the quantity theory of money. Of special importance in Hu's book are the ideas of the *Guanzi* and of the Legalist school, for instance with regard to employment. We shall discover that these conceptions also show up in the *Yantie lun*, but they are difficult to identify without prior knowledge of the contributions of the earlier authors. More visible are the philosophical positions of the Legalists (Fu 1996) and the Confucians, whose economic ideas have been discussed much earlier (Chen 1911; Böhme 1926). The *Yantie lun* is also a source for historians. For the general history of the period under consideration, see Loewe (1974). Here, the *Yantie lun* plays an important role in explaining the contrasting tendencies in China to conquer or to appease the peoples invading from the north, and the text is used to understand the changing understanding of cosmic principles and the corresponding cults at the imperial court. However, Loewe also explains how the modernists and their "critics" dealt with the central issues of monopoly and came to a conclusion with regard to these economic questions in section 41, which is translated as follows:

> The critics do not understand the issues facing the central government and mistakenly believe that the State's control of salt and iron is not expedient. We ask for the abolition of the State's monopoly for the production of spirits

in the provinces and for the withdrawal of the agencies of State that were established for the production of iron within the metropolitan area.

(Loewe 1974, p. 92)

The approval of this compromise vindicated the representatives of the government, in that the monopoly of salt was kept as a source for public revenue, which has often been used in many other countries, and the compromise largely left the control of iron production to the state, with its strategic importance for war and its economic significance for peaceful industry; it would essentially come to an end only when the centralised power of the realm fell apart.

Economic matters in the *Yantie lun*

There are rich discussions on economic matters in Chinese historical sources, and there were a number of terms which could be translated as "economic" or "economics", but what people meant by these terms did not fully coincide with how we interpret them (Zhao 2014, p. 67). The choice we make of what we regard as "economic" in a text such as *Yantie lun* is a matter of discretion. The more we adopt the modernist conception of seeing the economy as an autonomous force, as the classical economists did in the late eighteenth and early nineteenth century, the less we shall find in the form of explicit treatments; there are no models, no theory of value, no growth paths etc. If we take the belief of the actors seriously, that the state and its officials shape the political order by coercion or moral conviction, all aspects of economic life are touched and we arrive at a more fruitful interpretation. To make a choice, we look to what we regard ourselves as economically relevant; we therefore begin with (1) conceptions of development and the structure of production. We then discuss (2) market forms, (3) employment, (4) money, (5) public finance and (6) general and international policy, and we ask, in each case, how the parties involved in the debate formulate their views.

Conceptions of development and the structure of production

Mende (2002) points out that the economic chapters in the histories of Chinese dynasties typically deal with the following sequence of subjects: demography, agriculture, land tenure, silk production, state granaries, forms of taxation, transport by the state, the monopoly of salt and other forms of taxation, controls of markets and prices and monetary matters. This build-up of the concrete forms of production, state organisation and monetary exchange is represented in a similar manner in cameralist treatises in the West and emerges there out of the monographs on agriculture inherited from Greek and Roman antiquity (Schefold 1998, 2009). The *Yantie lun* is not so systematic, but there is awareness on both sides that recent development meant an extension of the monetary economy and that the personal services and the barter of old times have been replaced by a transition from feudal arrangements (labour services) to payments in kind and in money. In the historical reminiscences, the transformation is associated in particular with the Legalist Shang

Yang (fourth century BCE; Fu 1996, 17–19). The Literati argue in the first chapter of the *Yantie lun* that the monopolies were introduced in the preceding decades (see above) and helped to increase profit-seeking on the part of both the government and the people. Honesty dwindled, agriculture decayed and commerce and artisan production of "luxuries" increased. As it turns out later, they ascribe these deplorable tendencies to a lack of virtue on the part of the Court and the officials, and more specifically to increased difficulties in agricultural production due to the monopolies, which will be explained later, and to an attraction of commerce due to the increased predilection for luxuries which also encourage "useless" professions. The ruling elite should return to the path of virtue, and the monopolies, as part of the causes of decay, should be abolished. It seems to me that the Literati favour forms of production in which professions are inherited from father to son and from mother to daughter, be it in agriculture or in handicraft.[4] Inheritance of professions is not stressed explicitly, but it is a known way of thinking in archaic societies that one believes that good production is best served if the knowhow is transmitted within the family, possibly supported by guild organisations. Only if these ties are loosened is the path opened to pre-capitalist forms of production, which are clearly not in view here. Departure from the old ways is interpreted as decay and not as a precondition for upward mobility. But, as time went on, the Chinese state examination system led towards a meritocracy. In fact, Sang Hongyang already favours the appointment of officials on the basis of examinations, while the Confucians prefer virtue as the criterion (Mende 2002, p. 66).

Market forms

Sang Hongyang, as the spokesman of the modernists in the early part of the dialogue, argues for the monopolies with fiscal reasons, which in turn are based on the problem of power: he believes that it is necessary to push out the borders of the empire in order to be secure from barbarian invasions and that this necessitates the colonisation of inhospitable border regions, so that large expenses for the military and the semi-military forms of colonisation become necessary. But this is justified because the military extension also facilitates imports from more distant regions, and colourful descriptions of the imported luxury items are spread in the text. He refers to the *Guanzi*: if there is fertile land and people go hungry, it must be due to a lack of agricultural equipment; and if the land is rich in resources, but not the people, there must be a lack of merchants and artisans. The Confucian response is to reverse these arguments: if there is fertile land and people do not have enough to eat, commerce and industry have been developed excessively; if there are resources, but people do not have enough capital, production is not oriented towards basic needs and luxuries have needlessly been augmented. Sang Hongyang accordingly sees the problem of development, following *Guanzi*, somewhat as we interpret the problem of a poor county in Africa: if the second sector and the third are encouraged, the first can be modernised. The critics simply see the inequality, which they feel is rising in the rich empire of the Han. Both agree that the farmers need iron tools – we shall come back to this problem. Sang Hongyang insists that agriculture was not the only occupation even in the old times (see section on Employment below). This secondary sector is necessary not only to supplement the first, but also to facilitate exchanges with the countries beyond the borders: to get horses from the nomads in the north for silk, for instance. The critics judge that the goods so imported are expensive because of the costs of transportation, and are not more useful than what can be obtained domestically.

According to Wagner (2001), the monopolies were instruments of power. Vogel (2002, p. 83) explains that Sang Hongyang was not only concerned about the fiscal power of the state but also the political control. Before the monopolies existed, there was a local concentration of the might of the "lords of the mountains and swamps", i.e. of the entrepreneurs in iron production who had to concentrate capital and people somewhere in the wilderness to mine and process the iron (which required charcoal), and there, far from the centres of the administration, they established a local dominance which threatened local legal governments. Sang Hongyang was not against commerce and industry, but they had to be integrated into the system. This involved measures of redistribution.

Conditions of production were far from uniform. Vogel (2002, 88) mentions that the workers were in part free wage labourers, in part subject to feudal ties, in part conscripted by the state. Some were slaves. Planning of production probably was neither sophisticated nor detailed. The critics therefore pointed out that the instruments created were of bad quality and not adapted to the needs of the farmers, in particular not adapted to the different qualities of the soil and of the agricultural employments. The peasants therefore refused to buy or could not afford them. Many, apparently, returned to wooden implements. As expressed visually in the *Yantie lun*, they weeded by hand. The critics thus argued that the monopoly should be abandoned and repeated that the local power concentration of the entrepreneurs would not result, if the rites were followed. There would be an upswing of production in the countryside (chapters 5 and 31). We may here follow Zhong (2014) and distinguish "harmony of diversity" and great "uniformity": the Confucians want a harmonious society in which one is born and educated to perform a certain function and to pursue a course of life in accordance with the mores and one's potential, whereas Sang Hongyang believes in a celestial order that required the state to strengthen the bonds, to allocate goods by a combination of market and planning and to integrate people by using their economic interest, together with direct command and fear of punishment. Some redistribution is necessary – granaries are needed to provide for emergencies and to maintain the poor – but there must be freedom and opportunities for the strong to get some measure of riches. There are therefore elements of liberalism in both conceptions, constrained in different ways.

Employment

We start our consideration of employment policies with quotations from *Guanzi* (1998), because of their striking originality and the impact they seem to have had on the *Yantie lun*.

Rulers always desire to have their people employed. To bring this about, they must have laws established and their orders carried out. Therefore, for ruling a country and utilizing the masses, nothing is better than law: for preventing licentiousness and stopping violence, nothing is better than having criminal sanctions.

(p. 159)

Have the rich build grandiose tombs to employ the poor, construct highly elaborate grave sites to employ engravers and sculptors, use large coffins to provide work for carpenters, and prepare numerous sets of funerary clothing and coverlets to provide work for seamstresses . . . Doing this provides a source of living from which . . . all people benefit.

(p. 319)

If one were to limit the Son of Heaven's burial clothes to three hundred items, it would be too little. However, it would be fine to set this as a standard for the various great officers. What about it? . . . It is not something that an expert . . . would find acceptable.

(p. 415)

When great officers build their grave mounds high and their tombs elegant, they rob both farm and market place of labor. This is not a way to benefit a country. People should not be allowed to use silk coverings to drape over coffins and bury them in the ground. Those who are good at ruling a state simply depend upon the situation to relax or intensify their demands. This is to make use of financial calculations.

(p. 415)

The first quote expresses the responsibility of the Legalist for employment. It clearly is something that the market will not bring about spontaneously, in the view of the writer. The law must prevent people from employing themselves by becoming robbers or engaging in other illegal activities.

The second quote seems to indicate that the large funerals known from excavations of the remains of ancient China were consciously seen in the perspective of keeping up employment by providing, as it were, not for the infrastructure of the living, but for the dead. It was one of Keynes's great intuitions to realise this with respect to another despotic state:

Ancient Egypt was doubly fortunate, and doubtless owed to this its favoured wealth, in that it possessed *two* activities, namely, pyramid-building as well as the search for the precious metals, the fruits of which, since they could not serve the needs of man by being consumed, did not stale with abundance. The Middle Ages built cathedrals and sang dirges. Two pyramids, two masses for the dead, are twice as good as one; but not so two railways from London to York.

(Keynes 1967 [1936], p. 31)

Keynes understood that investment must be useful and that it is not possible to propose investment projects for employment in a capitalist society if they are not efficient. The Legalist despot seems not to be bound by such a consideration. I remember how cynical Keynes's words seemed to me, when I first read them as a student almost half a century ago. Could religion be associated with such mundane goals? Later I learnt that Pericles seemed to express similar ideas when he proposed to have the Parthenon built on the Acropolis. Plutarch (Schefold 2016b) mentions that Pericles pointed out the favourable effects on employment. Yet he did not build the Parthenon with the primary aim of creating employment.

But this seems to be precisely the content of the first part of the third quote: the funerary rites shall not be determined so as to create a ceremony which is dignified, but rather to have the desirable effect of maintaining employment. The end of the third and fourth quotes reveal that the Legalist nevertheless sees a limit to such creation of employment: it should not draw away labour from occupations which are more directly useful. We might say that the Legalist anticipates the danger of crowding-out – a consideration that seems so important in present-day discussions about Keynesianism.

In a sense, this precautionary remark underlines the pragmatism of the approach. It reveals an extreme form of employment policy that is probably not open to democratic states. The dilemma of the state in employment creation is that something should be done for the sake of the unemployed which is not really very useful, for otherwise, it would already have been decided to do it for the sake of the direct utility of the project and not for the indirect benefit of creating employment. The essence of Keynesian employment policy is to push towards the creation of something nearly useless – Keynes himself plays with the idea of filling bottles with dollar notes and burying them, in order to give others the opportunity to dig them up again (Keynes 1967 [1936], p. 129). Keynes adds: "It would, indeed, be more sensible to build houses and the like; but . . . the above would be better than nothing". Employment policies on the borderline between the useful and the redundant have been discussed from times immemorial. The merit of Keynes did not consist in the invention of this idea. The General Theory is not new because of such policy proposals, but because it criticised the neoclassical idea that full employment is restored automatically, if wages are flexible.[5]

This digression into modern economics may help to underline both the importance and the problematic of the suggestions made in the *Guanzi*. Shall the state order specific forms of behaviour for creating employment? If the state orders everyone to be tattooed, much employment will be created in the corresponding shops. The advantage over state projects to create employment would consist in the fact that the private individuals would have to dissave and to pay for their tattooing directly. The state therefore would not only save the cost for financing such investment into human "beauty" by means of incurring a debt or raising taxes, but the state's finances would actually benefit from the taxes paid out of the increased activity – of course, at the expense of individual freedom. Our question now is whether this extreme form of Legalist pragmatism also exists in the *Yantie lun*.

In fact, these ideas are in the *Yantie lun*, though less visible. Sang Hongyang quotes from Confucius (the citation is not in the writings of Confucius which have come down to us according to Gale 1931, p. 22): "One should not be too thrifty so as to be hard on one's inferiors". He explains what he means: "Without the embroidered ceremonial robes the seamstresses will have no occupation". Here, the sumptuous dress of the officials is defended with the argument that it creates employment. The employment means an enhanced expenditure of the state if it pays for the robes, but imitation may lead to more expenditure by others.

Sang Hongyang also defends his system of redistribution by the argument that the granaries require an administration so that people get employment or are "safeguarded from unemployment" (Ludwig 2002, p. 116; Gale 1931, p. 10). When the critics say that people abandon agriculture and are without employment, Sang Hongyang responds that they do not work because they prefer to receive the support for the poor from the granaries. The critics reply that absenteeism increases not because people are lazy, but because the impositions on work in the fields are too large. To this we shall return.

Here, we must consider the rites from the point of view of the Confucians. According to Richard Wilhelm (1930, p. 48):

> These rites are uneconomical in the highest degree. They are a weight on the time and the means of the living for the benefit of the past. But they are very much alive sociologically . . . they represent a triumph of the sociological perspective over the economic.
>
> (my translation)

Wilhelm wants to say that the rites are there because a value is attached to them in the sociological sense: to pursue them is virtuous, and that is seen as the opposite of the utilitarian point of view. Is it an exaggeration to say that the Confucians and traditionalists want the rites to be preserved for the good and the beautiful, while the Legalists let that pass and are prepared even to increase the luxuriousness of the activity, because that is useful by keeping power in place and maintaining employment?

Money

The *Yantie lun* contains more on the philosophy of money than on the practice of coinage or the mechanism of monetary exchange. The Mohists had said: "Shoes made to buy are shoes no more" (Schefold 2002a, p. 26). This is similar to the Aristotelian idea that the art of acquisition consists in production for use, and that production for exchange and the seeking of wealth for its own sake (the seeking of profits) is a different activity, the one involving value in use, the other value in exchange (Schefold 2016b; Hu 1988, pp. 80–81). The Confucians seem to prefer the clarity of value in use (see section on Public Finance), while Sang Hongyang pushes for monetisation, hence value in exchange (see his statement on the scheme for price equalisation in the "Introduction" chapter).

Early Chinese monetary thought is famous for the distinction between light and heavy coins, the former not counting much and associated with an inflationary tendency, the latter being of strong value and hence deflationary. This distinction, associated with Shan Qi, was used more to recommend policy than to analyse processes. For instance, if prices fall after a good harvest, wheat is "light" and money "heavy". So more money should be issued in order to facilitate the selling of the grain (Schefold 2002a, p. 22). This form of monetary policy also serves to lessen fluctuations in the *Guanzi* (Schefold 2002a, p. 27). Trust in the spontaneous self-regulation of the market develops only much later. When banknotes begin to get issued around the year 1000 CE, metallism is formulated in response; the great experiment with a vast economy based on fiat money is undertaken later under Mongol rule and becomes known in the West through Marco Polo (Schefold 2002a, p. 39). The conversation in the *Yantie lun* remains tied to the principles. Sang Hongyang quotes from the *Book of Changes* that exchange should be facilitated so that the people will be unflagging in industry (Ludwig 2002, p. 113; Yijing, Xici, 14). He is aware of stages in monetary history. He mentions cowry shells as money and turns to knife-money as a form of coins. He insists that the coins be issued by the State. It is counterfeiting if private persons issue coins. While the Confucians display a preference for older forms of exchange (barter) and indicate that money primarily circulates in the second sector, Sang Hongyang observes that it is necessary everywhere, also in agriculture. This is for him an occasion to return to his ideas of redistribution, for there is the danger that money corrupts the rich and that, as a reaction, the poor will also engage in corrupt practices of their own; his system is meant to ensure that all get provisions (*Yantie lun*, chapter 4). To dispel "doubts and suspicions", Sang Hongyang wishes to keep the production of coins under imperial control. He recalls that coinage was free under the government of Emperor Wen (179–157 BCE), but this led to local concentrations of power, to rebellions and illegal activities. He feels that the present arrangement is a return to the fundamental activities, i.e. the people are concerned with production. This seems to be a reference on the part of Sang Hongyang to the Confucian idea that the common people in a well-governed state should be concerned with the fundamental pursuits, that is, with agriculture. But the critics are not appeased by this allusion to one of their main principles; they reply that there had been different kinds of money, that commodities were traded and that the people were happy in earlier times. A new coinage makes it difficult for the peasants to distinguish good coins and bad coins. Traders exchange bad coins for good ones and "get the double" (*Yantie lun*, chapter 4). Apparently, the government was not able to maintain a strict standard for the coins and the farmers had difficulty distinguishing them, not because there were too many sorts in circulation, but because the coins of each sort were not of uniform quality. Hence the critics preferred private coinage, but it is not clear why the problem should be lessened thereby. The preference for private coinage was possibly just a consequence of the prejudice against state economic activity rather than a reasoned argument.

Public finance

In a restricted technical sense, the *Yantie lun* is about public finance, and the debates are fought by quoting precedents. For instance, the modernists argue that Shang Yang had been very successful as the minister in Qin who had controlled the people, was able to extend taxation widely while keeping taxes low, established monopolies which functioned well and made important conquests without putting too much strain on the people. In this same chapter 7, the critics respond that there were no monopolies at the time of Emperor Wen and that the people felt rich all the same. Now, since the monopolies have been introduced, the people are exhausted. And the critics deplore the harshness of Shang Yang. They admit that Shang Yang was successful in pushing back the barbarians and in subduing the vassals, but his conduct weakened the state and led ultimately to the decay of Qin.

The officials, exasperated, challenge the Literati as incompetent. These, to defend themselves from the reproaches of being dogmatic, of commenting on every issue without having been invited to do so, of never being informed about the facts, stand up and declare that they had rushed to get to the assembly at the imperial command in order to make clear that the wars have weakened the people and that they, narrow-minded Confucians who have come from the countryside, are very worried (*Yantie lun*, chapter 6). "This is the grievance of the people and the concern of your 'bigoted Confucianists'" (Gale 1931, p. 39). They return the challenge of the officials with ostentatious modesty. They complain that the people formerly paid taxes for what they knew and that they now have to pay for what they do not know. By this they mean that, earlier, the taxes were paid in kind, whereas now the peasants have to make payments in cash, hence they have to go to the market. The critics probably fear that the simple-minded peasants will be cheated by the merchants. Formerly, the men paid in wheat and the women by delivering textiles. The Secretary, representing the officials, responds that the previous Emperor had lowered the tax from one-tenth to one-thirtieth (chapter 15). The critics admit this but point out that the tax now is in proportion to the area cultivated, and not a fraction of the harvest actually made, so that the tribute is too low in good years and too high in bad ones. And there are, moreover, taxes per capita and forced labour. They conclude (chapter 15) that the rich families do not pay their due because they are strong and the tax officials do not dare to demand the full tax, while poor people abandon their land because it does not pay to work on it, given the impositions. As a result, the burden is concentrated on the middle class, which gets impoverished.

General and international policy

We return to the general situation. One of the Secretaries, in chapter 14, asserts that the introduction of the salt and iron monopolies let production in general grow and helped to improve not only the second sector but also the first (chapter 14). Sang Hongyang, in chapter 16, assures: "A wise man will not undertake a purposeless expedition and a sage King will not covet a useless land" (Gale 1931, p. 101). He adds that the previous Emperor did not keep all the conquered lands, but returned some to the Xiongnu and restricted the lands retained to the strategically important. He also says:

> La dynastie des Han a dépensé, depuis son avènement, des sommes exorbitantes en cadeaux offerts aux Khans barbares, afin d'acheter leur tranquillité e de nouer avec eux des relations pacifiques. Mais, oubliant nos largesses, ils reprenaient bientôt leurs exactions avec une ardeur renouvelée.[6]
>
> (Walter 1991 [1978], p. 215)

The modernists here defend themselves against the possible objection of the critics that not everything was tried to keep the nomads away by peaceful means, i.e. by giving them presents. Taken together, the officials maintain the position that their policies led to general prosperity and that the wars were inevitable. The critics argue that one should concentrate on the core regions of the country:

> Is it not probably true that there are vast areas lying uncultivated, much sowing without harrowing and much labour without fruit? Well may the odes say: Do not try to cultivate fields too large; – the weeds will only grow luxuriantly.
>
> (Gale 1931, p. 101)

The quote could be read to mean that the farmer should seek the optimal land–labour ratio; if the amount of labour is given, the optimum area of land will be that where output per head is a maximum. Hence, if land is divisible, not the entire area should be cultivated if the amount of labour does not warrant it. This technical point, stressed by Sraffa in his famous article about *Returns to Scale* in 1925 (Sraffa 1925), must here be interpreted as an intuition which can also be applied to the empire as a whole: there are ample opportunities to cultivate lands in the centre, avoiding the conflict with the barbarians.

Both sides share the conviction that the state should provide for the people; the only question is how it should be done. We might here speak of provisionism as the policy of a paternal head of state, who sees to it that the necessary sources are available; if necessary, imports have to be organised. The Confucians believe that imports are scarcely necessary, the empire being autarchic with respect to "necessaries", while Sang Hongyang opts for the import of luxury items made possible through the extension of the borders and the consequent contact with other countries. Neither side is mercantilist in that it would rely on the autonomous forces of the market, which would bring about the growth of an export sector capable of securing an income adequate to buy the imports without specific measures of protection. The attitude of provisionism is characteristic also of other despotic states. It has been shown by Fatih Ermis that it was part of the ideology of the Ottomans down to the eighteenth century, at a time when their Western rivals had become mercantilist (Ermis 2013). Provisionism was not exclusively an attitude of benevolent despots, however. We shall see that it also prevailed at Athens.

Comparisons

We now come to the cross-cultural comparison announced at the beginning of this chapter. In his path-breaking book, Hu Jichuang (1988) liked to compare the positions taken by early Chinese authors on economic matters with those of the classical Greek philosophers, in particular Aristotle. Hu was interested in the similarities between individual economic concepts and propositions as elements of early forms of economic theory in the Chinese and in the ancient European tradition. Our approach to the *Yantie lun* is broader than that taken by Hu to the texts considered by him. The *Yantie lun* has remained a classic document of how Legalist and Confucian thought interacted to form the Chinese ways of governance of the state and economy in later centuries. Hence our comparison will also have to be broader, transcending economic theory, but our comparison is much narrower insofar as it based on only a few texts.

In what spirit are forms of government and of running the economy related in the Chinese and in the Greek case? We have seen that the *Yantie lun* has remained a focus for the discussion of this relationship in China since it was written. Is there a similar continuity in the West?

The impact of early Greek ideas on later economic and political thought in Europe can obviously not be documented fully here for reasons of space, but we shall provide a striking and little known example of such continuity by referring to a cameralist author. We here provide only the main references as far as the Greek economic ideas and institutions are concerned; more details are to be found in Schefold (2016b).

We first compare the *Yantie lun* with the conceptions of the Greek historians and orators. The grand theme of Herodotus is the contrast between the Greek City States and the oriental empire of Persia, with their respective strengths and weaknesses. How were the City States, Athens in particular, with their democratic structures based on the political intercourse of the households of the citizens, able to withstand a much larger country? The political power at Athens was rooted in the popular assembly; the economic power rested on domestic production, supplemented by the market and maritime trade. The latter was absent in the land-based democracy of the citizens of Sparta, who had a stratum of free noncitizens as artisans and a relatively large stratum of slaves as their support. The history of Thucydides portrays the conflict between these two polar forms of City States. Both were provisionist, Sparta emphasising its autarchy. The Athenian economy was more open, but they lacked wheat, their land, Attica, being best suited for olive production. Hence, the Athenians in the classical period had a law that required each ship to help import grain on its return, and they maintained a close relationship with the Crimea, where Athenian colonies produced much of the grain consumed in the City. Public finance in Athens therefore could not rely on the revenues from large agricultural estates in the homeland. There were harbour taxes and other contributions, which the popular assembly imposed, but most characteristic was the system of liturgies, according to which citizens promised to maintain a certain service such as the payment for a warship for a year or the equipment for a choir in the theatre. It was therefore a gift-giving to the state which helped to sustain essential activities. The liturgies were not associated with formal coercion, but they were a matter of honour, which, in turn, could confer advantages. One used to distinguish between visible and invisible riches. Visible riches consisted of the houses, the fields and the olive trees which a household might have, while the invisible riches were credits outstanding and other monetary items which could not be seen and which therefore made it difficult to assess the wealth of the head of the house. The liturgies had to be based on what the household could afford to give, and hence comparisons had to be made on the basis of visible riches; each boasted to have given much in relation to the visible wealth owned, while one was tempted to conceal invisible riches. Provisionism therefore seems to be a characteristic of an earlier stage of development than mercantilism and not dependent on the political form of the state: a kind of provisionism is found both in classical Greece and in the world of the *Yantie lun*, especially among the Confucians, whose provisionism borders on autarkism. Nevertheless, though they had provisionism in common, the picture that emerges from the works of the historians and the orators indicates the specificity of the institutions of public finance and their connection with the political institutions and the economic conditions. The liturgies provided public goods without creating a large bureaucracy, and they strengthened the power of individual citizens. The Legalists in the *Yantie lun* cherish the ideal of a strong administration and the submissiveness of all except the emperor. Legalist language and some of the practices mentioned smack of despotism, which democratic Greeks loathed when they saw it operating in tyrannical City States, or in distant empires. However, the *Yantie lun* illustrates that the imperial rule was supposed to conform to monarchic ideals: observance of an order corresponding to the will of heaven, embedded in tradition, secured by old laws and developed, as the very dialogue of the *Yantie lun* shows, in consultation with the representatives of the people. Direct democratic rule by means of popular assemblies as in democratic City States was out of the question in a large empire.

Next, we compare the *Yantie lun* with a text in which systems of public finance are analysed directly, rather than with the philosophical texts on householding by Aristotle and Xenophon. A famous such text on public finance is the pseudo-Aristotelian *Oeconomica* II.[7] *Oeconomica* II, probably written around 300 BCE by Aristotelian scholars but not by the master himself, is on political economy, the term here meaning the householding of a City State. It discusses proposals to finance City States in emergencies and qualifies some of them as just and to be recommended and others as unjust and tyrannical, and to be rejected. This text was of special interest at the time of mercantilism and cameralism, when new forms of taxation were tried, when princes ceased to rely on the revenues of their domains and had to find new ways to finance increasing territorial states and soldiers. The problems treated therefore resemble those posed in the *Yantie lun*, but the solutions had to be different according to the different political systems. The Greek City States were provisionist and could be – but were not always – democratic. The cameralists mostly lived in monarchic states (kingdoms and principalities);

they tended towards mercantilism with regard to foreign trade and provisionism had been overcome.

Oeconomica II was, like the *Yantie lun*, reprinted and studied in early modern times. There were various sixteenth-century editions of the *Oeconomica* II, several in Latin, and a reprint of one of those Latin editions is found within the work of Kaspar Klock, *De Aerario*, of 1651 (Klock 2009). The book by Klock, a vast treatise published in 1651 but largely written during the Thirty Years War, deals with the finances of states and, in particular, principalities, from bottom up, discussing first agricultural and industrial production, coinage and monetary circulation, then a great variety of forms of taxation and finally maxims for the ruler on how to spend, all this in the early cameralist tradition. Klock's book follows the ample literature of his time on foreign countries and introduced his treatise with a book dedicated to the description of all the major countries of the world – European empires and nations, the Orient, the Americas, even sub-Saharan African kingdoms – with their systems of taxation, seen in relation to the specific "Reason of State" in each, the characteristics of the population, the economic arrangements, the social mores, explaining much through climate and geography, in order to demonstrate that the various aspects of the economic life of a country must fit together and that the systems of public finance have to be adapted to these characteristics. Klock's work is of double interest to us, for it deals with China, mainly on the basis of the reports of the Jesuits, and because it represents a unique seventeenth-century reflection on the historicity of public finance by comparing the modern views and those of antiquity on the basis of Klock's interpretation of *Oeconomica* II.

First a word about Klock's assessment of China. He treats the country as a closed world, intent to keep inner peace. Only the Great Wall reminds the reader of the times when the outer confines of China still had to be determined. Klock, who may have written this during one of the worst wars of history, praises Chinese peace, justice, benevolent government and the happiness of the state – no other country in the world and in history is more "political":

> ideo floret hîc Justitia, quietis mater, guberationis omnis bonitas, & Reipublicae felicitas . . . Non aliud regnum, nec Dominium antiquum, nec novum illo magis politicum est.
>
> (Klock 2009, XIX, 3)

Without going into details regarding population and the level of incomes, we note a key point made by Klock. Almost all taxes flow to the emperor in a realm in which there are no vassals and lords. Hence, it is essential that the emperor also spend as much so as to enable the people to pay taxes again in the following year. Klock explains this by means of the principle of communicating vessels, which is his illustration of equilibrium. Each other country study had given rise to the explanation of a bit of economic theory, not in abstract form, but by means of a visualisation. The Dutch, for instance, prosper because of share-holding trading companies, while the Grand Duke of Moskovy tries to keep the best trade for himself. China is used to illustrate a circular flow. And that this is what Klock means becomes clear when he goes a step further and asks what would happen if the emperor started to spend on foreign goods. He believes that this would mean a double imposition on the people, for they would have to spend the moneys for the taxes, but they would not have the hope of getting them back again by selling to the state. Literally and in the original:

> In Regno, dico; si enim extra Regnum expenderet, angariae (the impositions) dupliciter consumerent populum: Nam ex ejus manibus elaberentur pecuniae, facultatesque, neque spes superesset emolumenti, aut fructus alicujus.
>
> (Klock 2009, XIX, 18)

Klock does not speculate that an expenditure of the emperor abroad might lead to exports from China to other countries. The cameralist always fears the outflows due to imports and the successive export is not certain – his mercantilism lacks self-confidence. Although Klock portrays China at a period much later than that covered by the *Yantie lun*, his images of the working of the imperial system fits the realities described in the dialogue fairly well.

Oeconomica II (Kyrkos and Baloglou 2013) distinguishes householding according to four types of households: that of the Great King (meaning that of Persia), that of provincial governors, that of cities and finally that of private households. We may disregard the provinces. The householding of the cities is called οἰκονομία πολιτική (Aristotle 1346a6) – the term "political economy" appears here for the first time in history. The text affirms that the government of the King is the simplest, while that of the household is "difficult to reduce . . . to rules owing to the necessary variety of its aims" (Aristotle 1979 [1935], p. 349). Schefold (2016c) tries to explain this by pointing out that the monarch is one person in which all power is concentrated, while the household of the individual citizen must react to a variety of demands made on it according to the roles played by the head of the household. He must act according to the requirements of the City – for instance, paying liturgies; he may have duties in the military and be required to spend time with the army in a distant place; and he is a head of the family who ought to remain at home, to administer the estate and to keep the family fortune together. Greek philosophy revolves around the principles needed to make choices in contradictory situations. The modern solution, based on the separation of household and firm, consists in observing different ethical rules, depending whether one acts at home in the interest of the family, where one has to care also for weak family members, or in an enterprise where people have to be dismissed if they are inefficient. Max Weber thought that only this separation made *modern* capitalism possible (for other interpretations see Zoepffel 2006). *Yantie lun*, by contrast, emphasises the simple duties of the individual household and the complexity of the task of governing. What *Oeconomica* says about the "simplicity" of the household of the Great King of Persia is, one might say, the deliberate simplification of an outsider who only notices that tribute is being collected.

Oeconomica II mentions monopolies. The City of Byzantium, for lack of funds, created a banking monopoly. This is heavily criticised by Klock. To him, monopolies are granted by princes; they lead to prices being too high and are permissible only in special and extreme circumstances. Klock does not realise that if a popular assembly of citizens decides to create such a monopoly, it is a form of a self-imposed taxation, and that is why the people of Byzantium temporarily were ready to live with this expedient. The analogy with the *Yantie lun* consists in the fact that the monopolies discussed there have recognised costs for the public, in terms of extra profits made, for these serve as a mean of taxation. Moreover, the debate held according to the *Yantie lun* may be seen as a substitute for a consultation of the people which, in an empire, must be represented by individuals elected or chosen from above. Klock, although he is a Protestant, wants to be loyal to the catholic emperor and shows, despite his humanist admiration of the Ancients, little understanding for Athenian democracy.

There are several examples of monetary policies, which Klock seems to deplore and which are recounted in the original *Oeconomica* II as problematic. However, there are also more positive examples. The people of Clazomenae were, as a city, externally indebted and temporarily unable to pay back. They only could pay interest on their foreign debt. They decided to replace their currency of silver with one of iron, so that the purchasing power of the coins would not correspond to their intrinsic metal value anymore. These iron coins were distributed to the wealthy citizens who were invited to give silver for them, and the city promised to take back the iron coins and exchange them for silver again in the future, paying interest at the same time on the silver loan thus obtained from the wealthy. The silver so collected was used to pay back the foreign debt of the city. It was therefore an operation undertaken to finance the state by the issue of an undervalued currency, coupled with the promise to return to a currency of full value without loss to the public. The operation is reminiscent of the suspension of cash payments in Great Britain during the Napoleonic War, which was declared to be temporary and led to a return to the gold standard. In the British case, the trust that this would happen prevented a strongly inflationary outcome such as resulted in France, when the revolutionaries issued the Assignats.

The episode is remarkable because it demonstrates that already in Hellenistic times it was possible to conceive of the circulation of a fiat currency, nearly 2000 years before inconvertible paper notes began circulating in the West. Klock approves of the procedure and regards it as so interesting that he tries to add "modern" examples, one of them concerning the reign of Ferdinand and Isabella of Spain about 170 years earlier. If the principles of a fiat currency could be understood that early, why were they not used to replace the costly circulation in terms of silver by means of paper or leather or something similar? We saw above (section on Money) that notes in China began to appear around 1000 AD and were used systematically under the Mongol emperors.

The answer is clear: the weakness of the states and the rivalries among them in the West led to distrust in any kind of money that did not circulate at full value. Only exceptionally could such an experiment be tried. But European countries often resorted to the depreciation of coins, which represents an intermediate case. The larger and stronger the empire, the more it became a temptation to have coins of lower denomination circulating below full value. There then resulted the curious contrast between the inflation in terms of copper money, accompanied by deflationary tendencies in terms of silver and gold – opposing tendencies that could be observed in antiquity in the Roman Empire. The *Yantie lun* does not address this problematic directly. The wish to centralise monetary production by the Legalists may perhaps be explained in terms of the will on the part of the governing to manipulate the value of coins to some extent so as to achieve ends of monetary policy, which Sang Hongyang defends in terms of his schemes of redistribution. The Confucians seem to trust more if coins are privately issued on a decentralised basis. If the coins are under weight, they can be refused. Such coins would not be money according to Knapp's theory.

The comparisons could be continued. One might examine how economic principles are tied to philosophical views and religious convictions. But this and other speculations are now left for future research. It is clear that the major differences are related to the completely different structures of the countries and their economies: on the one hand, the vast empire, with the power concentrated in the imperial court, on the other the rivalry of a multiplicity of states, some with tyrants as governors, others democratic according to different constitutions. Visions of organising the economy and of thinking about it were formed in both cases, which would have an impact for a long time to come – possibly down to the present. Klock, as a humanist admiring antiquity and as a German a subject of the Holy Roman Empire, was a monarchist and stood in between. As we saw in the beginning, the *Yantie lun* is still a focus of debates on how to govern China and Aristotle's *Ethics* and *Politics* continue to inspire Western political and economic thought.

Notes

1 Other important economic themes are the equable marketing and balanced standard systems.
2 Legalism and Confucianism are here meant in the sense of broad philosophical traditions that helped to inspire and legitimise, and lend coherence to, political strategies. One should expect – and one in fact finds in the *Yantie lun* – that government officials tended to be Legalist and the Literati to be Confucians, but either side could, when it suited them, use the arguments of the other. Loewe shows in his book (Loewe 1974) how Confucianism eventually came to dominate as the ideology of a state which on occasions did not shy away from using Legalist measures. Historically speaking, this was the lasting outcome of the Han Empire.
3 Swann 1950, pp. 314–316; the original for this passage is in *Shiji* 30.
4 Mende draws attention to a passage in the *Yantie lun* which describes the lower ranks of society in the early phase of the Han Dynasty (Ludwig 2002, 177–178, and Mende, ibid., 178, footnote).
5 The flexibility of wage rates is important, because the lowering of the wage will lead to changes of methods of production in many industries, in such a way that more labour-intensive methods will come into use. Keynes showed that lowering the wage in this manner, if it were possible, would have countervailing macroeconomic effects: lowering money wages would also mean lowering money prices, and, with a lower price level, the deflation would reduce the inducement to invest and make a crisis worse. The critique of capital theory in recent decades has shown that lowering the real wage may not

even necessarily lead to the introduction of more labour-intensive methods of production because of capital reversing. I have been able to show that if the technology has certain random properties, reverse capital deepening will be excluded and lowering the wage does lead to the introduction of more labour-intensive techniques, but their number will be much smaller than expected. It is therefore questionable whether the neoclassical hope of restoring unemployment in this manner by means of efficient techniques will be feasible within reasonable ranges of a flexible real wage rate. Of course, one could always return to old techniques that employ more labour, like by replacing the plough by the spade, but such extreme measures would be inefficient even at very low wage rates (Schefold 2013a, 2013b).

6 My translation: "The dynasty of the Han has, since his inception, spent extraordinary sums in the form of gifts to the barbaric Khans in order to buy their acquiescence and in order to establish peaceful relations. But, forgetting our generosity, they soon took up again their claims with renewed verve".

7 This text is discussed in more detail in Schefold (2016c).

References

Aristotle. [1935] (1979). *Oeconomica*. In Aristotle in 23 volumes, vol. 18, with an English translation by G. Cyril Armstrong. Cambridge, MA: Harvard University Press.

Böhme, K. (1926). *Wirtschaftsanschauungen chinesischer Klassiker*. Hamburg: Ackermann und Wulff.

Chen, H. (1911). *The Economic Principles of Confucius and His School*. New York: Columbia University.

Ermis, F. (2013). *A History of Ottoman Economic Thought: Development before the Nineteenth Century*. Oxford and New York: Routledge.

Fu, Z. (1996). *Chinese Legalists: The Earliest Totalitarians and Their Art of Ruling*. Armonk and London: Sharpe.

Gale, E.M. (1931–34). *Discourses on Salt and Iron: A Debate on State Control of Commerce and Industry in Ancient China*. Chapters I–XIX. Leyden: Brill (1931). Chapters XX–XXVIII in *Journal of the North China Branch of the Royal Asiatic Society*, vol. 65. Shanghai: Kelly & Walsh (1934).

Guanzi Political, Economic and Philosophical Essays from Early China. (1998). A Study in Translation by W. Allyn Rickett, Vol. 2. Princeton: Princeton University Press.

Hu, J. (1988). *A Concise History of Chinese Economic Thought*. Beijing: Foreign Languages Press.

Keynes, J.M. [1936] (1967). *The General Theory of Employment, Interest and Money*. London: Macmillan.

Klock, K. (2009). *Tractatus juridico-politico-polemico-historicus De Aerario . . . Mit einer Einleitung hg. v. von Bertram Schefold* [pp. V*–CXIII* vorn im ersten Teilband]. Hildesheim: Olms. Reprint der Originalausgabe von 1651 in 2 Teilbänden. *Historia Scientiarum* (Wirtschaftswissenschaften). Ein Editionsprogramm der Fritz Thyssen Stiftung zur Geschichte der Wissenschaften in Deutschland.

Kyrkos, B.A. and Baloglou, C.P. (2013). *Oeconomica: Introduction, Translation and Commentaries*. Athens: Herodotos.

Loewe, M. (1974). *Crisis and Conflict in Han China 104 BC to AD 9*. London: Allen & Unwin.

Ludwig, S. (2002). "Huan Kuan: Yantie lun. Die Debatte über Salz und Eisen. Übersetzung von Sabine Ludwig, durchgesehen und annotiert von Erling von Mende". In Schefold (2002b).

Mende, E. von (2002). "Einleitung zum 'Yantie lun'". In Schefold (2002b).

Schefold, B. (1998). "Xenophons *Oikonomikos*: Der Anfang welcher Wirtschaftslehre?". In *Vademecum zu einem Klassiker der Haushaltsökonomie*. Kommentarband zum Faksimile-Nachdruck der 1734 erschienenen Ausgabe von Xenophon: *Oikonomikos*. Düsseldorf: Verlag Wirtschaft und Finanzen.

Schefold, B. (2002a). "Dauer im Wechsel. Das Selbstverständnis der chinesischen Wirtschaftswelt". In Schefold (2002b).

Schefold, B. (ed.). (2002b). *Vademecum zu dem Klassiker der chinesischen Wirtschaftsdebatten*. Kommentarband zum Faksimile des 1501 erschienenen Drucks (Hongzhi 14) von Huan Kuan: *Yantie lun*. Düsseldorf: Verlag Wirtschaft und Finanzen.

Schefold, B. (2009). "Einleitung". In Klock, K. (ed.), *Tractatus juridico-politico-polemico-historicus De Aerario . . . Mit einer Einleitung hrsg. v. Bertram Schefold* [pp. V*–CXIII* vorn im ersten Teilband]. Hildesheim: Olms.

Schefold, B. (2013a). "Approximate Surrogate Production Functions". *Cambridge Journal of Economics* 37 (5).

Schefold, B. (2013b). "Only a Few Techniques Matter! On the Number of Curves on the Wage Frontier". In S. Levrero, A. Palumbo and A. Stirati (eds.), *Sraffa and the Reconstruction of Economic Theory, Volume One: Theories of Value and Distribution*. London: Macmillan.

Schefold, B. (2016a). "History of Economic Thought and Economic History: Who Will Bring the Past to Life?". In Poettinger, M. and Tusset, G. (eds.), *Economic Thought and History: An Unresolved Relationship*. London: Routledge.

Schefold, B. (2016b). "Antiquity". In Faccarello, G. and Kurz, H. (eds.), *Handbook on the History of Economic Analysis*, volume 2. Cheltenham: Elgar.

Schefold, B. (2016c). "Political Economy in the Pseudo-Aristotelian Oeconomica II and the German Cameralist Klock". *History of Economic Thought and Policy* 2.

Sraffa, P. (1925). "Sulle relazioni fra costo e quantità prodotta". *Annali di economia* 2.

Swann, N.L. (1950). *Food and Money in Ancient China: The Earliest Economic History of China to A.D. 25*. Princeton, NJ: Princeton University Press.

Vogel, H.U. (2002). "'Das Yantie lun': Ereignisse und Rezeption". In Schefold (2002a).

Wagner, D.B. (2001). *The State and Iron Industry in Han China*. NIAS Reports, no.44, Chapter 3.

Walter, G. (ed.). [1978] (1991). *Dispute sur le sel et le fer. Yantie lun*. Paris: Seghers.

Wilhelm, R. (1930). *Chinesische Wirtschaftspsychologie*. Leipzig: Deutsche Wissenschaftliche Buchhandlung.

Zhao, J. (2014). "Fuguo Xue and the 'Economics' of Ancient China". In Cheng, L. Peach, T. and Wang, F. (eds.), *The History of Chinese Economic Thought*. London: Routledge.

Zhong, X. (2014). "Harmony of Diversity and Great Uniformity: Two Trains of Thought in the Economics of Ancient China". In Cheng, Peach and Wang (eds.), *The History of Chinese Economic Thought*. London: Routledge.

Zoepffel, R. (2006). *Oikonomika: Schriften zu Hauswirtschaft und Finanzwesen*. Aristoteles: *Werke* in deutscher Übersetzung, Band 10.2. Darmstadt: Wissenschaftliche Buchgesellschaft.

10 Sima Qian and *laissez-faire*

Satire on a "discordant and degenerate age"

Terry Peach[1]

Introduction

My purpose in this chapter is to challenge the view of Sima Qian as an advocate of a *laissez-faire* economic system in which individuals as consumers, producers and distributors (traders and merchants) are given unrestricted scope to relieve their desires through the pursuit of material wealth and profit, with resources allocated in response to price signals rather than state directives.[2] The point is not whether there are passages in Sima Qian's *Shiji* (*Records of the Grand Historian*)[3] that can be extracted in support of such a *laissez-faire* (or "free economy") reading, because such passages undoubtedly exist; rather, it is whether those passages can be taken at face value: a question I shall answer in the negative.

It has been perceptively remarked that readers of *Shiji* have, over the centuries, "often dislodged the overall structure and meaning of the [work] by focusing on a relatively small number of chapters".[4] As I shall argue, that stricture applies with particular force to a *laissez-faire* reading which is at its least implausible when attention is confined to one chapter alone (*Shiji* 129, "The Biography of the Money-Makers"). Even within that chapter, there are intimations, or clues, that the "literal" *laissez-faire* interpretation is not without its problems, but it is when one considers the material elsewhere in the *Shiji* that those problems become glaringly apparent.

Taken in the context of the work as a whole, *Shiji* 129 is unmasked as a bitingly satirical and sarcastic portrait of a "discordant and degenerate age" – Sima Qian's *own* age – in which people *did* seek the satisfaction of their own material desires, without thought or care for their impoverished brethren or, indeed, for anything except their own selfish material interests. Seen in this light, the behaviour and the personalities that are speciously worthy in *Shiji* 129 are one facet of an age that Sima Qian depicts elsewhere, albeit with subtle touches, as sliding further into "decay" under the impetus of his contemporary and nemesis, Emperor Han Wudi (r. 141–87 BCE).

Having succeeded to his father's post of *Taishi* ("Grand Historian") in 100 BCE, at or around the age of 45,[5] only one year was to pass before Sima Qian incurred Emperor Wu's displeasure (for speaking out in defence of General Li Ling, who had surrendered to the Xiongnu rather than dying in battle as was expected of him by Emperor Wu), underwent imprisonment and torture and was sentenced to castration.[6] At the time it would have been possible to have had the sentence commuted by payment of a fine but, as Sima Qian later explained, "my family was poor and lacked sufficient funds to buy commutation of the sentence. Of my friends and associates, not one would save me; among those near the emperor no one said as much as a word for me".[7] The other alternative was suicide, something he considered and rejected:

> the reason I have not refused to bear these ills and have continued to live, dwelling in vileness and disgrace without taking leave, is that I grieve that I have things in my heart that I have not been able to express fully, and I am shamed to think that after I am gone my writings will not be known to posterity.[8]

He continued:

> I wished to examine into all that concerns heaven and humankind, to penetrate the changes of the past and present, putting forth my views as one school of interpretation. But before I had finished my rough manuscript, I met with this calamity.[9]

It would not be surprising if, after suffering his ordeal, Sima Qian's revisions were to incorporate a harsh verdict on the person who may have been directly responsible for his punishment (Emperor Wu) and on the age that would countenance such unmerited barbarity.[10] But, without sight of the earlier manuscript we have no way of knowing the changes he introduced.

What we do have is a manuscript in which Sima Qian deploys an impressive battery of literary devices – including satire, of which he was a connoisseur,[11] irony, fictitious speeches attributed to historical figures, criticism of the present displaced to the past – that invite the reader to glimpse his bleak assessment of "the changes of the past and present".[12] As Burton Watson put it, the revelation "is not a pretty picture".[13]

The chapter is structured as follows. In the next section I review the main evidence from *Shiji* 129 in favour of Sima Qian's supposedly pro-*laissez-faire* stance. I then make a case against that interpretation, based mainly on material from elsewhere in the *Shiji*, after which I revisit *Shiji* 129 in the light of the contrary evidence. A brief conclusion follows. I then add a Postscript on what may have been the seminal recorded misunderstanding of *Shiji* 129 in the *Han shu*.

Sima Qian as an advocate of *laissez-faire*

The case for Sima Qian's advocacy of *laissez-faire* is based on a reading of passages from Chapter 129 in the *Shiji*, "The Biographies of the Money-Makers".[14] The chapter begins:

> Though only commoners with no special ranks or titles, they were able, without interfering with the government or hindering the activities of the people,

to increase their wealth by making the right moves at the right time. Wise men will find something to learn from them.[15]

Exactly what the "wise men" might learn is not disclosed at this point. Instead, Sima Qian moved on to describe the nature and extent of people's desires. As he put it:

> ears and eyes have always longed for the ultimate in beautiful sounds and forms, mouths have desired to taste the best in grass-fed and grain-fed animals, bodies have delighted in ease and comfort, and hearts have swelled with pride at the glories of power and ability. So long as these habits have been allowed to permeate the lives of the people, though one were to go from door to door preaching the subtle arguments of the Taoists, he could never succeed in changing them.[16]

Then, in what may appear to be an inference from the above, he wrote:

> Therefore the highest type of ruler accepts the nature of the people, the next best leads the people to what is beneficial, the next gives them moral instruction, the next forces them to be orderly, and the very worst kind enters into competition with them.[17]

The *laissez-faire* reading of the above passage[18] is that the "highest type of ruler" will not only accept the reality of people's multiple desires but will also endorse an economic system based on their unhindered efforts to satisfy those desires, both as consumers and as suppliers (manufacturers and merchants). In favour of such a reading, Sima Qian may appear to have put the matter beyond doubt:

> Society obviously must have farmers before it can eat; foresters, fishermen, miners, etc. before it can make use of natural resources; craftsmen before it can have manufactured goods; and merchants before they can be distributed. But once these exist, what need is there for government directives, mobilisations of labour, or periodic assemblies? Each man has only to be left to utilise his own abilities and exert his strength to obtain what he wishes. Thus, when a commodity is very cheap, it invites a rise in price; when it is very expensive, it invites a reduction. When each person works away at his own occupation and delights in his own business then, like water flowing downward, goods will naturally flow forth ceaselessly day and night without being summoned, and the people will produce commodities without having been asked. Does this not tally with reason? Is it not a natural result?[19]

Based on this passage alone it is little wonder that a *laissez-faire* interpretation has gained adherents. Motivated solely by a desire for profit that is portrayed as globally endemic ("Jostling and joyous, the whole world comes after profit; racing and rioting, after profit the whole world goes!"[20]), Sima Qian had sketched the outlines of an economic system in which producers and merchants supply the means to satisfy consumer demands (and desires) by responding to price signals rather than government directives. It might not have amounted to a *theory* of *laissez-faire*, but it could be construed as a first step in that direction.

The system Sima Qian had lightly sketched may well be one in which "goods will naturally flow forth ceaselessly day and night without being summoned", driven by profit-seeking behaviour on the part of producers and merchants, but, as he evidently realised, it is also one in which some people may end up being (considerably) richer than others. He pronounced:

> Poverty and wealth are not the sort of things that are arbitrarily handed to men or taken away: the clever have a surplus; the stupid never have enough.[21]

It is, it seems, their own fault – a result of their "stupidity" – if some people lose out in the "liberal" economic system. That message is apparently reinforced later in the chapter with reference to

> those impoverished men with aged parents and wives and children too weak or young to help them out, who have nothing to offer their ancestors at the seasonal sacrifice, who must depend upon the gifts and contributions of the community for food and clothing and are unable to provide for themselves.

Sima Qian continued: "if such men as these, reduced to such straits, still fail to find any shame or embarrassment, then they hardly deserve to be called human",[22] thus placing himself (so it seems) at an extreme, uncompassionate point on a pro-*laissez-faire* spectrum.[23]

As if in mitigation of the system's less attractive characteristics, a wealthy society is then commended (following *Guanzi*)[24] as one in which people can "appreciate rites and obligations" and, reminiscent of Aristotle's discussion of "liberality",[25] one in which the "superior men" who become rich will "delight in practicing virtue"; indeed:

> As fish by nature dwell in the deepest pools and wild beasts congregate in the most secluded mountains, so benevolence and righteousness[26] attach themselves to a man of wealth.[27]

Thanks to the benevolence of the wealthy, he may seem to suggest, perhaps not every person who "hardly deserves to be called human" will be left to perish under *laissez-faire*.

The rest, and the greater part of the chapter, is then taken up with accounts of individuals and entire states that had pursued various profit-seeking strategies in areas such as farming, animal-rearing, iron-smelting, mining, salt production, trade generally (including speculative activities) and money-lending. As Sima Qian stressed, all these endeavours were driven by a "natural" propensity – "the desire for wealth does not need to be taught; it is an integral part of all human nature"[28] – a desire shared by "wise men", reclusive "gentlemen", (corrupt) government officials, soldiers, criminals, prostitutes, doctors, magicians, farmers, craftsmen and merchants.[29] Some of his case-studies were taken from the distant past, while others referred to "worthy men of the present age" who were chosen "so that later generations may see how they did it [i.e. how they acquired great wealth] and select what may be of benefit to themselves".[30]

He concluded his survey, and the chapter, as follows:

> From this we may see that there is no fixed road to wealth, and money has no permanent master. It finds its way to the man of ability like the spokes of a wheel converging on the hub, and from the hands of the worthless it falls like shattered tiles. A family with 1,000 catties of gold may stand side by side with the lord of a city; the man with 100,000,000 cash may enjoy the pleasures of a king. Rich men such as these deserve to be called the "untitled nobility", do they not?[31]

It may seem that Sima Qian had almost answered the last question for us. Thus, among his roll-call of "rich men" (and one woman), Guan Zhong's wealth is reported to have "exceeded that of the lord of a great feudal kingdom";[32] the wealth of Zigong (Confucius's disciple) was such that "whatever state he visited the ruler never failed to descend into the courtyard and greet him as an equal";[33] Wuzhi Luo and the widow Qing, who had acquired wealth from trade and a monopoly of cinnabar caves, respectively, were both honoured by the First Emperor of Qin and "were treated with as much respect as though they had been the lords of a state of 10,000 chariots";[34] Mr Zhou of Shu, who made his fortune from iron-smelting, "grew so rich that . . . the pleasures he indulged in among his fields and lakes and on his bird and animal hunts were like those of a great lord";[35] the Kong family of Yuan, who also acquired wealth from iron-smelting, rode about "in carriages with a mounted retinue", visited the feudal lords, and "won a reputation for handing out lavish gifts in the manner of noblemen of leisure";[36] and the Ren family of Xuanqu, who originally made their fortune by stockpiling grain and reaping large profits from selling in times of shortage, "became leaders of the community and . . . enjoyed the respect of the ruler".[37] It was therefore in recognition of how such people behaved and were treated, as matters of fact, that they "may be called the 'untitled nobility'",[38] thus inviting, without strictly requiring, the retort that they *deserved* the appellation of "untitled nobility".[39] So interpreted, we appear to have an answer to the question posed in the chapter's opening paragraph: wise men should follow the examples of the "money-makers" in order to acquire wealth and high social status, and they should be allowed to do so in the context of a *laissez-faire* economic system, free of government interference, that is most conducive to their ends.

Laissez-faire and the money-makers: a different perspective

There are several indications within *Shiji* 121 itself that the apparently favourable treatment of an economic system (such as a *laissez-faire* system) driven by the unrestrained desire for wealth is deceptive. For example, the claim that "benevolence and righteousness attach themselves to a man of wealth" is directly contradicted by the later observation that "men [who] apply all their knowledge and use all their abilities simply in accumulating money . . . never have any strength left over to consider the question of giving some of it away".[40] Then there is the case of the people of Zou and Lu who were once "fond of Confucian learning and proficient in matters of ritual", but had later "abandoned scholarship and turned to the pursuit of profit" under the influence of travelling moneylenders and traders: a sign of progress, one might think, except that the "later days" are described as those in which "the state has declined".[41] Eyebrows could also rise at Sima Qian's inclusion of murder, theft, counterfeiting, prostitution and usurious money-lending (with interest of 1,000%) among his examples of profit-seeking activities,[42] and his description of "unusual schemes or methods" that "rich men have *invariably* employed . . . to get to the top",[43] including grave-robbing, gambling ("a wicked pastime") and various other "disgraceful" and "despicable" activities, as he describes them. Moreover, one might wonder if drawing attention to business schemes resulting in individuals and families owning vast numbers of slaves and "dominating" entire provinces was helpful to a *laissez-faire* cause.[44] However, although such instances may raise doubts about the sincerity of Sima Qian's embrace of *laissez-faire*, it is material elsewhere in the *Shiji* that should turn those doubts into disbelief.

It was in private correspondence written after his imprisonment and castration that Sima Qian explained that the purpose of his "useless writings" (as he self-deprecatingly referred to the *Shiji*) was to examine "the events of the past and [investigate] the principles behind *their success and failure, their rise and decay*".[45]

This view of history as a cyclical process of "rise and decay" was a defining feature of his work. To take his interpretation of the earliest recorded period of Chinese history (ca. 2355–619 BCE):[46]

> [In] times of peace and security, stress was laid upon the system of schools; agricultural pursuits, which are the basis of the nation, were honoured; secondary occupations such as trade were disparaged, and people were taught a sense of propriety and duty in order to discourage them from the search for profit. In periods of war and unrest, however, the opposite situation prevailed. When a thing has reached its height it must begin to decay.[47]

The "search for profits" and the development of "secondary" (non-agricultural) activities are taken, unequivocally, as manifestations of "decay": a position consistent with the description of Zou and Lu as entering a period of "decline" with the growing prevalence of profit-seeking behaviour,[48] but one that raises the question of why Sima Qian should wish to endorse a system that is actually *predicated* on "the search for profit".

The cycle of "rise and decay" is depicted as recurring until 770 BCE, when the Zhou Dynasty entered its own period of decay (or "weakness and decay")[49]. A prolonged period of "war and unrest" ensued, encompassing what has come to be known as the "Spring and Autumn Period" (770–480 BCE) and the "War-ring States Period" (480–221 BCE). Sima Qian described the latter period in desolate terms:

> the empire was torn by the strife of the warring kingdoms. Men honoured deceit and power and scoffed at benevolence and righteousness; they put wealth and possessions first and courtesy and humility last. Thus it happened that commoners grew so rich that their wealth was counted in the hundreds of millions, while among the poor there were those who could not even get enough dregs and chaff to fill their bellies.[50]

Clearly, there was nothing Sima Qian regarded as endearing about an age in which people sought wealth and possessions: it was, indeed, an age of "decay", both in virtue ("benevolence and righteousness"[51]) and in the living conditions of the poor. But what is truly remarkable about this passage is that the class of people who became fabulously rich, and who evidently could not care less about their starving fellow citizens, are the *same* class (of "commoners") who were seemingly held up in *Shiji* 129 as a shining example of those from whom "wise men" could find something to learn. Certainly, one thing they would not learn from *these* commoners is the compatibility of riches with "benevolence and righteousness".

Continuing with Sima Qian's historical narrative, the period of war, unrest, weakness and decay persisted until 221 BCE, when "the Qin finally united all the land within the four seas under a single rule".[52] An opportunity was thereby presented to put an end to decay and embark on a path of "righteous ways".[53] But it was an opportunity squandered. Instead of practicing (true) "benevolence and righteousness", the Qin endorsed and applied the prescriptions of "Legalists", thus ensuring its own downfall through a catalogue of failings: to employ "loyal and worthy men" as advisers; to use "ritual" as a means of ordering the empire; to reduce the severity of laws and punishments; to "succour the orphaned and lonely and those in dire poverty"; to lighten taxes and demands for corvée labour; to avoid warfare; and, more generally, to emulate the "benevolence and righteous-ness" of the sage rulers of antiquity.[54] After a mere 16 years, the Qin Dynasty was overthrown. Sima Qian remarked:

> Though men worked in the fields as hard as they could, they were unable to supply enough provisions [for the troops], and though the women wove and spun, they could not produce enough tents and hangings for the army. Soon the common people were exhausted; there was no surplus left to feed the orphans and widows, the children and the old people; and the roads were filled with the dead and dying. That is why the empire turned in revolt against the Qin.[55]

With the Qin replaced by the Han, a new phase of the cycle was to begin.

According to Sima Qian's account in *Shiji* 129, the early years of the Han were ones in which "the barriers and bridges were opened and the restrictions on the use of the resources of mountains and lakes were relaxed". He continued:

> As a result, the rich traders and great merchants travelled all around the empire distributing their wares to ever corner so that everyone could buy what he wanted.[56]

With *everyone* buying what they wanted, it might seem that the "rich traders and great merchants" were performing an admirable public service, fully in harmony with a pro-*laissez-faire* interpretation of Sima Qian's intentions. But in *Shiji* 30 a rather different story is told. There, the very same period is described as one of widespread poverty among the masses ("there was much hard work and little wealth"[57]), made *worse* by the activities of merchants:

> The laws and prohibitions of the Qin having been simplified or done away with, people who were intent upon making a profit by underhanded means began to hoard their wealth, buying up the commodities on the market, so that the price of goods [including the prime necessity, grain] shot up.[58]

As time passed, however, the situation gradually improved:

> In the reign of Emperor Hui and Empress Lü [195–180 BCE], the common people succeeded in putting behind them the sufferings of the age of the Warring States and ruler and subject alike sought rest in surcease of action. Therefore Emperor Hui sat with folded hands and unruffled garments and Empress Lü, though a woman ruling in the manner of an emperor, conducted the business of government without ever leaving her private chambers, and . . . the people applied themselves to the tasks of farming, and food and clothing became abundant.[59]

Moving closer to his own time, Sima Qian reports that by around 136 BCE, when

> the present emperor [Wudi] had been on the throne for a few years, a period of over seventy years had passed [in which] the nation had met with no major disturbance so that, except in times of flood or drought, every person was well supplied and every family had enough to get along on.[60]

Granaries were full, and the state treasury is reported as "overflowing". Moreover:

> Horses were to be seen even in the streets and lanes of the common people or plodding in great numbers along the paths between the fields, and any one so poor as to have to ride a mare was disdained by his neighbours and not allowed to join the gatherings of the villagers. . . . The local officials remained at the same posts long enough to see their sons and grandsons grow to manhood,

and the higher officials occupied the same positions so long that they adopted their official titles as surnames. As a result, men had a sense of self-respect and regarded it as a serious matter to break the law. Their first concern was to act in accordance with what was right and to avoid shame and dishonour.[61]

But the wheels of history were turning once again: "it has ever been the law of change that when things reach their period of greatest flourishing, they must begin to decay".[62]

The warning signs of decay at the beginning of Wu's reign were stated thus:

> At this time . . . because the net of the law was slack and the people were rich, it was possible for men to use their wealth to exploit others and to accumulate large fortunes. Some, such as the great landowners and powerful families, were able to do anything they pleased in the countryside, while the members of the imperial house and the nobility, the high officials and the lesser government officers, strove to outdo each other in luxurious living; there was no limit to how far each would go in aping the houses, carriages, and dress of his social superiors.[63]

The "period of greatest flourishing" was therefore marked not only by the relative abundance of necessities for the common people, but also by an orgy of conspicuous consumption among the higher classes. Less than two decades later, the empire would find itself on the brink of bankruptcy.

The problems that arose bear an uncanny similarity to those that had plagued the Qin, including costly (and unsuccessful) military operations against the Xiongnu;[64] other military adventures, prompted by megalomania and caprice on the part of Emperor Wu;[65] reliance on advice from the "wrong" ministers and generals, many of whom sought only their own profit;[66] massive public works projects (roads, canals, irrigation schemes), several of questionable benefit;[67] vanity projects, such as the building of palaces, lakes and parks;[68] and other hugely expensive indulgences on the part of Emperor Wu, including mass mobilisations in the delusional quest for spirit-beings who possessed the secret of immortality,[69] "frequent hunts and progresses about the empire, re-establishing the shrines of ancient times, carrying out the Feng and Shang sacrifices, and working to encourage the revival of rites and music".[70]

By around 120 BCE, "the funds of the government officials were completely exhausted".[71] But at least there was one group of people who were doing well for themselves:

> The rich merchants and big traders . . . were busy accumulating wealth and forcing the poor into their hire, transporting goods back and forth in hundreds of carts, buying up surplus commodities and hoarding them in the villages; even the feudal lords were forced to go to them with bowed heads and beg for what they needed. Others who were engaged in smelting iron and extracting salt from sea water accumulated [vast] fortunes.[72]

Just like their predecessors in the Warring States period,[73] these rich merchants and industrialists "did nothing to help the distress of the nation, and the common people were plunged deeper and deeper into misery".[74] Meanwhile, "idle and unscrupulous landlords" were acquiring "huge estates", and within a couple of years, as demands to bankroll the state intensified, the rich were united in "scrambling to hide their wealth".[75] The "benevolent and righteous" profit-seekers, seemingly commended by Sima Qian in *Shiji* 129, had vanished from the pages of history.

It seems impossible to reconcile the apparently positive depiction of gain-seeking economic activities in *Shiji* 129 with the wholly negative treatment elsewhere in the book, where the search for profit is taken as symptomatic of "decay" and those who benefit from it are portrayed as pathologically indifferent to the well-being of anyone but themselves. Moreover, it is the *disparagement* of efforts to satisfy desire – by individuals and entire states, in all contexts – that stands out as one of the main themes in the *Shiji*,[76] so why Sima Qian should wish to exempt from censure a prominent genus of that behavioural species, in one solitary chapter, is even more puzzling. Evidently, *Shiji* 129 calls for further consideration.

Shiji 129: reconsideration

According to the "free market" or "*laissez-faire*" interpretation of the opening paragraphs of *Shiji* 129, Sima Qian accepted that people were driven to satisfy their various desires and commended a ruler (the "highest type of ruler") who would allow them to do so. But such a reading is difficult to reconcile with what he had written elsewhere in *Shiji:* the "highest type of ruler" would surely *not* countenance behaviour that is symptomatic of an age of "decay". On closer inspection, however, although the *laissez-faire* reading, or inference, may have accorded with Sima Qian's rhetorical intent, the opening passages are also consistent with the idea of a "highest ruler" who would *constrain* desire-seeking behaviour.

Recognition of the "nature of the people" as being driven to satisfy their many desires was almost commonplace in Sima Qian's time. It was something accepted by "Legalists" and by "Confucians". But that acceptance did not entail indulgence. For the "Legalists", it meant restricting the opportunities, or "gates", through which people "can attain their desire", the sanctioned opportunities being confined to agriculture and warfare.[77] For the "Confucians", and for Xun Qing's version of "Confucianism" in particular, it meant using ritual principles "to train men's desires" involving detailed specification of permissible levels of material consumption, all graded according to social status. As recorded in *Xunzi*, in language strikingly similar to Sima Qian's:

> As for people's natural dispositions, their eyes desire the utmost in sights, their ears deserve the utmost in sounds, their mouths desire the utmost in favours, their noses desire the utmost in smells, and their bodies desire the utmost in comfort. These "five utmosts" are something the natural dispositions of people cannot avoid desiring.[78]

However, although the "utmosts" are "something the natural dispositions of people cannot avoid desiring", their efforts to satisfy desires can and must be limited:

> People's nature is bad . . . they are born with a fondness for profit in them. If they follow along with this, then struggle and contention will arise . . . They are born with desires of the eyes and ears, a fondness for beautiful sights and sounds. If they follow along with these, then lasciviousness and chaos will arise . . . So, it is necessary to await the transforming influence of teachers and models and the guidance of ritual and *yi* [rightness, or righteousness].[79]

Thus, according to Xunzi's "Confucianism", the "highest type of ruler" would indeed accept that people naturally seek profit and the satisfaction of desires, but would then educate them in ritual principles in order to limit such behaviour.

Assuming that the people *can* be educated, with the result that "*yi* defeats profit", we would have what Xunzi termed "an ordered age". Whereas, if "profit overcomes *yi*", then it is a chaotic age"[80] or, as Sima Qian expressed it, an "age of decay". Dong Zhongshu, under whom Sima Qian is reported to have studied,[81] held essentially the same position:

> The present age has abandoned regulations [that set] limits so that each person indulges his or her desires. When desires have no limits, then the vulgar act without restraint. When this tendency persists without end, the powerful people worry over insufficiencies above; the little people fear starvation below. Thus, the wealthy increasingly covet profit and cannot act righteously; the poor daily disobey prohibitions and cannot be stopped. This is why the present age is difficult to govern.[82]

As with Xunzi, Dong's "highest type of ruler" would recognise that people have a natural inclination to "follow their desires" but would "cultivate officials" to take "charge of instruction and training, striving to transform the people with virtue and goodness".[83] He would *not* allow people to indulge their desires without restraint.

In writing that "the highest type of ruler accepts the nature of the people", it follows that Sima Qian was not committing *himself* to the position that people should be unhindered in their efforts to satisfy their desires. Rather, it allowed him to satirise a ruler – Emperor Wu – who was presiding over an age in which "profit overcomes yi", and who qualified as "the highest type of ruler" only through an inversion of orthodox ethical standards.

Sima Qian's apparent disparagement of the poor in *Shiji* 129 can be seen as similarly deceptive. His declaration that "the clever have a surplus, the stupid never have enough" is almost a direct quotation from the *Guanzi*: "Capable rulers will have more than enough [of grain, weapons and money], while those who are stupid will suffer shortages".[84] As with his ironic description of "the highest type of ruler", his choice of expression can also be read as a veiled criticism of Emperor Wu, whose extravagant policies had brought the empire to the point of bankruptcy, not as an indictment of the poor as sub-human victims of their own stupidity.

It is of course true that later passages in *Shiji* 129 *do* assert that the impoverished in society "hardly deserve to be called human".[85] But this was a sentiment that Sima Qian evidently associated with "Legalists", whose views he abhorred. Thus, in *Shiji* 87 he gives Li Si[86] the following lines: "I say, there is no greater disgrace than being mean and lowly, and no greater sorrow than poverty and want".[87] And in *Shiji* 122 he reports the views of a "harsh official" – a member of a group he also despised[88] – in these terms: "An official who can't advance to a salary of 2,000 pictuls or a merchant who can't make at least 10,000,000 cash is not fit to be called a man!"[89] In *seeming* to share the sentiments of those he regarded as deplorable human beings, utterly devoid of virtue, he was being ironic; he was not expressing views that he personally endorsed.

I turn to the rhetorical suggestion at the conclusion to *Shiji* 129 that the rich may deserve to be called "untitled nobility": something that might appear to confer merited applause, but only if "nobility" is itself a badge of true merit. And that was certainly not Sima Qian's own position.

As he observed in *Shiji* 18:

> When I read the records of the distinguished followers of Gaozu [the first emperor of Han] who were enfeoffed as marquises, and observe the reasons for which their descendants were deprived of the fiefs of their fathers, I am struck by how different the situation is from what I have heard concerning ancient times . . . [when nobles] held their positions . . . [for] a period of over 1,000 years, and fulfilled their duties as guardians of the Son of Heaven.

As to the reason for the difference in "situation": "Was it not because they [the nobles of antiquity] were diligent in virtue and attendant to the laws of their superiors?" – the clear implication being that the later nobles possessed none of those qualities.[90]

It had all started to go wrong in the period of "weakness and decay" as the "Zhou dynasty began to wane, and rites and music fell into disuse; the feudal lords conducted themselves as they pleased . . . [and] evil ways flourished".[91] By the time we reach Wu's reign, just before the empire took another cyclical nose-dive, the "members of the imperial house and the nobility" were striving "to outdo each other in luxurious living; there was no limit to how far each would go in aping the houses, carriages, and dress of his social superiors".[92] For Sima Qian, "nobility" was evidently not a badge of merit.

The contrast between the latter-day nobility, titled and untitled, and people of *true* merit is exposed starkly in *Shiji* 124, "The Biographies of the Wandering Knights". Sima Qian explained his purpose in writing the chapter as follows:

> Saving others in distress, helping those who cannot help themselves – is this not what a benevolent man does? Never betraying a trust, never going back

on one's word – this is the conduct of a righteous man. Thus I made "The Biographies of the Wandering Knights".[93]

The proclaimed merits of these people had nothing to do with wealth. Rather:

among the knights of the common people there are men who are fair in their dealings and true to their promises, who will risk death for others without a thought for their own safety, and who are praised for their righteousness a thousand miles around. . . . [They] do not simply strive to get ahead at any price.[94]

Here are "commoners" who really do deserve praise. And, just in case we fail to see the contrast with the imposters to virtue, Sima Qian makes it for us:

On the other hand, when it comes to those who band together in cliques and powerful family groups, pooling their wealth and making the poor serve them, arrogantly and cruelly oppressing the weak and helpless, giving free reign to their own desires and treating people any way they please – such men the wandering knights despise even as others do.[95]

He may not have written "as I do", but he seems to leave little doubt as to his own position.

Perhaps, after all, rich commoners really do "deserve to be called the 'untitled nobility'", if that is taken to signify greedy, self-indulgent specimens of human- ity who are strangers to "benevolence and righteousness". But, if so, what *should* wise men "learn from them"? Perhaps the unvarnished lesson comes down to this: that wealth is esteemed in itself, and as a means of conferring the (debased) status of nobility, but only in an age of weakness and decay.

Where, then, does this leave Sima Qian's vision of a society in which

each person works away at his own occupation and delights in his own busi- ness, [and in which] like water flowing downward, goods will naturally flow forth ceaselessly day and night without being summoned, and the people will produce commodities without having been asked?

The blunt answer is, in a quandary. If desires are extinguished or severely con- strained, so too are incentives to respond swiftly, if at all, to price signals, unless people are motivated by quite different considerations such as the "public good". In the latter case, there might be a *laissez-faire* system of sorts, but not one that produced the likes of the "untitled nobility" in *Shiji* 129.

Conclusion

I have argued that Sima Qian was not an advocate of a *laissez-faire* system that would be populated by "money-makers" of the type who figure in *Shiji* 129, and whether he could approve of *any laissez-faire* system, even one in which the actors play for small stakes, is uncertain. The appearance of a contrary position is down to his rhetorical skill, but there are indications even within *Shiji* 129 that the appearance may be deceptive, while the reality of that deception becomes (or should become) clear in the light of material elsewhere in the *Shiji*.

It would seem that several commentators have had an inkling of something slightly strange about their interpretations, particularly when it came to crediting Sima Qian with cool indifference towards inequality. Hence the textually unsupported attributions of a "hope" that everyone might prosper under *laissez-faire* or, in Chen Huanzhang's case, a curious interpretation of the conclusion to *Shiji* 129 to a similar end.[96] What they could be said to have realised, if only vaguely, was the difficulty in reconciling the allegedly pro-*laissez-faire* Sima Qian of *Shiji* 129 with the other Sima Qian who wrote the rest of the book. My resolution to their dilemma is simple: the pro-*laissez-faire* Sima Qian is an illusion created by the historian himself.

As I interpret it, *Shiji* 129 amounts to chapter-length treatment of people who Sima Qian despised. There was nothing remotely admirable about them but, as a (recurring) historical phenomenon, they fully merited consideration in his work. In his judgement, however, the respect and admiration which they were accorded as a matter of fact was symptomatic of the warped values of the "discordant and degenerate age" in which they, and he, lived: an age presided over by an Emperor whose own value system was similarly compromised. True to his own literary tastes, and doubtless with some apprehension of the damage to his posthumous reputation that a more direct critique might bring, he therefore followed Sima Xiangru's example[97] by constructing his own brilliantly satirical reprimand to an age of selfishness, unbridled desire and wanton extravagance. He was not inscribing a manifesto for a utility-maximising system of *laissez-faire*.

Postscript: the *Han shu*

The *Han shu* (*Book of Han*), compiled in the first century CE by Ban Gu (32–92) using a draft written by his father, Ban Biao (3–54), and with contributions from his sister, Ban Zhao (ca. 48–116), provides evidence of what may be (on the reading offered here) the first misinterpretation of Sima Qian's *Shiji* 119, grounded in a blinkered and unswervingly literal comprehension of that chapter alone. In that regard it set a trend that was to continue until present times.

Ban Biao was unimpressed with *Shiji* 129, which he believed "slights justice and attaches shame to poverty".[98] His son dutifully followed suit: "In narrating the money-makers, he [Sima Qian] honours those whose situation is such that they make a profit and finds shame in the lowly and poor".[99] In composing his own chapter on "money-makers", *Han shu* 91, Ban Gu thoroughly revised the material from the *Shiji* in a way better to convey his pious "Confucian" morality.

In place of Sima Qian's curt introduction to his chapter,[100] Ban Gu opens his by returning to the halcyon days of the "Ancient Kings", when "the people had a sense of shame and, moreover, of respect; they highly esteemed rightness, but disesteemed profit".[101] But those values were forgotten, according to Ban, when "the House of Zhou became decadent". Thereafter, "those who practiced trickery and deceit, and who committed crimes and felonies, enjoyed a sufficiency . . . [while those] who maintained the (proper way) *Dao* and observed the *li* did not escape hardships of hunger and cold". Hence the point of Ban's chapter, "to transmit changes of [different] generations" and enumerate "what persons did" *in the period of decline.*[102]

Of course, we already know what they did: they "practiced trickery and deceit and . . . committed crimes and felonies". In a word, they all became *decadent*, and that is explicitly the damning judgement passed by Ban Gu on various individuals and families from whom Sima Qian had averred, "wise men will have something to learn".[103] Some of these social miscreants had "overstepped the law of the land" in their quest for "excessive gains and profits",[104] while the iron-smelting Zhou of Shu and Kong of Yuan, together with Dian Qian of Qi who profited from his employment of slaves, had

> unlawfully dared [to collect what rightly were] government revenues [on resources] of mountains and streams, on copper, iron, fish, salt, and marketplaces, and who, by manipulating the counting sticks, on the one hand strove to obtain the profits belonging to the sovereign and, on the other hand, seized [for their own interests] occupations of the ordinary common people – all [such wealthy families] sunk into the evils of lawlessness, excess, and usurpation.[105]

Then, in the conclusion to his chapter, Ban Gu singled out "persons such as Tian Shu, Huan Fa and Long Lechang,

> who became rich through robbing graves, gambling, robbery, and perpetrating [other] crimes, yet stood [equal with the good as] stand upper front teeth. [Such people not being discriminated in society] injure civilisation, and destroy [good] usages. It is the road to grave [social] disorder."[106]

Unlike Sima Qian's conclusion – "rich men such as these deserve to be called the 'untitled nobility', do they not?" – Ban's was devoid of any trace of subtlety and rhetorical ambivalence. The reader was to be left in no doubt that "rich men" were a positive menace to society, and the only lesson "wise men" should learn from *his* account of their activities is that they deserved neither praise nor emulation. But what Ban Gu apparently failed to realise, on a spectacular scale, was that he was only making explicit the judgements Sima Qian had left implicit. The whole exercise was nothing more than an unintended tribute to Sima Qian's use of irony.

Notes

1 A previous version of this chapter was presented at the 48th annual UK History of Economic Thought Conference, held at Shanghai University of Finance and Economics,

China, 1–4 September 2016. I should like to thank the conference participants for helpful comments and encouragement.

2 Interpretations along these lines have been advanced by Chen Huanzhang (1911), pp. 176–179; Spengler (1964); Hu Jichuang (1988), pp. 240–248; Young (1996); Ma Tao [1998] (2014); Tang Renwu [1996] (2014); and Zhou Jing [2001] (2014).

3 My references will be to Burton Watson's three-volume translation of the *Shiji*, designated hereafter as *Qin, Han* I and *Han* II.

4 Nienhouser (2011), p. 482.

5 Sima Qian's lifespan is usually given as ca. 145–89 BCE.

6 See Watson, *Han* I, p. x.

7 Letter to his friend, Ren An, *Qin*, p. 232.

8 Ibid., p. 235.

9 Ibid., p. 236.

10 "Obviously a man who had suffered such a punishment would have every reason to hate a ruler who inflicted it" (Watson, *Han* II, pp. x–xi). Nienhouser suggests that "the sentencing of Qian seems to have been Emperor Wu's own design" (2011, p. 268 n.26), while Rickett states baldly that Sima Qian "held a bitter hatred to Emperor Wu" (1998, p. 355).

11 This is evidenced by *Shiji* 117, a biography of the poet Sima Xiangru, in which high praise is bestowed on the poem "Sir Fantasy", described by Sima Qian as "a satirical reprimand" of wanton extravagance. The satire is intensified by Sima Qian's report that Emperor Wu was "exceedingly pleased" with a revised version of the poem that had held up the emperor's *own* extravagance for reprimand.

12 Sima Qian's deployment of satire was noted by Needham (1956, p. 5). Watson also draws attention to Sima Qian's use of satire (*Han* II, p. 373 n.1), and to irony (*Han* I, p. 425 n.3), the use of the past to criticise the present (*Han* II, pp. xviii–xix), the tactic of portraying individuals in different lights between chapters (*Han* II, p. xv), and the use of guarded language in veiled attacks on Emperor Wu (*Han* I, p. 310, *Han* II, pp. 85 n.17, 162). Lewis observes, "the multi-voiced nature of the work . . . serves to offer historical lessons, through an ironic interplay between quoted assertions and factual narrative" (2007, p. 216). See also Nienhouser (2011).

13 *Han* II, p. xii.

14 The literal translation of the Chinese title for the chapter, *Huozhi,* is "wealth increasing".

15 *Han* II, p. 433.

16 Ibid., pp. 433–434.

17 *Han* I, p. 434.

18 As given, for example, by Ma Tao (2014) [1998], p. 159.

19 Han I, p. 434.

20 Ibid., p. 436.

21 Ibid., p. 435.

22 Ibid., pp. 448–449.

23 Cf. "if a man is not a gentleman of unusual character who has deliberately sought retirement from the world, and if he grows old in poverty and lowliness and still insists upon talking about his 'benevolence and righteousness', he ought to be thoroughly ashamed of himself" (ibid., p. 449).

24 "When the granaries are full, they [the people] will know propriety and moderation. When their clothing and food is adequate, they will know the distinction between honour and shame". From the opening paragraph of *Guanzi*, repeated in Rickett (1998, XXIII.80, p. 460).

25 Aristotle, *The Nicomachean Ethics*, IV.i.

26 I suggest that Sima Qian's use of "benevolence and righteousness" in this context is sardonic. For the contrast with *true* "benevolence and righteousness" see below, p. 7 n.51.

27 Han I, p. 436.

28 Ibid.
29 Ibid., pp. 446–447.
30 Ibid., p. 450.
31 Ibid., p. 454.
32 Ibid., p. 435.
33 Ibid., p. 438.
34 Ibid., p. 440.
35 Ibid., p. 450.
36 Ibid., p. 451.
37 Ibid., p. 452.
38 Ibid., p. 447.
39 Cf. Hu Jichuang's reading, according to which Sima Qian "had glorified some famous rich men . . . with the honorary title of 'sage' and told the story of their lives . . . in order to let posterity study and follow their methods of pursuing wealth . . . Sima Qian not only affirmed the inevitable existence of the inequality of wealth distribution, but also eulogised the rich merchants as 'sages' and actively taught their way of wealth-making" (1998, p. 247).
40 *Han* II, p. 447. Among the 20 or so individuals and families who are singled out by Sima Qian as successful "money-makers", the rich men who "delight in practicing virtue" are numbered at precisely one (ibid., p. 438).
41 Ibid., pp. 444, 451.
42 Ibid., pp. 446–447, 452–453.
43 Ibid., p. 453, my emphasis.
44 See ibid., pp. 450–451, 453.
45 Letter to Ren An. *Qin*, p. 236, emphasis added.
46 Sima Qian takes as his sources *The Book of Documents* and *The Book of Odes*, both revered as canonical texts, particularly by self-declared "Confucians".
47 *Shiji* 30, *Han* II, p. 84.
48 See above, p. 6.
49 *Shiji* 30, *Han* II, p. 84.
50 Ibid., pp. 84–85.
51 "Benevolence and righteousness" are used by Sima Qian as shorthand for basic "Confucian" values, although a distinction should be made between *genuine* "benevolence and righteousness" and its hypocritical, disingenuous namesake (as in *Shiji* 119, *Han* II, pp. 435–436, quoted above p. 9). Sima Qian's approval of those (genuine) values is evidenced throughout the *Shiji*, in some cases through the speeches and writings attributed to his historical characters, in others more directly. The "benevolent and righteous" person would care for the welfare of others and esteem honesty, loyalty and sincerity. At the level of the state, the ruler would model himself on the "sage kings" of antiquity by employing "loyal and worthy" gentlemen as his advisers, he would set a virtuous example and use ritual rather than harsh punishment as a means of influencing behaviour and, above all, his abiding concern would be for the welfare of his people. The state would come to the aid of the disadvantaged in times of need, taxes and demands for corvée labour would be minimised, and agriculture would be favoured over other ("secondary") economic activities. (See: *Shiji* 6, *Qin*, pp. 76–82; *Shiji* 15, *Qin*, p. 85; *Shiji* 79, *Qin*, p. 153; *Shiji* 87, *Qin*, pp. 201–202; *Shiji* 88, *Qin*, p. 213; *Shiji* 97, *Han* I, pp. 226–227; *Shiji* 10 (in which Emperor Wen is praised at length for his approximation to the "Confucian" sage); *Shiji* 17, *Han* I, p. 426; *Shiji* 10, *Han* II, p. 162; and *Shiji* 20, *Han* II, p. 202).
52 *Shiji* 30, *Han* II, pp. 84–85.
53 *Shiji* 6, *Qin*, p. 83.
54 Ibid., p. 82. The principal exponents of "Legalist" methods of governance were Shang Yang (390–338 BCE) and Han Fei (280–233). Li Si (d. 208), who became Chief

Minister in the Qin Dynasty, was an enthusiastic supporter, and enforcer, of "Legalist" policies. Sima Qian did not disguise his antipathy to "Legalist" doctrine and its proponents (see *Shiji* 68, *Qin*, p. 99 and *Shiji* 87, *Qin*, pp. 205–206).

55 *Shiji* 112, *Han* II, p. 195. Cf. the account in *Shiji* 30: "At that time [i.e. during the Qin], the ruler was busy driving back the barbarians . . . while within the empire he was carrying out various construction works and projects, so that although the men who remained at home worked the fields, they could not supply enough to eat, and though the women wove and spun, they could not produce enough clothing" (*Han* II, p. 85).

56 *Han* II, p. 400.

57 Ibid., p. 61.

58 Ibid. It is made clear in what immediately follows that these "people" were indeed merchants, whose "underhanded" behaviour resulted in an order "forbidding [them] to wear silk or ride in carriages", and in higher taxes on their profits. These laws were subsequently relaxed under the reign of Emperor Hui and Empress Lü (195–180 BCE). Ibid., pp. 61–62.

59 *Shiji* 9, *Han* I, p. 284.

60 *Shiji* 30, *Han* II, p. 63. Commenting on essentially the same passage in *Han shu* 24, it has been suggested that the claim of plenty in the early years of Wu's reign was greatly exaggerated (Loewe 2011, p. 105). If so, it would represent a rhetorical ploy to bring the folly of Wu's policies into sharp relief.

61 Shiji 30, Han II, p. 63.r

62 Ibid.

63 Ibid.

64 *Shiji* 110, *Han* II, pp. 149–160.

65 Such as the deployment of over 60,000 troops to attack Dayuan (East Uzbekistan) and capture a number of their horses ("twenty or thirty of their choicest horses" and others "of less high quality", as it turned out) for which the emperor had developed "a great liking" (*Shiji* 123, *Han* II, p. 245); and an enormously costly military incursion to the land of "the southwestern barbarians" which, on Sima Qian's laconic account, "came about because someone saw some *ju* berry juice" (something unavailable in the "central kingdom") (*Shiji* 116, *Han* II, p. 258).

66 *Shiji* 110, *Han* II, p. 162; *Shiji* 112, *Han* II, p. 202; *Shiji* 120, *Han* II, pp. 309–312; *Shiji* 84, *Han* I, p. 439; *Shiji* 107, *Han* II.

67 *Shiji* 29, *Han* II; *Shiji* 103, *Han* I, p. 481.

68 *Shiji* 30, *Han* II, p. 78.

69 *Shiji* 28.

70 *Shiji* 103, *Han* I, 481.

71 *Shiji* 30, *Han* II p. 68.

72 Ibid.

73 See above, p. 7.

74 Sima Qian reports that a couple of years earlier the Chancellor of Han, Gonsung Hong, had "made a point of using course bedding and refusing to eat highly spiced food, hoping to set an example for the empire. His efforts, however, had no effect upon the customs of the time and men only devoted themselves with greater energy to the pursuit of [private] reward and gain" (*Shiji* 30, *Han* II, p. 67).

75 Ibid., p. 74.

76 See *Shiji* 6, *Qin*, p. 69 and *Shiji* 87, *Qin*, pp. 171, 191 on the problem of desire in the Qin; for the baleful effects on various individuals of seeking to satisfy their desires, see *Shiji* 79, *Qin*, pp. 152–153, *Shiji* 89, *Han* I, p. 145, *Shiji* 92, *Han* I, p. 178; in his letter to Ren An, Sima Qian makes the general point that "no more severe misfortune can come to a man than to be driven by covetous desire" (*Qin*, p. 229).

77 According to *Shangjun shu* (*Book of the Lord Shang*) the "desire of people for riches and honour does not generally cease before their coffins are closed" (Duyvendak 1928, p. 144). Therefore, "it is necessary to examine whence fame and profit spring.

If the profit comes [only] from the soil, then people will use their strength to the full; if fame results [only] from war, then they will fight to the death" (ibid., p. 113).

78 *Xunzi* Ch. 11. Hutton (2014), p. 104.
79 Ibid., Ch. 23, p. 248.
80 Ibid., Ch. 27, p. 304.
81 That is, according to Watson (*Han* II, p. 370 n.19), although Loewe questions whether Dong Zhongshu and Sima Qian had ever been in direct contact with each other (2011, p. 44).
82 *Chunqiu fanlu* (*Luxuriant Gems of the Spring and Autumn*) Ch. 27.1. Queen and Major (2016), p. 271.
83 From Dong Zhongshu's "Reply to the Third Imperial Instruction" as recorded in *Han shu* 56. Queen and Major (2016), p. 637.
84 *Guanzi*, p. 422 (Rickett 1998, p. 422). The *Guanzi* (*Master Guan*) takes its name from Guan Zhong, who was an adviser to Duke Huan of Qi (685–643 BCE). According to the account in *Shi ji* 30: "Duke Huan . . . following the advice of his minister Guan Zhong, initiated the system of buying up goods when the price was low and selling when it was high, and of exploiting the resources of the mountains and seas, until he had the other feudal lords paying court to him . . . [and] had won for himself the title of dictator" (*Han* II, pp. 84–85). The *Guanzi* mostly dates from the late third to the first century BCE. Sima Qian quotes from a version that must have been available at his time in *Shiji* 119, *Han* II, p. 436.
85 See above, p. 4.
86 Li Si is the Qin statesman who infamously proposed that "all records of the historians other than those of the state of Qin be burned", that anyone "who ventures to discuss the *Odes* or *Documents* shall be executed in the marketplace" and that anyone "who uses antiquity to criticise the present shall be executed along with his family". Sima Qian noted laconically, "An imperial decree granted approval of the proposal" (*Shiji* 6, *Qin*, p. 55).
87 *Qin*, p. 179.
88 As he stated in *Shiji* 122, "The Biographies of the Harsh Officials", "good government depends on virtue, not harshness" (*Han* II, p. 380). Sima Qian was himself a recipient of the measures dished out by harsh officials during his imprisonment (cf. Watson, *Han* II p. 406 n.13).
89 *Han* II, p. 383. This attitude was expressed very clearly in the *Han Feizi*: "If men start out with equal opportunities and yet there are a few who, without having suffered from some calamity like famine or sickness, still sink into poverty and destitution, it must be due either to laziness or to extravagant living. The lazy and extravagant grow poor; the diligent and frugal get rich" (from Watson 2003, p. 122). Han Fei (280–233 BCE) is usually portrayed as a representative of the "Legalist school". He is reported to have been a student of the Xun Qing, with Li Si as his classmate.
90 *Han* I, pp. 427–428.
91 *Shiji* 121, *Han* II, p. 355.
92 *Shiji* 30, *Han* II, p. 63.
93 *Han* II, p. 409.
94 Ibid., p. 411.
95 Ibid., p. 412.
96 Hu Jichuang attributed to Sima Qian the "naïve hope that everybody might get rich" (1988, pp. 246, 248), an assertion also made by Spengler (1964, p. 234). Chen Huan-zhang was obviously troubled by the apparent "acceptance" of inequality, which clashed with his view of Sima Qian as a "Confucian". In a bizarre move, he therefore interpreted the final line of *Shiji* 119 as a disavowal of everything that had gone before, allowing him to claim that Sima Qian supported an equal distribution, in spite of everything that had been written in the chapter seemingly to the contrary (1911, p. 179).
97 See above, p. 5 n.11.
98 Quoted by Durrant (2011), p. 488.

194   *Terry Peach*

99   Ibid., pp. 496–497.
100 Quoted above p. 3.
101 In Swann (1950), p. 417.
102 Ibid., p. 419.
103 The characters discussed by Ban Gu are the same as those who feature in *Shiji* 129 with the addition of others who had succumbed to "decadence" in later times. The discussion here refers only to comments made by Gu on the former class.
104 Swann notes that the "overstepping" had arisen from "Monopolistic practices according to common law, customs, good usage, as much as governmental decrees" (1950, p. 461 n.298).
105 Ibid., p. 461.
106 Ibid., pp. 461–462.

References

Chen, H. (1911) *The Economic Principles of Confucius and His School* (New York: Columbia University Press).

Durrant, S.W. (2011) "The Han Histories". In Felder, A. (ed.), *The Oxford History of Historical Writings* (vol. 1) (Oxford: Oxford University Press).

Duyvendak, J. (1928) *Book of the Lord Shang (Shangjun shu)* (London: Arthur Probsthain).

Hu, J. (1988) *A Concise History of Chinese Economic Thought* (Beijing: Foreign Languages Press).

Hutton, E.L. (2014) *Xunzi* (Princeton, NJ: Princeton University Press).

Lewis, M.E. (2007) *The Early Chinese Empires: Qin and Han* (Cambridge, MA: Harvard University Press).

Loewe, M. (2011) *Dong Zhongshu, a 'Confucian' Heritage and the Chunqiu Fanlu* (Leiden: Brill).

Ma, T. [1998] (2014) "Confucian Thought on the Free Economy". In Cheng, Peach and Wang (eds.), *The History of Ancient Chinese Economic Thought* (London: Routledge).

Needham, J. (1956) *Science and Civilization in China* (vol. 2) (Cambridge: Cambridge University Press).

Nienhouser, W.H. (2011) "Sima Qian and the *Shiji*". In Felder, A. (ed.) (2011).

Queen, S.A. and Major, J.S. (2016) *Luxuriant Gems of the Spring and Autumn (Chungqiufanlu)* (New York: Columbia University Press).

Rickett, W.A. (1998) *Guanzi* (Princeton, NJ: Princeton University Press).

Spengler, J.J. (1964) "Sima Qian, Unsuccessful Exponent of Laissez Faire". *Southern Economic Journal*, 30.3, pp. 224–243.

Swann, N.L. (1950) *Food and Money in Ancient China* [Han shu 24 and 91] (Princeton, NJ: Princeton University Press).

Tang, R. [1996] (2014) "A Comparison between Confucian and Daoist Economic Philosophies in the Pre-Qin Era". In Cheng, Peach and Wang (eds.), *The History of Ancient Chinese Economic Thought* (London: Routledge).

Watson, B. (1993) *Sima Qian: Records of the Grand Historian in 3 Volumes (Qin, Han I and Han II)* (New York: Columbia University Press).

Watson, B. (2003) *Han Feizi: Basic Writings* (New York: Columbia University Press).

Young, L. (1996) "The Tao of Markets: Sima Qian and the Invisible Hand". *Pacific Economic Review*, 1, pp. 137–145.

Zhou Jing [2001] (2014) "*Fu Guo Xue* and the 'Economics' of ancient China". In Cheng, Peach and Wang (eds.) (2014), *The History of Ancient Chinese Economic Thought* (London: Routledge).

Index

Note: Page numbers in italics indicate figures and in bold indicate tables on the corresponding pages.

For Product Safety Concerns and Information please contact our EU
representative GPSR@taylorandfrancis.com
Taylor & Francis Verlag GmbH, Kaufingerstraße 24, 80331 München, Germany

www.ingramcontent.com/pod-product-compliance
Ingram Content Group UK Ltd.
Pitfield, Milton Keynes, MK11 3LW, UK
UKHW021028180425
457613UK00021B/1120